Current Issues in Business Management 2024

Ela Sibel Bayrak Meydanoglu, Riza Öztürk,
Dilek Zamantili Nayir and Müge Klein (eds.)

Current Issues in Business Management 2024

PETER LANG

Berlin · Bruxelles · Chennai · Lausanne · New York · Oxford

Bibliographic Information published by the Deutsche Nationalbibliothek
The Deutsche Nationalbibliothek lists this publication in the Deutsche Nationalbibliografie; detailed bibliographic data is available in the internet at http://dnb.d-nb.de.

Library of Congress Control Number: 2025033858

ISBN 978-3-631-93848-5 (Print)
ISBN 978-3-631-93838-6 (E-PDF)
ISBN 978-3-631-93849-2 (E-PUB)
DOI 10.3726/b22936

Published by Peter Lang GmbH, Berlin (Germany)

info@peterlang.com

This publication has been peer reviewed.

www.peterlang.com

Contents

Figures

Tables

Preface

Rapid technological progress, profound transformations in global markets, and the growing importance of sustainable value creation models characterize current developments in both business and society. Companies and institutions face the challenge of developing effective strategies to address these issues while simultaneously driving forward-looking change. Here, emerging technologies such as Artificial Intelligence (AI) and blockchain play a significant role, alongside questions regarding financing models, governance frameworks, and consumer behavior in an increasingly interconnected world.

In this context, the Turkish-German University, in collaboration with Bielefeld University of Applied Sciences and Arts, hosted a conference focusing on innovative perspectives and practice-oriented research at the intersection of finance and business administration, technology adoption, and sustainable development. Researchers discussed central topics, including the role of AI and generative technology in finance and accounting, the dynamics of virtual teamwork, responsible financing, new marketing and consumer approaches, and organizational challenges in modern corporate structures. The contributions presented during the conference form the core of this edited volume.

Mehmet Hakan Özdemir, Tolga Tuzcuoğlu, and Erencan Yavrucu open the volume with "Integrating Generative Artificial Intelligence in Finance: Enhancing Financial Reporting and Quantitative Decision Making." They explore how modern AI models can be leveraged to automate and streamline financial reporting. The authors present AI-based tools designed to accelerate decision-making processes and improve the quality of financial analyses.

Nevertheless, they highlight the ethical, regulatory, and data protection challenges that businesses must address when adopting such systems.

Ferhat Sayın, Hilmi Berkay Abbasoğlu, and Serdar Salih Durmuşoğlu investigate the psychology behind purchasing decisions in digital marketplaces in "The Impact of FOMO-Laden Limited Time Offers on Customer Behavior: The Moderating Role of Curved vs. Sharp Angled Presentation." They argue that limited-time offers, combined with intentionally enticing or provocative visual designs, can significantly increase impulsive buying tendencies. However, they also emphasize that consumers' fear of missing out can vary greatly across different target groups.

Abdulrahman AlAbdeh and Mehtap Öner explore "The Influence of Financing Decisions on Financial Performance and Value of Manufacturing Companies: Evidence from Turkey." Using panel data, the authors investigate how different forms of capital structure affect the performance of listed manufacturing companies. Their findings point to a notably negative correlation between high levels of debt financing and key metrics such as Return on Assets and market value.

Eliza Starke, Angelina Egbers, Lia Bo Josephs, Alina Neumann, Judith Quiring, Manuel Stegemann, and Jan Schilling present "Battling the Pink Tax: How Awareness Campaigns Shape Fairness and Brand Perception." This study shows how gender-specific price differences affect consumer behavior and highlights the role of media campaigns in raising awareness about this issue. Particular attention is paid to how transparent and fair pricing strategies can have a positive impact on brand perception.

Andreas Uphaus and Tim Kampe discuss "Artificial Intelligence in Finance and Accounting of Small and Medium-Sized and Family-Owned Companies—Use Cases, Opportunities, and Risks." Drawing on expert interviews and literature research, they identify specific AI-based approaches that can unlock considerable optimization potential in financing, accounting, and controlling, particularly within smaller family-owned enterprises. However, they also point to critical questions of data security, practical implementation, and workforce readiness.

Dorothee Wilm and Alexander Förster examine "Lessons Learned? The Challenges of Generative AI and Large Language Models (LLM) Implementation Projects Within the Corporate Office World." They analyze whether the hurdles faced in earlier Web 2.0 projects are mirrored in today's efforts to adopt generative AI and LLMs. Their findings stress the importance of well-considered implementation strategies and comprehensive change-management processes to ensure long-term productivity gains from innovative technologies.

Margareta Teodorescu and Ela Sibel Bayrak Meydanoğlu concentrate on "Unraveling Regenerative Finance: Economic Insights into Blockchain's Disruptive Potential." The chapter illustrates how blockchain technology can promote more transparency and efficiency in financial systems by embracing sustainable, public-welfare-oriented principles. Additionally, the authors discuss challenges such as scalability, regulatory uncertainties, and market acceptance.

Hüseyin Hayri Nuroğlu addresses "Investment Franchising: Is It a Viable Solution for Small Investors Facing Governance Problems in Emerging Markets?" The chapter explores how alternative franchising models—particularly in smaller investor groups—are evolving and the role that ownership and decision rights play in franchise networks. The analysis points to the growing need for clear governance structures and financing concepts to minimize conflicts between franchisors and franchisees.

Moritz Martin Botts and Ömer Hurmacı close the volume with "Marketing Public Goods to Citizens: A Psychological Ownership Perspective on Urban Parks." Building on the concept of Psychological Ownership, the authors show how citizens can be encouraged to adopt more environmentally responsible behavior when they feel that a public area "belongs to us all." This emphasis on collective responsibility underscores how public goods can be sustainably maintained and enhanced if local communities are actively engaged.

These contributions represent the current state of research on technological, financial, and organizational innovations that support a sustainable, fair, and efficient advancement of our society. As such, this edited volume offers practitioners and academics alike valuable insights into the emerging topics that will shape economic structures and value chains in the coming years.

Editors:
Ela Sibel Bayrak Meydanoglu, Riza Öztürk,
Dilek Zamantili Nayir, and Müge Klein
10th November 2024, Istanbul

1. Integrating Generative Artificial Intelligence in Finance: Enhancing Financial Reporting and Quantitative Decision Making

Mehmet Hakan Özdemir, Tolga Tuzcuoğlu,** and Erencan Yavrucu**

ABSTRACT

This study investigates the integration of generative artificial intelligence (GenAI) in the field of finance, specifically focusing on enhancing financial reporting and quantitative decision making through AI-driven tools. The study highlights two key applications, which are the Financial Statement Analysis Assistant and the Financial Benchmarking Tool. These applications emphasize advanced chatbots operated by GenAI to improve efficiency, accuracy, and decision making in companies. In addition, they automate the analysis and presentation of financial data, potentially reducing reliance on human financial analysts while offering real-time insights and customized reports for stakeholders. The results show the capacity of GenAI to transform financial reporting by ensuring regulatory compliance and minimizing errors, and to enhance strategic planning. This study offers significant insights for practitioners and researchers, demonstrating how GenAI can be seamlessly integrated into financial operations to improve operational efficiency, decision making, and competitiveness.

Keywords: Generative artificial intelligence, Finance, Financial reporting, Quantitative decision making

Introduction

AI has experienced significant growth in recent years owing to advancements in hardware and software technologies (Kalota, 2024). Nonetheless, despite the extensive and interdisciplinary body of literature in Artificial Intelligence (AI), a universally accepted definition remains absent (Stone et al., 2022). Nilsson (2010) offered this helpful definition: "Artificial intelligence is that activity devoted to making machines intelligent, and intelligence is that

*Faculty of Economic and Administrative Sciences, Department of Business Administration, Turkish-German University, Istanbul, Turkey.
**Robert Bosch GmbH
Email: <hakan.ozdemir@tau.edu.tr>

quality that enables an entity to function appropriately and with foresight in its environment." Another definition was provided by Jaggia et al. (2023): "Artificial Intelligence is used to describe computer systems that demonstrate human-like intelligence and cognitive abilities, such as deduction, pattern recognition, and the interpretation of complex data." These definitions are actually similar in that they place a strong focus on machines behaving "intelligently" like humans. For computers and machines to behave intelligently, they must acquire knowledge, thus, the phrase machine learning. Machine learning constitutes a subset of AI (Kalota, 2024). However, rather than predicting anything based on a pre-existing dataset, GenAI might be compared to a machine learning model that is trained to generate new data. A system that learns to generate additional items similar to the training data is referred to as a GenAI system (Zewe, 2023). GenAI utilizes machine learning, neural networks, and various methodologies to analyze patterns and information from training data to generate new content (such as text, images, and music). Consequently, GenAI can now be employed for diverse tasks, including generating customized content and optimizing business operations (Ooi et al., 2023).

The basic purpose of financial reporting is to offer high-quality financial reporting information concerning economic entities, generally financial in nature, helpful for economic decision making. Due to the fact that it will positively affect capital providers and other stakeholders in making decisions regarding investment, credit, and other similar resource allocations, providing high-quality financial reporting information is vital since it will enhance the overall efficiency of the market (Beest et al., 2009).

Numerous recent studies examine the application of GenAI in the financial sector. In a study, Chen et al. (2023) investigate the recent advancements of GenAI in the financial and business sectors, mention its beneficial applications, present examples of current GenAI tools, and illustrate its potential to transform data analysis in academic and business contexts. To evaluate the capacity of GenAI in facilitating decision making inside financial markets, they use ChatGPT to ascertain business opinions toward environmental policies by analyzing language derived from corporate financial statements. The results show that ChatGPT sentiment scores can predict stock return performance and a company's risk management capability. GenAI's limitations and challenges are also highlighted in the study. Rane (2023) examines the roles and challenges of GenAI in finance and accounting. In the financial sector, ChatGPT facilitates customer interactions by providing personalized advice, real-time market analysis, and investment strategies. ChatGPT optimizes algorithmic trading, risk management, and fraud detection by managing substantial volumes of data. In accounting, AI models reduce operational expenses and human errors by automating data entry, categorization, and report generation. But using ChatGPT and other AI technologies in finance and accounting brings up some ethical concerns, such as data privacy, security, and biased decision-making algorithms. Although AI systems need to develop in order to work in financial markets, they have a lot of potential in these fields. Krause (2023a) examines GenAI and large language models (LLMs) in finance. The study concentrates on ChatGPT, Bard, and Bing AI because they improve financial analysis, automate processes, and provide insights. Natural language processing (NLP), financial analysis, and decision making are optimized by language generation through these models. The focus is to efficiently prompt and validate the AI-generated results to assess the strengths and limitations of each model. AI models in finance can be evaluated based on ROUGE, BLEU, accuracy, precision, and perplexity. Issues of context awareness, factual accuracy, bias, fairness, and domain adaptation require attention regardless of ability. Future goals for AI models in finance include domain adaptation, knowledge integration, explainability, interpretability, and ethics. In their study, Demyttenaere et al. (2023) discuss GenAI's ability to transform financial processes, improve decision making, and increase risk management. AI has already improved finance teams' content creation and research, but the article predicted that AI "copilots" will work alongside humans. The authors also discuss accuracy, data security, and privacy issues that must be addressed to fully utilize AI in financial operations. Gopika (2024) discusses how GenAI transformed accounting and finance. The study highlights how generative tools are transforming accounting procedures, such as automating payroll, audits, and financial forecasting, which overall improves efficiency and precision. AI can analyze large datasets to identify trends and make predictions. However, there may also be drawbacks such as data security, job loss, and excessive use of AI. The study emphasizes that despite the many advantages of AI, human judgment is still needed to overcome challenges in business. The study by Linkon et al. (2024) discusses the transformative role of GenAI and LLMs in different sectors. Increasing use of GenAI can solve real-world problems in various sectors, such as finance, manufacturing, and healthcare. The study underscores the importance of employing AI for the benefit of humanity while contributing to the discourse on AI ethics, governance, and regulation. The report by Zec (2024) examines the integration of GenAI within the fintech sector. GenAI improves customer interactions, as well as financial services. This results in the development of customized financial products and the improvement of operational efficiency. This study again highlights the ethical and legal issues that may arise from the use of AI. A balance must be established between innovation and risk management to foster compliance and trust within the fintech sector. As in previous studies, Cassidy and Hittner (2024) also mention the impact of GenAI on financial reporting and accounting in their study. As GenAI automates many routine tasks, professionals have more time for strategic decision making. However, the study emphasizes the necessity of human oversight in checking the accuracy of the outputs generated by AI, and it is mentioned that comprehensive training should be provided to optimize the use of GenAI in financial reporting and decision making. Liu and Wang (2024) investigate the adoption of GenAI in the provision of virtual financial advice and financial market analysis. GenAI's ability to generate creative content and deliver accurate predictions has the potential to influence financial decision making. The study compares GenAI with traditional models to emphasize the advantages, and subsequently explores emerging trends. It also explains how GenAI can be used in finance for decision making, intelligent investment guidance, and risk evaluation.

To summarize, owing to advancements in GenAI, the finance world has experienced a vast change in the fields of financial reporting, strategic decision making and daily operations. The implications of GenAI have been mainly used in process automation, predictive analytics and chance and risk evaluation. In addition, it can be concluded that the current body of literature mainly focuses on how GenAI-based solutions are applied in the daily routine of financial management. Likewise, it has been observed that recent studies discussed the advantages and challenges of GenAI applications in the financial sector and how it is likely to develop in the future.

This study aims to contribute to the current literature by addressing the gaps concerning the practical application of GenAI to financial reporting and quantitative decision making. While existing research has focused on the theoretical potential and ethical considerations of GenAI, fewer studies have elaborated on its operational implementation in the field of finance. Accordingly, by discussing concrete examples of how GenAI can be used as an instrument in daily financial operations, this study wants to showcase the potential of GenAI for operational efficiency, regulatory compliance, and decision-making accuracy in an effort to provide a basis for future research in financial transformation.

Method

This study qualitatively investigates the application of GenAI in finance. Two potential use cases were identified to show how GenAI can improve financial reporting and quantitative decision making in organizations.

The two use cases are methodically examined in detail regarding their financial importance, expected benefits, implementation requirements, and potential obstacles. To this end, literature and practical experiences are put together to illustrate the practical and strategic implications of integrating GenAI into financial operations. The study thus aims to provide valuable insights for academics, practitioners, and policy makers interested in the future of financial technology.

Findings

In this study, the Financial Statement Analysis Assistant and the Financial Benchmarking Tool were selected as practical examples to show the application of GenAI in finance. The reason for this preference exclusively on these two applications was due to their representation of key functions in corporate finance and financial management, which are financial reporting and performance comparison, respectively. In addition, it was concluded that the selected application areas offered improvement potentials in terms of financial analysis and decision making. In addition, the implementation of the Financial Statement Analysis Assistant and the Financial Benchmarking Tool underlined the long-term benefits of GenAI as they addressed the importance as well as the need for automation, efficiency, and accuracy in diverse financial operations.

Financial Statement Analysis Assistant

The rapid evolution of GenAI has marked an exciting new era that allows the implementation of modern technology to transform and enhance profitability in various spheres of finance (Krause, 2023b). The Financial Statement Analysis Assistant is one of the most impressive innovations, which provides executive reports based on executive summaries from numerous financial statements. This particular use case would be especially relevant for organizations wishing to streamline their internal processes of financial reporting, improve the quality of decisions made, or reduce the amount of time and resources that go into manual, judgment-driven analysis.

Though they are a basic component of companies' financial communication worldwide, financial statements play an important role in informing stakeholders about the financial viability, performance, and focus of the company. For so many years, extracting high-level summaries out of such documents has proven to be a time-consuming task that requires vast resources. The Assistant, however, applies GenAI in regard to the proactive summarization of relevant financial information, which is significant considering the fast pace of doing business today. This is, however, more targeted towards executives and decision makers who need to quickly assess the financial position of an organization without having to get into the details of the financial statements.

The Financial Statement Analysis Assistant improves the decision-making process for the stakeholders by providing short and clear summaries. This application is relevant for financial analysts because it allows them to lessen the use of data analysis so that they can perform tasks that are more important, like planning and managing risk for the organization.

The usage of the Financial Statement Analysis Assistant comes with various advantages, some of which stand to improve further the productivity and the performance of financial management in any given company (Qiu et al., 2024).

1. Time Efficiency: One of the key advantages of the Financial Statement Analysis Assistant relates to the reduction in the time that would have been spent on carrying out the analysis of the financial statements. Whereas such processes in the past may have taken a number of hours or even days to perform, today, that entire process can take only a few

minutes. This kind of efficiency is particularly important, especially for businesses operating in dynamic industries where decisions have to be made quickly.
2. Consistency and Accuracy: Financial statements are prone to being biased, especially when a single person manually evaluates all financial documents, since human judgment may be erroneous. To some extent, the Financial Statement Analysis Assistant reduces this by providing consistent and accurate reports so that the users do not have to rely on incorrect information.
3. Enhanced Positional Assessment: Executives and managers are able to utilize the information and complete the appropriate response in a timely manner by organizing the complex financial information into meaningful, short, and actionable information. The tool provides management with appropriate information whenever required, whether to present the company's status in a meeting or to analyze the financial status of the company before a big investment.
4. Scalability: The Financial Statement Analysis Assistant is able to scale up or down to fit the needs of companies of different sizes. AI algorithms of the tool's platform can handle a lot of information effectively and accurately, whether it involves financial statement analysis for a small company or a huge international corporation.

The successful implementation of the Financial Statement Analysis Assistant entails various critical technical and organizational factors.

1. Format and Document Management: The tool requires suitable structural documentation, such as financial statements that may be kept in different forms and on various systems. Organizations should put in place appropriate document management and retrieval systems that the tool will use effectively. Furthermore, it is important to ensure the quality of financial data in terms of accuracy, completeness, and up-to-dateness.
2. AI Model Training and Development: Behind the Financial Statement Analysis Assistant are its major components, which are AI models, most of which are NLP-based. These models need to be effective from the perspective of providing focused summarization of information and, as such, should be trained on a wide range of various varying financial statement documents. Continuous training of the model and its updates

will be critical in making sure that the tool is in line with the changes in financial reporting policies and practices.

3. User Interface Design: It is imperative that the tool is equipped with capabilities that allow users to simply use the finance documents to upload them to the software and view the summaries generated. The interface ought to be easy to operate with maximum lack of effort for training before use. In addition, it must have functional and change capabilities that allow it to be changed according to users' needs.
4. Compliance and Security: Given the private environments of financial data, the Financial Statement Analysis Assistant must deploy conforming to strict security protocols. Data encryption, secure storage options, and access controls are part of this process in order to avoid breaches or unauthorized access. Furthermore, organizations need to make sure that the tool is compliant with relevant regulations, especially those related to financial reporting and data protection.

However, there are several challenges that an organization has to deal with when implementing the Financial Statement Analysis Assistant, even though it brings in a lot of advantages.

1. Data Quality and Formatting: The tool's summaries depend to a large extent on the quality, format, and accuracy of the input data. Financial statements that have not been well formatted or whose records are inconsistent can make summary outputs inaccurate or incomplete. Therefore, it is imperative for organizations that any financial documentation uploaded within the application follows proper order and established formats.
2. Making sense of AI models: In NLP technology, AI models can produce overly complex and ambiguous outputs. This creates a continuous need to revise the models in use as people have trouble understanding how the AI-based summaries relate to the content of the original documents.
3. User Adoption: The success of the Financial Statement Analysis Assistant lies in how well it will be accepted by the different groups of users. Trust in AI-generated summaries may be challenging for generic users who are used to doing financial reports in a more classical manner. Therefore, organizations should provide training and demonstrate both reliability and accuracy of the technology used to enhance trust in its outputs.

4. Compatibility with existing processes: The system has to integrate well within the current finance systems and processes within an organization. This could mean major changes to already implemented processes, which may result in resource wastage and disruption. In this context, companies should try to gradually reduce the discomfort that may occur during the adaptation process.

The Financial Statement Analysis Assistant is one of the early tools that fundamentally departs from earlier instances by shedding light on a new use of GenAI in the financial services domain. Thus, this instrument assists in the extraction and summarization of financial information in an automated way and accordingly offers many benefits, such as saving time, providing accurate information, and improving decision making. However, before these systems are deployed, it is important to understand as well as address issues related to the quality of data, the AI model, user interface, and regulatory requirements. The organizations, once faced with the above problems, can market the Financial Statement Analysis Assistant to enhance the process of financial reporting and decision making faster than their competitors.

Financial Benchmarking Tool

As a compilation of competitors' financial statements and annual reports, the Financial Benchmarking Tool is a commercial application of GenAI technology. In the process of performing the comparative analysis, this tool generates assessments of key financial theories and other trends and directs them to facilitate the growth of the organization in the competitive sphere.

Financial benchmarking is a process where rival companies or organizations are used to gauge the financial productivity of a particular organization, assessing its strengths, weaknesses, opportunities, and threats. Often, however, this activity is very labor-intensive, requiring the gathering, processing, and sub-analysis of the fiscal document statistics from various financial institutions. Tasks are automated with the Financial Benchmarking Tool to make use of GenAI in improving the work instead of and the quality of insights provided (Brito et al., 2019).

In an environment that is constantly changing, whether due to new technology or new competitors, an individual always has to know where his or her organization is relative to other organizations within the same field. When using this tool, finance professionals receive relevant information in time that is correct concerning trends; hence, they ascertain advanced decision making on investment policies, reducing unnecessary expenses, or enhancing the productivity or performance of the processes of the organization. In addition, because of bringing in AI technologies, it goes without saying that this tool will be able to cover even more sophisticated trends in such economic indicators and metrics that would be overlooked if the traditional analysis were relied upon, thereby shedding more light on what is happening in the economy.

The Financial Benchmarking Tool's implementation has a lot of noteworthy benefits that can boost financial performance and improve strategic decision making in organizations.

1. Superior Strategy Development: By providing an in-depth analysis of rival companies' financial statements, this tool enables businesses to assess their performance against industry benchmarks. Such analysis may inform strategic decisions on how to position themselves in the market, adjust pricing policies, or allocate resources. For instance, if it indicates that one competitor is achieving better profit margins through effective cost management, then similar practices can be looked into by the organization.
2. Enhanced Financial Performance: The useful insights drawn from the tool may lead to significant positive changes in the financial results. The tool may pinpoint poorly performing sectors compared with rivals; therefore, management would have to investigate them and solve any problems found therein. On the other hand, it can also emphasize some areas where they are ahead of the competition, showing that those advantages could still be exploited even further.
3. Time and Cost Efficiency: Automation changes the way time and resources are used in financial benchmarking by automating data analysis. For example, conventional benchmarking practices often involve manual data collection, complicated calculations, and detailed analysis, which make them laborious and prone to human errors. GenAI-enabled tools make such activities faster, more accurate, and with less human input.
4. Informed Decision Making: This tool is able to extract key financial measures and trends for decision makers; hence, enough information

is provided for them concerning strategic options. This is very helpful, especially in unpredictable industries with rapidly changing financial situations or competitive environments. The tool produces prompt insights so that decisions are based on the latest relevant information available.

There are a few important technical and operational factors that should be taken into consideration by organizations coping with implementing of the Financial Benchmarking Tool efficiently.

1. Raw Data Availability and Assimilation: The tool requires a number of inputs of financial data to be in place, which include annual statements and reports belonging to the competition. Such systems for sourcing and merging all these types of information probably involve contracting out to data providers or harvesting articles and press releases from the Internet to obtain the required financial data. In order for the tool to function properly, it suffices to claim that all the inputs are clean and all the data employed are accurate.
2. Superior AI Algorithms: The Financial Benchmarking Tool seeks the deployment of GenAI models, which are at the center of this tool and will be able to undertake complicated analytical tasks such as finance report summarization using NLP, spotting trends through machine learning, and suggesting actions to be taken. To ensure proper use, these models should first be loaded with large amounts of data that are related to what they will be modeling. Also, continuous improvements through re-training have to be done to ensure that precision and relevance are kept at very high levels.
3. User Interface Design: The quality design will enhance the usability of the tool. The interface should permit the users to upload the financial documents with ease, alter the parameters for benchmarking, and follow the insights it provides further. Indirectly, it should also facilitate the preparation of templates for reports, which could then be supplied to different relevant persons.
4. Compliance and Security: As mentioned in the previous paragraphs of this study, financial reports and data are very valuable elements that, especially, global companies try to protect with care and very strict measures. This demands the adherence to and application of very high encryption and access control levels to the data in the system to guard

it against unauthorized access or invasion. In addition, organizations should also guarantee the alignment between the use of the tool and established compliance guidelines in the industry in question, especially on the challenges of using some information, for instance, financial information in the banking or health sectors.

Organizations must address solutions for challenges that are encountered when trying to implement the Financial Benchmarking Tool as a way of improving the benchmarking process.

1. Data Quality and Availability: As with any software and system involving AI, the quality and accuracy of input data in the Financial Benchmarking Tool are the most important element for the proper functioning of the system. There might be instances of erroneous conclusions and advice as a result of either incomplete or faulty financial records. Hence, there is a need for proper investment in data management practices.
2. Model Interpretability and Bias: Despite the strengths of the AI models, it is inevitable that there are some results that cannot be easily explained or that come out as negative biases. If there is bias in the data used to train the AI or if it favors certain sectors or regions, it will affect the smooth functioning of the system. So, it becomes necessary for such institutions to periodically update and enhance the AI models so that the output is legal and non-biased.
3. Integration with Existing Workflows: Operating with the Financial Benchmarking Tool may involve a radical change in processes or systems. Finance practitioners attached to the conventional model may stand a chance to oppose this change, and thus, this innovation will be adopted slowly. Therefore, it is crucial that companies not only integrate appropriate operational instructions for end-users but also deliver adequate training materials that support the solution application within designated decision-making contexts.
4. Regulatory Considerations: The regulators' interest regarding AI is nowadays shifting toward its capabilities in financial analysis. It is a duty for the organizations to try to ensure that the tool works according to the laws and regulations in place for that particular country, encompassing the proper use of data, standards of financial reporting, and mainly ethical concerns on the usage of AI. Failure to do so

will unfortunately attract lawsuits to damage the reputation that the organizations hold.

The Financial Benchmarking tool is an illustrative example of how GenAI can greatly impact the financial sector through strategic optimization, efficiency in operations, as well as making informed choices. It is essential for any company using this tool to consider the following factors in order to have all its benefits: data quality management strategies; the development process for AI models; user interfaces that are easy and simple to use; and compliance with legal requirements related to using that technology. If these issues are taken into account by firms, they will have the capacity to use the benchmarking tool to outperform their peers and achieve improved financial outcomes over an extended period.

Table 1 summarizes the comparison between the Financial Statement Analysis Assistant and the Financial Benchmarking Tool across several dimensions.

Table 1: Comparison of GenAI financial tools

Dimension	Financial Statement Analysis Assistant	Financial Benchmarking Tool
Predictive analytics	Moderate—Focuses on summarizing past data rather than future predictions	High—Identifies trends and patterns for competitive analysis
Risk assessment	Limited—Primarily helps with positional assessment rather than risk forecasting	Moderate—Aids in assessing industry risks by benchmarking against competitors
Time efficiency	High—Significantly reduces time in manual data review	High—Automates time-intensive benchmarking process
Consistency and accuracy	High—Automates consistency and reduces error in financial summaries	Moderate—Dependent on input data quality for accuracy
Scalability	High—Scalable to different organizational sizes	High—Scalable across diverse organizational and industry needs
User interface	User-friendly, enables easy upload and summary view	Customizable interface for detailed benchmarking options
Compliance and security	Strong focus on compliance, with secure data protocols	Strong focus on compliance, with secure data handling protocols

Discussion and Conclusions

With regard to finance, the advancement brought by GenAI is very visible in the reporting and the decision-making procedures. The two potential applications, the Financial Statement Analysis Assistant and the Financial Benchmarking Tool, were targeted in this study. Both these applications illustrate how GenAI can help enhance business activities involving finances and how organizations relate to such services.

The Financial Statement Analysis Assistant exhibits how GenAI improves the processes of extracting and summarizing financial information, thereby achieving time, cost, and quality benefits. The executive management summary generator tool extracts summarization from the financial statements, hence meeting the basic need for accurate and timely information that reduces the amount of time spent by decision makers on analysis as opposed to strategic thinking. The extent to which the tool can be used and the speed of producing the same outputs make it even more important in the financial world. In the same manner, the Financial Benchmarking Tool illustrates the operational benefits of GenAI that allow in-depth comparison of the financial statements of competing firms. In broad terms, it can be said that this software simplifies and speeds up a management task associated with benchmarking while providing the management with better knowledge of the competitive landscape where the company operates, and so enhancing the quality of strategic management, hence better returns. With the ability to identify patterns and generate insights out of large sets of data, the tool can become a key resource for organizations that seek to leverage competition.

Despite the clear benefits, the implementation of GenAI tools such as the Financial Statement Analysis Assistant and the Financial Benchmarking Tool requires thorough preparation and consideration. The essential elements comprise ensuring high-quality and accessible data, developing and maintaining advanced AI models, and designing user-friendly interfaces. Organizations must address the complexities of data security, regulatory compliance, and model interpretability to fully utilize the potential of GenAI in finance. This study clearly describes several formal and informal current barriers that organizations are likely to encounter in the process of deploying these tools. In order for these changes to be successful, issues such as insufficient data quality and availability, model bias, low user adoption, and lack of integration with existing systems and processes must be resolved. It can be noted that the enforcement of regulations around AI and indeed technology as a whole, especially within the scope of finance, is a dynamic affair which will require constant adjustments.

Future research should be directed towards the advancement of these tools as their precision, reliability, and user acceptance can be improved. It is also essential to look into how AI in finance operates concerning ethics, particularly in ensuring fairness, transparency, and accountability in AI-driven decision making.

In conclusion, the integration of GenAI into financial reporting and quantitative decision making holds immense promise for the financial sector. The Financial Statement Analysis Assistant and Financial Benchmarking Tool, as explored in this study, are indicative of the broader potential of AI to revolutionize financial practices. However, realizing this potential requires a balanced approach that addresses both the opportunities and challenges presented by AI. Through careful implementation and ongoing adaptation, organizations can leverage GenAI to achieve greater efficiency, accuracy, and strategic insight, ultimately driving their success in a competitive and rapidly evolving financial landscape.

Bibliography

Beest, F. V., Braam, G. J. M., & Boelens, S. (2009). *Quality of financial reporting: Measuring qualitative characteristics.* <https://repository.ubn.ru.nl//bitstream/handle/2066/74896/74896.pdf>.

Brito, E., Sifa, R., Bauckhage, C., Loitz, R., Lohmeier, U., & Pünt, C. (2019). A hybrid AI tool to extract key performance indicators from financial reports for benchmarking. In *Proceedings of the ACM Symposium on Document Engineering 2019 (DocEng '19)*. Association for Computing Machinery, New York, NY, USA, Article 36, pp. 1–4. <https://doi.org/10.1145/3342558.3345420>.

Cassidy, B., & Hittner, R. (2024, August 4). Empowering accounting professionals: The transformative role of Generative AI in accounting and financial reporting. *Deloitte.* <https://www2.deloitte.com/us/en/blog/accounting-finance-blog/2024/generative-ai-in-financial-reporting.html>.

Chen, B., Wu, Z., & Zhao, R. (2023). From fiction to fact: the growing role of generative AI in business and finance. *Journal of Chinese Economic and*

Business Studies, 21(4), 471–496. <https://doi.org/10.1080/14765284.2023.2245279>.

Demyttenaere, M., Roos, A., Sheth, H., Rodt, M., Harris, M., Khodabandeh, S., Fehling, R., Martines, D., & Grabowski, J. (2023, August 22). Generative AI in the finance function of the future. *BCG.* <https://www.bcg.com/publications/2023/generative-ai-in-finance-and-accounting>.

Gopika, S. S. (2024). Artificial intelligence in accounting and finance. *Recent Trends in Management and Commerce, 5*(2), 59–62. <https://doi.org/10.46632/rmc/5/2/12>.

Jaggia, S., Kelly, A., Lertwachara, K., & Chen, L. (2023). *Business analytics: Communicating with numbers* (2nd ed.). New York, NY, USA: McGraw Hill.

Kalota, F. (2024). A primer on generative artificial intelligence. *Education Sciences, 14*(2), 172. <https://doi.org/10.3390/educsci14020172>.

Krause, D. (2023a). Large language models and generative AI in finance: an analysis of ChatGPT, Bard, and Bing AI. *Bard, and Bing AI.* <http://dx.doi.org/10.2139/ssrn.4511540>.

Krause, D. (2023b). *Proper Generative AI Prompting for Financial Analysis* (May 20, 2023). Available at SSRN: <http://dx.doi.org/10.2139/ssrn.4453664>.

Linkon, A. A., Shaima, M., Sarker, M. S. U., Badruddowza, Nabi, N., Rana, M. N. U., Ghosh, S. K., Esa, H., & Chowdhury, F. R. (2024). Advancements and applications of generative artificial intelligence and large language models on business management: a comprehensive review. *Journal of Computer Science and Technology Studies, 6*(1), 225–232. <https://doi.org/10.32996/jcsts.2024.6.1.26>.

Liu, Y., & Wang, J. (2024). Analysis of financial market using generative artificial intelligence. *Academic Journal of Science and Technology, 11*(1), 21–25. <https://doi.org/10.54097/y17mrj84>.

Nilsson, N. J. (2010). *The Quest for Artificial Intelligence: A History of Ideas and Achievements.* Cambridge University Press.

Ooi, K. B., Tan, G. W. H., Al-Emran, M., Al-Sharafi, M. A., Capatina, A., Chakraborty, A., Dwivedi, Y. K., Huang, T. L., Kar, A. K, Lee, V. H., Loh, X. M., Micu, A., Mikalef, P., Mogaji, E., Pandey, N., Raman, R., Rana, N., P., Sarker, P., Sharma, A., Teng, C. I., Wamba, S. F., & Wong, L. W. (2023). The potential of generative artificial intelligence across disciplines: Perspectives and future directions. *Journal of Computer Information Systems*, 1–32. <https://doi.org/10.1080/08874417.2023.2261010>.

Qiu, Y., Duvvuri, V. C., Yadavalli, P., & Prasad, N. (2024). Evaluation of generative AI Q&A chatbot chained to optical character recognition models for financial documents. In *Proceedings of the 2024 8th International Conference on Machine Learning and Soft Computing (ICMLSC '24)*. Association for Computing Machinery, New York, NY, USA, pp. 101–110. <https://doi.org/10.1145/3647750.3647766>.

Rane, N. (2023). Role and challenges of ChatGPT and similar generative artificial intelligence in finance and accounting. *SSRN Electronic Journal*. <https://doi.org/10.2139/ssrn.4603206>.

Stone, P., Brooks, R., Brynjolfsson, E., Calo, R., Etzioni, O., Hager, G., Hirschberg, J., Kalyanakrishnan, S., Kamar, E., Kraus, S., Leyton-Brown, K., Parkes, D., Press, W., Saxenian, A., Shah, J., Tambe, M., & Teller, A. (2022). *Artificial intelligence and life in 2030: The one hundred year study on artificial intelligence*. <arXiv preprint arXiv:2211.06318>.

Zec, J. (2024, June 26). New "Genai Fintechs" are driving AI further into financial services—here's how. *Citi Ventures*. <https://www.citi.com/ventures/perspectives/opinion/genai-fintechs.html>.

Zewe, A. (2023). Explained: Generative AI. How do powerful generative AI systems like ChatGPT work, and what makes them different from other types of artificial intelligence? *MIT News*. <https://news.mit.edu/2023/explained-generative-ai-1109>.

2. The Impact of FoMO-Laden Limited Time Offers on Customer Behavior: The Moderating Role of Curved vs. Sharp Angled Presentation

Ferhat Sayın, Hilmi Berkay Abbasoğlu,* and Serdar Salih Durmuşoğlu***

ABSTRACT
Nowadays, companies frequently use scarcity strategies to attract customers' attention and help them make faster decisions. Scarcity strategies, which are frequently used especially by e-commerce platforms, both give customers an advantage and increase the company's sales. Scarcity strategies with quantity or time constraints trigger customers' impulsive purchase intentions. This study investigates the effect of limited-time offers with different visual designs (curved and sharp-angled) on customers' fear of missing out and impulsive purchase intentions. Perceived attractiveness, perceived value, and fear of missing out are used as mediating variables in the study. Measuring the effect of limited time offers in different visual designs (curved and sharp-angled) will make both practical and theoretical contributions to the marketing world. The research is still in the development stage, and no data has been collected.

Keywords: Limited time offers, FoMO, Perceived attractiveness, Perceived value, Impulsive buying tendency, Visual design

Introduction

Scarcity strategies (limited time offers, limited quantity offers) are frequently used by marketing professionals. They are to increase demand from customers by limiting the supply of products or services that are already available. Sometimes these strategies are created by making the product or service available for purchase at a certain price for a limited period of time, sometimes by limiting sales to stocks (Cialdini, 1993). In fact, these scarcity strategies are based on a psychological phenomenon called the scarcity effect (Brock, 1968). This phenomenon, known in academic literature as the scarcity principle,

*Turkish-German University, Faculty of Economics and Business Administration, Department of Business Administration, Istanbul, Turkey
**Fonksiyonel Holding
Email: <ferhat.sayin@tau.edu.tr>

suggests that when people realize that something is scarce, the demand for it will increase.

Scarcity leads customers to find the product or service more attractive (Aggarwal et al., 2011) and subsequently perceive it as more valuable (Cialdini, 2009). There may be an increase in customers' fear of missing out (FoMO) as limited time offers encourage customers to make quick decisions, which may lead them to make unplanned purchases. FoMO has been defined as the FoMO on a rewarding event that has emerged with the increase in digitalization (Przybylski et al., 2013). In the marketing context, FoMO is frequently used to trigger customers and lead them to purchase behavior (Hodkinson, 2016). There are many studies investigating the FoMO level of users in digital environments (Alt, 2015; Hattingh et al., 2022; Jabeen et al., 2023). Good and Hyman (2020), in their study investigating the antecedents of FoMO in the marketing context, suggest that FoMO positively affects the purchase likelihood.

Customers have shifted from physical to digital markets. Digital advertising spending was over 600 billion dollars in 2023 and is expected to exceed 800 billion dollars in 2026 (Statista, 2023). While there are many techniques that appeal to customers' senses in physical stores, appealing to the senses is limited in digital stores. Digital stores affect customers' visual senses. Hoegg and Alba (2007) argue that the visual senses are a dominant sense that affects other senses. This makes it important how different visual designs offered on e-commerce sites affect customers. Previous research on limited time offers has investigated the message salience of the offer (Peng et al., 2018), the impact of the validity period of the offer on customers (Gierl et al., 2008), and its comparison with limited quantity offers (Jha et al., 2019). Customers' click behavior towards limited-time offers with different visual designs has not yet been investigated in the literature. The reason for investigating click behavior in limited-time offers is that sharing services platforms among e-commerce sites try to attract customers with limited-time offers. The growing number of sharing services that offer scarcity-based services that trigger a customer's FoMO, such as cars, bicycles, motorcycles, houses, rooms, etc. Due to the heavy use of limited-time offers in the sharing services industry, it is important to investigate the clicking behavior of customers towards visual designs in order to increase the sales figures of companies. Most sharing service companies offer limited-time offers to their customers, triggering the FoMO level of the customers and leading them to purchase. The research model examines customers' behavior towards limited time offers with different visual designs (curved vs. sharp angled) within the framework of the S-O-R model.

The research will make both theoretical and practical contributions by examining the effects of visual designs in limited-time offers on FoMO and impulsive buying behavior. This research is a developmental paper, and therefore, data have not yet been collected.

Literature Review

Scarcity strategies make the perception of existing products more valuable. Peng et al. (2018) argue that the phrase "valid for a limited time" increases the perceived value of the product by customers. Similarly, limited-time offers create a sense of urgency in consumers, leading to increased purchase intentions (Hanna et al., 2016). Aggarwal et al. (2011) argue that message salience (valid for 24 hours) influences purchase intentions more than message ambiguity (valid for a certain period of time) in limited-time offers. Another study on limited time offers examined the effects of the length of the limited time period on customers and found that too long a limited time period (e.g., 2 weeks) leads to procrastination, while too short a time period (e.g., five minutes) leads to dissatisfaction (Gierl et al., 2008). Gierl et al. (2008) also argue that limited-time offers increase the attractiveness of the product. Aggarwal and Vaidyanathan (2003) argue that limited-time offers increase the enthusiasm to purchase and decrease the motivation to switch to alternative products. Since limited-time offers usually include additional values such as discounts and free shipping, they are also seen as a financial gain by the customer (Wu & Hsing, 2006). Limited-time offers are more effective than quantity scarcity as they contain price indicators (Jha et al., 2019). Since limited-time offers increase perceived value, the research model suggests that perceived value will increase FoMO level.

FoMO has been defined as the fear of missing out on a rewarding event that has emerged with the increase in digitalization (Przybylski et al., 2013). FoMO, which is one of the topics studied especially in psychology literature, has been associated with depression (Elhai et al., 2016), smartphone addiction (Sha et al., 2019), sleep problems (Adams et al., 2016), decreased self-confidence (Buglass et al., 2016), scarcity on social media (Parveen et al., 2022), and excessive consumption behavior (Zhang et al., 2020). In the context of marketing, FoMO is considered as a temporary emotional state (Good & Hyman, 2021). Hodkinson (2016) defines FoMO as a process that affects customers' decision-making and suggests that younger customers experience FoMO more than older customers. While FoMO cognitively creates anxiety about missing out on a product or service during shopping, emotionally it can cause regret and anxiety (Hodkinson, 2016). Especially with the increase in digitalization, FoMO has become an effective phenomenon in customers' decision-making processes. This study suggests that different visual designs will affect FoMO differently.

Visual elements play a dominant role in the formation of responses to stimuli (Hoegg & Alba, 2007). Willis and Todoroc (2006) argue that reactions to visual stimuli are usually unconscious. Bar et al. (2006) suggest that visual stimuli influence judgments. Longstreet et al. (2021) suggest that the perceived aesthetics of a stimulus is related to visual attractiveness. In this case, if an image is attractive, the visual system automatically focuses on following the relevant image (Berridge, 2009). Visual attractiveness creates rewarding benefits for the individual, leading to a higher value attribution to the object. Orth and Crouch (2014) suggest that visual attractiveness increases attention and purchase intention. There are many studies on curved and sharp angles in the literature. Bertamini et al. (2015) argue that curved designs are more preferred over sharp angled designs. Curved design is often associated with friendliness (Bar & Neta, 2006), harmony (Gomez-Puerto et al., 2016), and softness (Becker et al., 2011). Wang et al. (2021) suggest that curved designs are associated with a feeling of rightness in customers. Sharp angled designs are often associated with harshness (Jiang et al., 2015), threat (Zhang et al., 2006), and difficulty (Westerman et al., 2012). Larson et al. (2007), while acknowledging the emotions associated with sharp angled design, argue that it is more attention-grabbing in a marketing context.

In their study on curved and sharp-angled designs on websites, Biswal et al. (2023) argue that curved designs affect the visual appeal, and this increases the click-through rate. Although the literature suggests that curved designs elicit more positive emotions in individuals, sharp angled designs may be more effective than curved designs in attention-grabbing offers, such as limited time offers. Furthermore, understanding the effects of these two designs on FoMO may provide practical solutions in terms of marketing strategies.

Theoretical Framework

Theoretical Underpinning: S-O-R Theory and Proposed Research Model

Before the S-O-R model emerged, stimuli and responses were used in the literature. Mehriban and Russell (1974) proposed the S-O-R model by adding the organism part to the S-R model. The organism part refers to the emotional and cognitive processes of individuals between stimuli and response. The S-O-R model has primarily been used in the field of psychology. Housten and Rothschild (1977) first used the S-O-R model in the marketing context. Watson et al. (2018) state that the S-O-R model can be used to explore stimuli in the marketing context and to understand experiential retailing and consumer behavior. In this research, limited-time offers with different visual designs are considered as stimuli (Figure 1). The study uses perceived attractiveness, perceived value, and FoMO in the organism part and impulsive purchase intention in the response part. The S-O-R model is an appropriate model to measure the effect of different visual designs on customers.

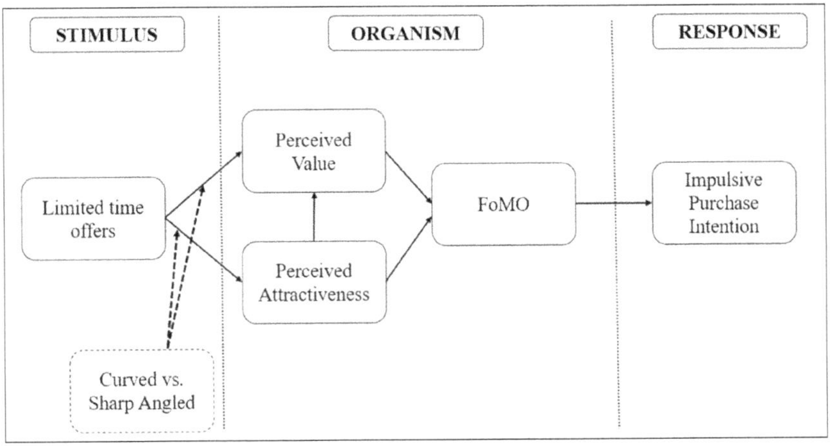

Figure 1: Proposed research model.

Limited-Time Offers

The concept of scarcity is defined in marketing literature as a situation in which products or services are not available in sufficient quantity or time to meet the needs of customers (Brock, 1968). Cialdini (1993) argues that scarcity can be used to persuade customers in marketing campaigns and categorizes scarcity into two groups: time and quantity scarcity. While quantity scarcity refers to the limited number of offers, time scarcity refers to the fact that the offer is valid for a certain period of time (Aggarwal et al., 2011; Cialdini, 1993). The focus of this study is on limited-time offers as a scarcity strategy. In limited-time offers, the offer is valid for a certain period of time (Aggarwal et al., 2011). While both supply and demand are determinants in quantity scarcity, time-based scarcity varies according to supply (Gierl & Huettl, 2008). For this reason, the competition between consumers that occurs in quantity scarcity does not occur in limited-time offers (Aggarwal et al., 2011; Jang et al., 2015).

Limited time offers differ from other scarcity strategies in that they are associated with scarcity of supply or offer rather than scarcity of product or service (Aggarwal et al., 2011). Customers feel the need to make decisions quickly in order not to miss the offer (Abendroth & Diehl, 2006). Limited-time offers provide benefits such as discounts, free shipping, and extra products for products that can be purchased within a certain period of time.

Perceived Attractiveness

Perceived attractiveness is a psychological phenomenon that explains how aesthetic attributes are evaluated based on certain criteria (Rubenstein, 2005). Scarcity strategies evoke a perception of quality in customers and trigger the feeling that the offer has an unmissable value compared to a normal offer (Brannon & Brock, 2001; Lynn, 1989). Vermallen and Robben (1994) argue that scarcity is used by customers as a heuristic shortcut. Therefore, scarcity strategies are perceived as more attractive by customers (Garnefeld et al., 2018). Aggarwal et al. (2011) argue that offers created with scarcity strategies increase attractiveness because they create a sense of winning in customers. The main reason why customers feel a sense of winning is the increase in perceived social utility due to the restriction of others' access to the offer, which leads customers to feel a sense of uniqueness (Aggarwal et al., 2011). Limited-time offers increase perceived attractiveness as they are part of scarcity strategies.

Therefore, we hypothesize as follows:

H_1: Limited-time offers have a positive effect on perceived attractiveness.

Perceived Value

Perceived value is defined as the customer's evaluation of the benefits provided by the product or service in relation to the costs incurred (Zeithaml, 1988). The value of the product has been explained in different ways, such as product quality (Buzzell & Gale, 1989), comparison of all products purchased (Sawyer & Dickson, 1984), and comparison with cost (Porter, 1985). When customers are convinced that a product or service is scarce, perceived value increases (Cialdini, 2009). Due to their nature, limited-time offers require the customer to make a purchase within a certain period of time in order to purchase the product. Aggarwal et al. (2011) argue that time-based scarcity strategies cause customers to make faster decisions, which positively affects perceived value.

The scarcity of a product or service increases the perceived value of the product or service according to commodity theory (Brock, 1968). Limited-time offers increase the perceived value of the product or service as they are temporarily available to customers (Broeder & Wentink, 2022).

Therefore, we hypothesize as follows;

H_2: Limited-time offers have a positive effect on perceived value.

Aggarwal et al. (2011) argue that offer attractiveness creates a sense of uniqueness for the customer. Since the feeling of uniqueness increases perceived value (Knight & Kim, 2007), perceived attractiveness plays a mediating role between limited time offers and perceived value in the model.

Therefore, we hypothesize as follows:

H_3: Perceived attractiveness positively affects perceived value.

Fear of Missing Out

Fear of Missing Out is a psychological phenomenon defined as the fear that individuals have of missing out on rewarding experiences that do not involve them (Przybylski et al., 2013). FoMO, which is linked to self-determination theory, arises when individuals' psychological needs for a sense of belonging and enough freedom are not met (Przybylski et al., 2013). Hodkinson (2016) argues that FoMO has a greater impact on purchase processes, especially for younger consumers. Customers believe that products are more attractive as a result of scarcity strategies (Caminal & Vives, 1996). However, customers who get the chance to own products offered through scarcity strategies may more easily believe that they are envied by other people (Gierl & Huettl, 2010). Previous studies suggest that the perception of scarcity increases perceived value (Gierl & Huettl, 2010; Wu et al., 2012). Since FoMO is defined as the fear of missing out on rewarding experiences, it can be expected to occur when perceived value and perceived attractiveness are high.

Therefore, we hypothesize as follows:

H_4: Perceived value has a positive effect on Fear of Missing Out.
H_5: Perceived attractiveness has a positive effect on Fear of Missing Out.

Impulsive Buying Tendency

Impulsive purchase intention is defined as the sudden and unplanned purchase of products by customers with an existing strong desire to buy (Rook & Fisher, 1995). Piron et al. (1991) consider impulsive buying behavior as buying behavior that occurs as a result of hedonic emotions triggered by a stimulus. Kacen and Lee (2002), on the other hand, define impulsive buying behavior as quick decision making and the desire to have the product quickly. Piron et al. (1991) consider impulsive buying behavior as buying behavior that occurs as a result of hedonic emotions triggered by a stimulus. Karen and Lee (2002), on the other hand, define impulsive buying behavior as quick decision making and the desire to have the product quickly. Verplanken and Herabadi (2001) propose that transient emotional interactions such as pleasure seeking, self-soothing, and individual reward expectancy underlie impulsive buying behavior. Defining FoMO as the fear of missing out on a rewarding experience satisfies the reward expectancy created by impulsive buying behavior. Individuals who experience FoMO are likely to be unable to make rational decisions. Zhang et al. (2020) argue that FoMO can affect impulsive purchase intention and that an increase in the FoMO level of an individual distances the individual from rationality. If an individual's FoMO level increases, both his/her interest in the product and willingness to pay increase (Good & Hyman, 2022; Zhang et al., 2020; Dinh & Lee, 2021). Aggarwal et al. (2011) argue that scarcity messages persuade customers to purchase more quickly.

Therefore, we hypothesize as follows:

H_6: Fear of Missing Out has a positive effect on impulsive buying tendency.

Visual Design (Curved vs. Sharp Angled) as a Moderator

Visual elements play a more dominant role in decision making than other stimuli (Hoegg & Alba, 2007). Reactions to visual stimuli are usually unconscious (Willis & Todoroc, 2006). Bar et al. (2006) suggest that judgments are influenced by visual elements. In the literature, curved designs are claimed to evoke positive emotions (Bar & Neta, 2006; Becker et al., 2011; Bertamini et al., 2015; Biswal et al., 2023; Gomez-Puerto et al., 2016; Wang et al., 2021), while sharp angled designs trigger more negative emotions (Jiang et al., 2015; Westerman et al., 2012; Zhang et al., 2006). However, Larson et al. (2007) argue that sharp-angled designs are more attention-grabbing in a marketing context. Gable and Harmon-Jones (2008) argue that visually appealing adaptations reduce attention and increase interest in the object. Corr and McNaughton (2012), in their research in the field of neuroscience, state that the attractiveness of visual stimuli triggers approach or avoidance behavior. In this research, visual design (curved vs. sharp angled) is used as a moderator to examine how visual design will affect individuals' FoMO level and whether this will increase impulsive purchase intention.

Therefore, we hypothesize as follows:

H_7: Virtual design (curved vs. sharp-angled) elements moderate the impact of limited-time offers on perceived value and perceived attractiveness.

Methodology

Research Design

This study aims to examine the effect of limited-time offers with different visual designs (curved and sharp-angled) on FoMO and impulsive buying intention through the S-O-R model. Due to its quasi-experimental design, the study aims to measure the response of randomly selected participants in a laboratory setting to limited-time offers with different visual designs (curved and sharp-angled). At the end of the research model, where perceived value and perceived attractiveness are used as mediators between limited time offer and FoMO, purchase likelihood will be measured. The study is a developmental research in which data have not yet been collected.

Structured manipulations may be investigated using a quasi-experimental design, which is more practical than using randomized assignment as in complete experimental investigations (Creswell, 2014). The experimental manipulation of the study is limited-time offers with different visual designs. Participants will be divided into two groups as experimental and control groups. The experimental group will be offered limited-time offers with curved design while the control group will be offered limited-time offers with sharp design.

Shiv and Fedorikhin (1999) argue that customers tend to underreact to discounts and promotional offers for products they are not interested in. For this reason, 10 products will be shown to the participants at the beginning of the experiment, and they will be asked to choose the product they are interested in. In this way, the results of the experiment will be prevented from being manipulated due to the participants' lack of interest in the product.

Data Collection

In the quasi-experimental study, half of the participants will be presented with limited-time offers with curved design while the other half will be presented with limited-time offers with sharp angled design. Afterwards, the participants will be given a questionnaire including perceived attractiveness, perceived value, FoMO, and impulse purchase intention questions, and asked to fill it out. This method is used in customer behavior research (Dholakia, 2000). The reason for conducting the research in a laboratory setting is to minimize external influences on the participants (Bagozzi, 1975).

Sampling Strategy

Hodkinson (2016) argues that FoMO has a greater impact on purchase processes, especially for younger consumers. For this reason, the convenience sampling method will be used in the study, and the sample will be selected from university students. All participants will be subjected to the experiment in a laboratory setting under equal conditions. Participants will be asked whether they have been exposed to limited-time offers in the last three months.

Measurement

The questionnaire to be given to the participants consists of manipulation control (Wu et al., 2012), perceived scarcity (Lee et al., 2015), perceived attractiveness

(Fuchs et al., 2015), perceived value (Sweeney & Soutar, 2001), FoMO (Zhang et al., 2020), and impulsive purchase intention (Rook & Fisher, 1995).

Data Analysis

Within the scope of the research, limited-time offers and their visual designs (curved and sharp-angled) will be used as experimental manipulations. Participants will be examined in two different groups according to the visual design. In this study, different statistical methods will be used to understand the effects of limited-time offers with different visual designs on FoMO and impulsive purchase intention (Field, 2013). An independent sample *t*-test will be used to determine whether there is a significant difference between the two groups.

There are four dependent variables (perceived attractiveness, perceived value, FoMO, and impulsive purchase intention). In order to examine these dependent variables simultaneously, multivariate analysis of variance (MANOVA) will be used (Hair et al., 2014). If the results of the MANOVA test are statistically significant, ANOVA will be applied for each variable.

Structural equation modeling and moderation analysis will be applied to examine the effects in more detail due to the manipulation of limited time offers and the visual design (curved and sharp-angled) of the offers as independent variables (Kline, 2015). In moderation analysis, differences between groups will be tested with multiple-group structural equation modeling. If the difference is statistically significant, Cohen's d effect size will be calculated to assess the magnitude of the differences (Cohen, 1988).

Anticipated Results and Contributions

Expected Findings

This study examines the impact of limited-time offers on FoMO. The fact that the offer is valid for a short period of time may create a sense of urgency in customers and thus increase FoMO and the tendency to make unplanned purchases. Among the expected findings of this study are the extent to which limited-time offers affect FoMO and whether this translates into an unplanned purchase tendency.

Another important expected finding is the extent to which perceived value and perceived attractiveness affect FoMO. Perceived attractiveness is the emotional state created by the way the product or offer is presented (Bloch, 1995). When the aesthetic factors of the way the offer is presented are attractive to the consumer, the possibility of missing the offer may trigger a strong FoMO feeling in consumers. Perceived attractiveness can increase perceived value. Perceived value can strongly trigger FoMO both because the offer is offered for a limited time and the customer benefits from the price, and because of the attractiveness of the aesthetic elements of the offer.

Previous research on limited-time offers has investigated the message salience of the offer (Peng et al., 2018), the impact of the validity period of the offer on customers (Gierl et al., 2008), and its comparison with limited quantity offers (Jha et al., 2019). This research investigates to what extent limited-time offers with different visual designs affect the FoMO level of the customer and subsequently how they affect unplanned purchases.

Finally, studies on the extent to which limited-time offers increase purchase intention are available in the literature. However, this study will reveal the effects of FoMO on unplanned purchases by trying to measure the unplanned purchase tendency through FoMO.

Theoretical Contributions

This study adds a new perspective to the literature by examining the effects of limited-time offers on FoMO in depth. It will examine in detail how FoMO-laden offers, which are frequently used by marketers with the widespread use of the Internet, affect consumer behavior.

On the other hand, it will make a new theoretical contribution by revealing the extent to which limited-time offers with different visual designs (curved and sharp angles) affect FoMO and by linking FoMO to the importance of visual presentations in marketing strategies. How visual design affects limited-time offers has not yet been investigated. This study will contribute to more efficient scarcity strategies by examining limited-time offers in different visual designs.

The effects of FoMO on impulsive purchase intention will contribute to a better understanding of consumers' purchasing psychology and reveal consumers' tendency to make unplanned decisions.

Managerial Implications

The findings of the study provide valuable insights for marketing professionals. The perception created by the differences between the visual designs of limited-time offers will increase the effectiveness of limited-time offers. Understanding which design is more effective for FoMOs will help to successfully convert offers into sales.

Impulse buying behavior is a topic that requires detailed examination in marketing strategies. Jabeen et al. (2023) in their study on the effects of FoMO on social media platforms state that social media platforms, businesses, and advertisers that pursue a FoMO-laden strategy will lead their customers or users to fatigue and then discontinuity in the medium and long term. It should be noted that excessively increasing the level of FoMO may cause negative emotional reactions in the medium and long term. Marketers should consider long-term customer satisfaction when using these strategies.

Conclusion

There are detailed studies on limited-time offers from different perspectives in the literature. This study contributes to more effective offers by measuring the impact of limited-time offers with different designs on FoMO. In addition, the extent to which FoMO increases the tendency to make unplanned purchases is another contribution of the study. Although this study contributes to increasing the effectiveness of FoMO-laden strategies, marketers should always consider medium and long-term customer satisfaction.

Bibliography

Abendroth, L. J., & Diehl, K. (2006). Now or never: Effects of limited purchase opportunities on patterns of regret over time. *Journal of Consumer Research*, *33*(3), 342–351. <https://doi.org/10.1086/508438>.

Adams, S. K., Williford, D. N., Vaccaro, A., Kisler, T. S., Francis, A., & Newman, B. (2016). The young and the restless: Socializing trumps sleep, fear of missing out, and technological distractions in first-year college students. *International Journal of Adolescence and Youth*, *22*(3), 337–348. <https://doi.org/10.1080/02673843.2016.1181557>.

Aggarwal, P., & Vaidyanathan, R. (2003). Use it or lose it: Purchase acceleration effects of time-limited promotions. *Journal of Consumer Behaviour, 2*(4), 393–403. <https://doi.org/10.1002/cb.116>.

Aggarwal, P., Jun, S. Y., & Huh, J. H. (2011). Scarcity messages. *Journal of Advertising, 40*(3), 19–30. <https://doi.org/10.2753/joa0091-3367400302>.

Alt, D. (2015). College students' academic motivation, media engagement and fear of missing out. *Computers in Human Behavior, 49*, 111–119. <https://doi.org/10.1016/j.chb.2015.02.057>.

Bagozzi, R. P. (1975). Social exchange in marketing. *Journal of the Academy of Marketing Science, 3*(2), 314–327. <https://doi.org/10.1177/009207037500300222>.

Bar, M., & Neta, M. (2006). Humans prefer curved visual objects. *Psychological Science, 17*(8), 645–648. <https://doi.org/10.1111/j.1467-9280.2006.01759.x>.

Bar, M., Neta, M., & Linz, H. (2006). Very first impressions. *Emotion, 6*(2), 269–278. <https://doi.org/10.1037/1528-3542.6.2.269>.

Becker, L., Van Rompay, T. J., Schifferstein, H. N., & Galetzka, M. (2010). Tough package, strong taste: The influence of packaging design on taste impressions and product evaluations. *Food Quality and Preference, 22*(1), 17–23. <https://doi.org/10.1016/j.foodqual.2010.06.007>.

Berridge, K. C. (2009). Wanting and liking: Observations from the neuroscience and psychology laboratory. *Inquiry*, *52*(4), 378–398. <https://doi.org/10.1080/00201740903087359>.

Bertamini, M., Palumbo, L., Gheorghes, T. N., & Galatsidas, M. (2015). Do observers like curvature or do they dislike angularity? *British Journal of Psychology, 107*(1), 154–178. <https://doi.org/10.1111/bjop.12132>.

Biswas, D., Abell, A., & Chacko, R. (2023). Curvy digital marketing designs: Virtual elements with rounded shapes enhance online click-through rates. *Journal of Consumer Research*. <https://doi.org/10.1093/jcr/ucad078>.

Bloch, P. H. (1995). Seeking the ideal form: Product design and consumer response. *Journal of Marketing, 59*(3), 16. <https://doi.org/10.2307/1252116>.

Brannon, L. A., & Brock, T. C. (2001). Scarcity claims elicit extreme responding to persuasive messages: Role of cognitive elaboration. *Personality and Social Psychology Bulletin*, *27*(3), 365–375. <https://doi.org/10.1177/0146167201273010>.

Brock, T. C. (1968). *Implications of Commodity Theory for Value Change* (pp. 243–275). Elsevier eBooks. <https://doi.org/10.1016/b978-1-4832-3071-9.50016-7>.

Broeder, P., & Wentink, E. (2022). Limited-time scarcity and competitive arousal in E-commerce. *The International Review of Retail Distribution and Consumer Research, 32*(5), 549–567. <https://doi.org/10.1080/09593969.2022.2098360>.

Buglass, S. L., Binder, J. F., Betts, L. R., & Underwood, J. D. (2016). Motivators of online vulnerability: The impact of social network site use and FOMO. *Computers in Human Behavior, 66*, 248–255. <https://doi.org/10.1016/j.chb.2016.09.055>.

Buzzell, R. D., & Gale, B. T. (1989). The PIMS principles: Linking strategy to performance. *Long Range Planning, 22*(3), 153. <https://doi.org/10.1016/0024-6301(89)90028-9>.

Caminal, R., & Vives, X. (1996). Why market shares matter: An information-based theory. *The RAND Journal of Economics, 27*(2), 221. <https://doi.org/10.2307/2555924>.

Cialdini, R. B. (1993). *Influence: The Psychology of Persuasion*. <http://cds.cern.ch/record/2010777>.

Cialdini, R. B. (2009). We have to break up. *Perspectives on Psychological Science, 4*(1), 5–6. <https://doi.org/10.1111/j.1745-6924.2009.01091.x>.

Cialdini, R. B. (2009). *Influence: Science and practice* (Vol. 4). Boston, MA: Pearson education.

Cohen, J. (1988). *Statistical Power Analysis for the Behavioral Sciences* (2nd ed.). Hillsdale, NJ: Lawrence Erlbaum Associates, Publishers.

Corr, P. J., & McNaughton, N. (2012). Neuroscience and approach/avoidance personality traits: A two stage (valuation–motivation) approach. *Neuroscience & Biobehavioral Reviews, 36*(10), 2339–2354. <https://doi.org/10.1016/j.neubiorev.2012.09.013>.

Creswell, J. W. (2014). *Research Design: Qualitative, Quantitative and Mixed Methods Approaches* (4th ed.). Thousand Oaks, CA: Sage.

Dholakia, U. M. (2000). Temptation and resistance: An integrated model of consumption impulse formation and enactment. *Psychology & Marketing, 17*(11), 955–982. <https://doi.org/10.1002/1520-6793(200011)17:11<955::AID-MAR3>3.0.CO;2-J>.

Dinh, T. C. T., & Lee, Y. (2021). "I want to be as trendy as influencers" – how "fear of missing out" leads to buying intention for products endorsed by social media influencers. *Journal of Research in Interactive Marketing, 16*(3), 346–364. <https://doi.org/10.1108/jrim-04-2021-0127>.

Elhai, J. D., Levine, J. C., Dvorak, R. D., & Hall, B. J. (2016). Fear of missing out, need for touch, anxiety and depression are related to problematic smartphone use. *Computers in Human Behavior, 63*, 509–516. <https://doi.org/10.1016/j.chb.2016.05.079>.

Field, A. (2013). *Discovering Statistics Using IBM SPSS Statistics: And Sex and Drugs and Rock "N" Roll* (4th ed.), Los Angeles, London, New Delhi: Sage.

Fuchs, C., Schreier, M., & Van Osselaer, S. M. (2015). The handmade effect: What's love got to do with it? *Journal of Marketing, 79*(2), 98–110. <https://doi.org/10.1509/jm.14.0018>.

Gable, P. A., & Harmon-Jones, E. (2008). Approach-motivated positive affect reduces breadth of attention. *Psychological Science, 19*(5), 476–482. <https://doi.org/10.1111/j.1467-9280.2008.02112.x>.

Garnefeld, I., Böhm, E., Klimke, L., & Oestreich, A. (2018). I thought it was over, but now it is back: customer reactions to ex post time extensions of sales promotions. *Journal of the Academy of Marketing Science, 46*(6), 1133–1147. <https://doi.org/10.1007/s11747-018-0600-y>.

Gierl, H., & Huettl, V. (2010). Are scarce products always more attractive? The interaction of different types of scarcity signals with products' suitability for conspicuous consumption. *International Journal of Research in Marketing, 27*(3), 225–235. <https://doi.org/10.1016/j.ijresmar.2010.02.002>.

Gierl, H., Plantsch, M., & Schweidler, J. (2008). Scarcity effects on sales volume in retail. *The International Review of Retail Distribution and Consumer Research, 18*(1), 45–61. <https://doi.org/10.1080/09593960701778077>.

Gómez-Puerto, G., Munar, E., & Nadal, M. (2016). Preference for curvature: a historical and conceptual framework. *Frontiers in Human Neuroscience, 9*. <https://doi.org/10.3389/fnhum.2015.00712>.

Good, M. C., & Hyman, M. R. (2020). Direct and indirect effects of fear-of-missing-out appeals on purchase likelihood. *Journal of Consumer Behaviour, 20*(3), 564–576. <https://doi.org/10.1002/cb.1885>.

Hair, J. F., Sarstedt, M., Hopkins, L., & Kuppelwieser, V. G. (2014). Partial least squares structural equation modeling (PLS-SEM). *European Business Review, 26*(2), 106–121. <https://doi.org/10.1108/ebr-10-2013-0128>.

Hanna, R. C., Swain, S. D., & Berger, P. D. (2016). Optimizing time-limited price promotions. *Journal of Marketing Analytics, 4*(2–3), 77–92. <https://doi.org/10.1057/s41270-016-0006-y>.

Hattingh, M., Dhir, A., Ractham, P., Ferraris, A., & Yahiaoui, D. (2022). Factors mediating social media-induced fear of missing out (FoMO) and social media fatigue: A comparative study among Instagram and Snapchat users. *Technological Forecasting and Social Change, 185*, 122099. <https://doi.org/10.1016/j.techfore.2022.122099>.

Hodkinson, C. (2016). 'Fear of Missing Out' (FOMO) marketing appeals: A conceptual model. *Journal of Marketing Communications, 25*(1), 65–88. <https://doi.org/10.1080/13527266.2016.1234504>.

Hoegg, J., & Alba, J. W. (2007). Taste perception: More than meets the tongue. *Journal of Consumer Research, 33*(4), 490–498. <https://doi.org/10.1086/510222>.

Houston, M. J., & Rothschild, M. L. (1977). *A Paradigm for Research on Consumer Involvement.*

Jabeen, F., Tandon, A., Sithipolvanichgul, J., Srivastava, S., & Dhir, A. (2023). Social media-induced fear of missing out (FoMO) and social media fatigue: The role of narcissism, comparison and disclosure. *Journal of Business Research, 159*, 113693. <https://doi.org/10.1016/j.jbusres.2023.113693>.

Jang, W. E., Ko, Y. J., Morris, J. D., & Chang, Y. (2015). Scarcity message effects on consumption behavior: Limited edition product considerations. *Psychology and Marketing, 32*(10), 989–1001. <https://doi.org/10.1002/mar.20836>.

Jha, S., Dutta, S., & Koksal, A. (2019). Effectiveness of monetary discounts: Comparing quantity scarcity and time restriction. *Journal of Consumer Marketing, 36*(7), 901–910. <https://doi.org/10.1108/jcm-07-2018-2763>.

Jiang, Y., Gorn, G. J., Galli, M., & Chattopadhyay, A. (2015). Does your company have the right logo? How and why circular- and angular-logo shapes influence brand attribute judgments. *Journal of Consumer Research, 42*(5), 709–726. <https://doi.org/10.1093/jcr/ucv049>.

Kacen, J. J., & Lee, J. A. (2002). The influence of culture on consumer impulsive buying behavior. *Journal of Consumer Psychology, 12*(2), 163–176. <https://doi.org/10.1207/s15327663jcp1202_08>.

Kim, E. Y., & Knight, D. K. (2007). A path analytic exploration of consumer information search in online clothing purchases. *Journal of the Korean Society of Clothing and Textiles, 31*(2), 1721–1732.

Kline, R. B. (2015). *Principles and Practice of Structural Equation Modeling.* Guildford Press.

Knight, D. K., & Young Kim, E. (2007), "Japanese consumers' need for uniqueness: Effects on brand perceptions and purchase intention," *Journal of Fashion Marketing and Management, 11*(2), 270–280. <https://doi.org/10.1108/13612020710751428>.

Larson, C. L., Aronoff, J., & Stearns, J. J. (2007). The shape of threat: Simple geometric forms evoke rapid and sustained capture of attention. *Emotion, 7*(3), 526–534. <https://doi.org/10.1037/1528-3542.7.3.526>.

Longstreet, P., Valacich, J., & Wells, J. (2021). Towards an understanding of online visual aesthetics: An instantiation of the composition perspective. *Technology in Society, 65*, 101536. <https://doi.org/10.1016/j.techsoc.2021.101536>.

Lynn, M. (1989). Scarcity effects on desirability: Mediated by assumed expensiveness? *Journal of Economic Psychology, 10*(2), 257–274. <https://doi.org/10.1016/0167-4870(89)90023-8>.

Mehrabian, A., & Russell, J. A. (1974). *An Approach to Environmental Psychology.* <http://ci.nii.ac.jp/ncid/BA0718977X?l=en>.

Orth, U. R., & Crouch, R. C. (2014). Is beauty in the aisles of the retailer? Package processing in visually complex contexts. *Journal of Retailing, 90*(4), 524–537. <https://doi.org/10.1016/j.jretai.2014.05.004>.

Parveen, H., Ajina, A. S., Habbas, N. S. M., Al-Faryan, M. a. S., & Khaled, A. S. (2022). Buy now or regret later: Social media-induced panic buying of medical supplies during COVID-19. *Innovative Marketing, 18*(3), 197–206. <https://doi.org/10.21511/im.18(3).2022.17>.

Peng, L., Zhang, W., Wang, X., & Liang, S. (2018). Moderating effects of time pressure on the relationship between perceived value and purchase intention in social E-commerce sales promotion: Considering the impact of product involvement. *Information & Management, 56*(2), 317–328. <https://doi.org/10.1016/j.im.2018.11.007>.

Piron, F. (1991). Defining impulse purchasing. *Advances in Consumer Research, 18*, 509–514.

Porter, M. E. (1985). *Competitive Advantage: Creating and Sustaining Superior Performance*. <http://ci.nii.ac.jp/ncid/BA00852365>.

Przybylski, A. K., Murayama, K., DeHaan, C. R., & Gladwell, V. (2013). Motivational, emotional, and behavioral correlates of fear of missing out.

Computers in Human Behavior, 29(4), 1841–1848. <https://doi.org/10.1016/j.chb.2013.02.014>.

Rook, D. W., & Fisher, R. J. (1995). Normative influences on impulsive buying behavior. *Journal of Consumer Research, 22*(3), 305. <https://doi.org/10.1086/209452>.

Rubenstein, A. J. (2005). Variation in perceived attractiveness. *Psychological Science, 16*(10), 759–762. <https://doi.org/10.1111/j.1467-9280.2005.01610.x>.

Sawyer Alan G., & Dickson Peter R. (1984), Psychological perspectives on consumer response to sales promotion. In E. Jocz Katherine (Ed.) *Research on Sales Promotions: Collected Papers*. Cambridge, MA: Marketing Science Institute, pp. 1–21.

Sha, P., Sariyska, R., Riedl, R., Lachmann, B., & Montag, C. (2018). Linking Internet communication and smartphone use disorder by taking a closer look at the Facebook and WhatsApp applications. *Addictive Behaviors Reports, 9*, 100148. <https://doi.org/10.1016/j.abrep.2018.100148>.

Shiv, B., & Fedorikhin, A. (1999). Heart and mind in conflict: The interplay of affect and cognition in consumer decision making. *Journal of Consumer Research, 26*(3), 278–292. <https://doi.org/10.1086/209563>.

Statista (2023), Digital advertising spending worldwide from 2021–2026. *Statista*, Last Accessed September 25, 2024. <https://www.statista.com/statistics/237974/online-advertisingspending-worldwide/>.

Sweeney, J. C., & Soutar, G. N. (2001). Consumer perceived value: The development of a multiple item scale. *Journal of Retailing, 77*(2), 203–220. <https://doi.org/10.1016/s0022-4359(01)00041-0>.

Verhallen, T. M., & Robben, H. S. (1994). Scarcity and preference: An experiment on unavailability and product evaluation. *Journal of Economic Psychology, 15*(2), 315–331. <https://doi.org/10.1016/0167-4870(94)90007-8>.

Verplanken, B., & Herabadi, A. (2001). Individual differences in impulse buying tendency: Feeling and no thinking. *European Journal of Personality, 15*(1_suppl), S71–S83. <https://doi.org/10.1002/per.423>.

Wang, J., Zhang, X., & Jiang, J. (2021). Healthy-Angular, unhealthy-circular: Effects of the fit between shapes and healthiness on consumer food preferences. *Journal of Business Research, 139*, 740–750. <https://doi.org/10.1016/j.jbusres.2021.10.012>.

Watson, A., Alexander, B., & Salavati, L. (2018). The impact of experiential augmented reality applications on fashion purchase intention. *International Journal of Retail & Distribution Management, 48*(5), 433–451. <https://doi.org/10.1108/ijrdm-06-2017-0117>.

Westerman, S. J., Gardner, P. H., Sutherland, E. J., White, T., Jordan, K., Watts, D., & Wells, S. (2012). Product design: Preference for rounded versus angular design elements. *Psychology and Marketing, 29*(8), 595–605. <https://doi.org/10.1002/mar.20546>.

Willis, J., & Todorov, A. (2006). First impressions. *Psychological Science, 17*(7), 592–598. <https://doi.org/10.1111/j.1467-9280.2006.01750.x>.

Wu, C., & Hsing, S. (2006). Less is more: How scarcity influences consumers' value perceptions and purchase intents through mediating variables, *Journal of American Academy of Business, 9*(2), 125–132.

Wu, W., Lu, H., Wu, Y., & Fu, C. (2012). The effects of product scarcity and consumers' need for uniqueness on purchase intention. *International Journal of Consumer Studies, 36*(3), 263–274. <https://doi.org/10.1111/j.1470-6431.2011.01000.x >.

Zeithaml, V. A. (1988). Consumer perceptions of price, quality, and value: A means-end model and synthesis of evidence. *Journal of Marketing, 52*(3), 2–22. <https://doi.org/10.1177/002224298805200302>.

Zhang, Y., Feick, L., & Price, L. J. (2006). The impact of self-construal on aesthetic preference for angular versus rounded shapes. *Personality and Social Psychology Bulletin, 32*(6), 794–805. <https://doi.org/10.1177/0146167206286626>.

Zhang, Z., Jiménez, F. R., & Cicala, J. E. (2020). Fear of missing out scale: A self-concept perspective. *Psychology and Marketing, 37*(11), 1619–1634. <https://doi.org/10.1002/mar.21406>.

3. The Influence of Financing Decisions on Financial Performance and Value of Manufacturing Companies: Evidence from Turkey

Abdulrahman AlAbdeh and Mehtap Öner***

ABSTRACT

The underlying objective of this study is to explore the consequences of financing decisions on the financial performance and value of 138 manufacturing companies traded on Borsa Istanbul during the 2009–2022 time span. By utilizing a panel data framework, two dependent variables were adopted. While return on assets (ROA) is used as an accounting-fit benchmark of financial performance, market capitalization (MARKET CAP) is used as a market-fit benchmark of the firm value. The total debt to total assets ratio is used as an indicator for the capital structure (CS), which represents financing decisions of the selected companies. In addition, three control variables, namely current ratio, size, and age are also embraced in the study. The outcomes of the evaluation demonstrated that a significant adverse correlation exists between financing decisions and the two dependent variables, namely, ROA, and MARKET CAP. As for the control variables, size, and age have a significant direct correlation with ROA and market capitalization. As a conclusion of the study's findings, it can be asserted that financing decisions have a substantial inverse impact on companies' financial performance and value, which is in line with the Pecking Order Theory.

Keywords: Capital structure, Financing decisions, Firm performance, Firm value, Panel data

Introduction

In the pursuit of enhancing a company's value, the mix of debt and equity financing, which constitutes the capital structure of a firm, plays a crucial role in wealth creation. Efficient and dynamic combinations lead to increased company worth and reduced capital costs (Bhaduri, 2002). On the other hand, improper financing decisions may hinder operations and resource utilization (Adesina et al., 2015).

---

*Business Development Officer, TouristPay, Istanbul, Turkey
**Assoc. Prof. Dr., Marmara University, Faculty of Business Administration, Istanbul, Turkey
Emails: <abdeh@touristpay.com.tr>, <mehtap.oner@marmara.edu.tr>

Debt, which can be short or long term, is simply the outcome of borrowing and is something that needs to be paid back. In contrast to debt funding, equity funding is anticipated to stay with the firm for an unlimited extent of time. One of the most important advantages of debt financing is that, compared to equity, debt is cost-effective due to the tax savings it provides. But at the same time, increasing the debt level in the capital structure also increases financial risk, hence the probability of bankruptcy. Therefore, companies generally aim toward carrying on an efficient funding mix that stabilizes the advantages of tax savings and bankruptcy risks, yet large amounts of debt can raise the capital cost and, accordingly, lead to lower financial performance and value (Desai, 2007).

The association between financing decisions, performance, and value has been explored since before the famous Modigliani and Miller (1958) prepositions. Prior to Modigliani and Miller (1958), capital structure theories were categorized as basic or traditional, aiming to ascertain a business's most efficient debt-to-equity ratio. The Net Income, Net Operating Income, and Traditional approaches were known as classical theories. Net Income Theory (Durand, 1952) posited that an organization's worth surges with higher financial leverage, assuming constant costs of debt and equity, no taxes, and a lower risk structure for debt. Critics argued that increased financial leverage leads to higher costs. On the other hand, according to the Net Operating Income approach, an enterprise's market value abides unaltered by capital structure changes. It is assumed that debt costs do not influence leverage and the outlay of debt is lower than equity. Critics highlighted that increased financial leverage leads to higher investor returns. The Traditional Theory of Capital Structure (Solomon, 1963) proposed an optimal structure between the theories of Net Income and Net Operating Income, assuming constant debt costs up to a point, debt as a lower-cost means of funding relative to ownership capital, and an optimal structure reducing total capital costs. Critics argued that beyond a certain point, increased debt raises costs, nullifying benefits. Modigliani and Miller's (M&M) Theory (1958), which is accepted as a cornerstone in the related literature, states that in an ideal market, a business's worth is independent of its financing decisions, with propositions addressing value and cost implications with and without taxes. M&M's argument faced criticism for not considering real-world imperfections, and subsequent research challenged their applicability.

The Modigliani and Miller (1958) study serves as the pillar for the contemporary configuration of capital structure philosophies, albeit with idealized assumptions. Subsequent philosophies, like Trade-Off, Pecking Order, Agency Cost, Signaling, and Market Timing, have emerged to address practical market considerations. The Trade-off rationale, stemming from Modigliani and Miller's discord, advocates for a harmony in weighing the benefits and costs of debt financing, with the optimal debt level seen as a balance between tax benefits and financial risk. Moreover, the Dynamic Trade-off Theory introduces time-dependent adjustments, recognizing that optimal capital structure can change with evolving financial plans. Pecking Order Theory contends that information asymmetry leads firms to adopt, first retained earnings, then debt, and finally equity for financing. Agency Cost Theory acknowledges conflicts of interest and suggests that debt disciplines managers (Jensen, 1986). Signaling Theory posits that managers use leverage as an effective signaling tool for prospective investors to give them insights about a firm's true value, while the Theory of Market Timing, nominated by Baker and Wurgler (2002), challenges efficient market assumptions and suggests that firms adjust capital structure based on equity market conditions. In conclusion, these diverse capital structure theories offer nuanced perspectives on financing decisions, considering tax advantages, information asymmetry, agency conflicts, signaling, and market dynamics, emphasizing the need for a comprehensive understanding of firms' financing choices in real-world scenarios. No specific methods ensure optimal capital structure, but arguments like Pecking Order, Trade-off, Agency Cost, Market Timing, and Signaling, offer varied perspectives (Frank & Goyal, 2009).

Literature Review

Post Modigliani and Miller (1958) scholars delved into the intricate connection between companies' financing decisions and financial outcomes, revealing conflicting perspectives. While some studies indicate a substantial adverse correlation between the performance of a company and its capital structure, some others indicate a positive one. This section aims to present insights from prior research regarding different economies with respect to the influence of funding strategies on financial performance and firm value. The emphasis will be on research conducted in emerging markets, rather than developed ones, that might share more similarities with the Turkish market. A dedicated section will also spotlight explorations specifically conducted in the Turkish market that contributes to the evidence related to the financing choices and performance in this context.

Evidence Regarding the Impact of Financing Decisions on the Financial Performance of the Companies

In an extensive exploration of the association between capital structure and financial performance on a global scale, the evidence indicates varying results. Krishnan and Moyer (1997) found that the state of origin significantly impacts financing decisions and fiscal performance. Majumdar et al. (1999) discovered a momentous inverse association between debt levels in the financial composition and the financial performance of Indian companies. On the other hand, Abor (2005) reported that financial performance and interim debt are substantially positively associated for the selected firms indexed on the Ghana Stock Exchange, while Zeitun and Tian (2007) disclosed an inverse consequential repercussion of financing choices on all market and accounting measures used to assess performance for non-financial Jordanian companies. Similarly, El-Sayed Ebaid (2009), who studied non-financial organizations traded on the Stock Exchange of Egypt, observed an inverse effect on the profitability of the studied sample with respect to debt levels. As for the Nigerian context, the evidence was similar that Chinaemerem and Anthony (2012) reported a significant adverse correlation between financing decisions and firms' financial performance. However, Ajibola et al. (2018) identified a positive substantial association between debt level and ROE for Nigerian manufacturing companies. For Iranian firms, while Pouraghajan et al. (2012) reported a strongly adverse correlation between the leverage ratio and financial performance, for Vietnam firms, Le and Phan (2017) found that the distress cost of external financing exceeds the benefit of tax saving, culminating in an inverse correlation between financing decisions and company performance. Furthermore, with respect to India, Chadha and Sharma (2015) observed that debt does not influence financial performance criteria when the proxies were Tobin's Q and return on assets (ROA) but it is inversely associated with the profitability indicator of ROE. In Pakistan, Aziz and Abbas (2019) uncovered a substantially inverse correlation between debt financing and firms' performance. A more recent study by Ayaz et al. (2021) for Malaysian firms concluded that financial leverage reinforces company performance, serving as an efficient approach to prevent managerial empire-building, with this advantage exceeding the cost of debt financing. However, in Saudi Arabia, Boshnak's (2023) results disclosed significantly adverse relationships between various debt measures and companies' operational, financial, and market performance.

Evidence Regarding the Impact of Financing Decisions on Firm Value

A thorough inspection of how financing decisions impact firm value in different economies also shows conflicting results. Examining the nexus between financing decisions and company value across different markets, Antwi et al. (2012) discovered that non-current liabilities present a crucial part in demonstrating a company's value, emphasizing its significance for corporate executives in funding business activities. The study recommends a preference for long-term debt over equity capital, attributing a better influence on a company's overall value to the former. Adetunji et al. (2016) echoed the importance of financial leverage, asserting its significant influence on firms' value in the Stock Exchange of Nigeria. The research emphasizes the superiority of leverage over equity for funding long-term initiatives and suggests optimizing financial leverage to maximize a company's value. Conversely, Vo and Ellis (2017) explored Vietnamese companies and revealed that external financing has a detrimental effect on shareholder wealth, suggesting that for Vietnamese firms, the costs of debt financing outweigh its benefits. Additionally, low-leveraged companies were identified as having a higher potential to create value for shareholders. Hirdinis (2019) studied Indonesian mining companies, revealing a significantly positive influence of financing decisions on company value. In the situation of the Amman Stock Exchange, Al-Slehat (2019) reported that Tobin's Q is adversely associated with debt; however, debt had no effect on firms' value. Nevertheless, both the size and structure of assets positively influenced firms' value, emphasizing the need for firms to carefully balance capital composition for long-standing sustainability and growth.

Turkish Market Evidence Regarding the Impact of Financing Decisions on Financial Performance and Firm Value

Analyzing the correlation between funding composition and the financial performance of businesses in the Turkish setting, a multitude of research has offered diverse insights. While Sayılgan et al. (2006) identified an adverse effect of gearing on profitability in Turkish manufacturing businesses; Albayrak and Akbulut (2008) disclosed an adverse correlation between financing decisions and ROA but a positive correlation with ROE. Additionally, Birgili and Düzer (2010) reported an adverse association between debt and firms' worth. Contrarily, Uluyol et al. (2014) discovered sector-specific variations, where leverage negatively affected ROE in certain sectors but had a positive effect in the construction sector. Furthermore, Nassar (2016) indicated a significantly inverse interrelation between financial structure and companies' financial efficacy. Abdulqader (2022) uncovered a complex scenario, with current liabilities and non-current liabilities exhibiting a substantially direct association with ROE but a substantially inverse relationship with ROA. Rashid (2022) extended the exploration to the Turkish and German manufacturing sectors, discovering an adverse effect of total and non-current liabilities on profitability. Together, these studies underscore the nuanced dynamics of financing decisions and their repercussion on Turkish firms' value and financial performance across diverse sectors and periods.

Research Design and Methodology

Research methodology reflects the approaches, procedures, and means utilized to gather and examine data to address a research subject or hypothesis. Numerous research methodologies exist, encompassing the quantitative approach, qualitative approach, and mixed-methods. Each approach has its advantages and disadvantages, and the selection of methodology is influenced by the subject of the study, the nature of data that must be gathered, the resources that are accessible, and the methodological framework.

In this passage of the study, the distinguishing characteristics of panel data methodology will be highlighted, and a brief discussion of the commonly accessible forms of data utilized in an empirical study will be given. The most suitable estimation technique for this investigation will be chosen depending on the nature of the dataset by evaluating several estimation approaches to utilize the panel data approach.

Panel Data Methodology

Panel data, encompassing time series and cross-sectional dimensions, serves as a robust form of empirical analysis, allowing researchers to examine relationships among variables over various time periods and across different sample units simultaneously (Gujarati, 2003; Wooldridge, 2003). The edge of the panel data approach over time series and cross-sectional data is notable. Unlike time series and cross-sectional analyses, panel data acknowledges and handles heterogeneity, making it suitable for studying countries, companies, and individuals with specific characteristics (Baltagi, 2001). It provides increased variability, informative data, greater degrees of freedom, reduced collinearity between variables, and improved econometric measures. Panel data also diminishes the ramification of excluded factors, offering insights into both intertemporal behavior and individual uniqueness, thereby mitigating the effects of omitted or unnoticed factors (Gujarati, 2003; Hsiao, 2007). Notably, panel data is adept at recognizing effects that might be overlooked in classic time series and cross-sectional analyses. The micro-level focus of panel data, commonly on individuals and companies, allows for more accurate evaluation of numerous parameters and eliminates biases caused by aggregation over entities (Baltagi, 2001; Gujarati, 2003). In light of these advantages, embracing panel data frameworks becomes essential for enhancing empirical analysis beyond the limitations of time series or cross-sectional data.

Data and Variables Description

The study, conducted on 138 manufacturing entities publicly traded on Turkey's stock exchange from 2009 to 2022, utilizes data from the Thomson Reuters database to assess the implications of financing decisions on financial performance and value of the selected companies. ROA serves as a dependent variable for financial performance, while market capitalization is adopted as an indicator of firm value. ROA, a profitability ratio, gauges a company's operating efficiency and is widely recognized in previous studies as a key performance indicator (Albayrak & Akbulut, 2008; Boshnak, 2023; Chadha & Sharma, 2015; Krishnan & Moyer, 1997; Le & Phan, 2017; Zeitun & Tian, 2007). On the other hand, market capitalization, representing market worth, is adopted as a market-based indicator of firm value in line with established literature (Boshnak, 2023; Le & Phan, 2017; McConnell & Servaes, 1990; Zeitun & Tian, 2007). The key independent variable is the financing decision proxied by total debt to total assets, aligning with findings from former research (Aziz & Abbas, 2019; El-Sayed Ebaid, 2009; Gill et al., 2011; Le &

Phan, 2017; Salim & Yadav, 2012). Three control variables—size (natural log of total assets), age (number of years since incorporation), and current ratio (current assets over current liabilities)—are also considered based on past research (Aziz & Abbas, 2019; Chadha & Sharma, 2015; Haron, 2014; Majumdar et al., 1999; Pathak & Chandani, 2023; Pouraghajan et al., 2012; Zeitun & Tian, 2007).

All the variables utilized in the analysis are demonstrated in Table 2 with their acronyms and explanations.

Table 2: The variables utilized in the study and their explanations

Variable	Acronym	Explanation
Dependent variables		
Return on assets	ROA	Net income/Total assets
Market capitalization	MARKETCAP	Multiplying the specified share category by the most recent closing price
Independent variable		
Capital structure	CS	Total debt to total assets
Control variables		
Size	Size	Natural log of total assets
Age	Age	Sum of the years from the firm's founding year to each within the examined time span
Liquidity	CR	Current assets over current liabilities

In the following subsections, the hypothesis development and the research design will be thoroughly explained.

Hypothesis Development

The outcomes of evidence-based investigations examining the link between financing decisions and company performance and value are both diverse and conflicting. Given that most capital structure studies and empirical research carried out in developed nations claim a positive linkage between financing decisions and company financial performance/value (Berger & Bonacorsi Di Patti, 2006; Gill et al., 2011). Some of the investigations looking into this connection in transitional economies demonstrates a detrimental link (Majumdar et al., 1999; Zeitun & Tian, 2007). In this analysis, we expect that financing decisions will exert a statistically substantial effect on the companies' financial performance and value; therefore, it is hypothesized that:

H1: Capital structure affects the financial performance of firms.
H2: Capital structure affects the firm value.

Research Design

The current investigation strives to explore the influence of financing decisions on companies' financial performance and value. To empirically examine the hypothesis generated, two models were developed. Equation (1) which represents the first model (Model 1) is established to discover the significance of financing decisions represented by the leverage ratio on company financial performance proxied by ROA. Model 2 which is represented by Equation (2) is established to assess the influence of financing decisions demonstrated by the leverage ratio on company value proxied by market capitalization. The numerical representation of the models developed can be seen below:

$$ROA_{it} = \beta_0 + \beta_1 \mathrm{CS}_{it} + \beta_2 SIZE_{it} + \beta_3 \mathrm{AGE}_{it} + \beta_4 \mathrm{CR}_{it} + \varepsilon_{it} \quad (1)$$

$$\mathrm{MARKETCAP}_{it} = \beta_0 + \beta_1 \mathrm{CS}_{it} + \beta_2 SIZE_{it} + \beta_3 \mathrm{AGE}_{it} + \beta_4 \mathrm{CR}_{it} + \varepsilon_{it} \quad (2)$$

In the early stages of the study, the problem of multicollinearity was assessed by utilizing the Variance Inflation Factor (VIF) testing, revealing VIF values below 5, indicating an absence of multicollinearity (Lopez, 2021). The Likelihood-ratio inspection identified the existence of unit and time ramifications in Model (1), and unit effect in Model (2) emphasizing their significant role in shaping the dependent variables of ROA and market capitalization (Tatoğlu, 2020). The Hausman test determined the model as a two-way fixed effects model, considering both time-specific features and the unique properties of units in the panel data. Subsequent tests evaluated fundamental assumptions: the Jarque-Bera normality test confirmed normal distribution; the Wald test detected heteroskedasticity; Pesaran, Friedman, and Frees tests revealed a lack of cross-sectional independence; and Durbin-Watson and Baltagi's LBI tests identified autocorrelation. To address these issues, the panel data model was re-estimated using Driscoll-Kraay standard errors, accounting for cross-sectional dependency, autocorrelation, and heteroskedasticity, aiming for more accurate estimations (Longhi & Nandi, 2014; Lopez, 2021; Tatoğlu, 2020). The study employs fixed effects estimation, robust standard errors, and appropriate techniques to ensure parameter accuracy and effectiveness in dealing with panel data nuances.

Empirical Findings

Descriptive Statistics

Table 3 demonstrates descriptive statistics for 138 non-financial companies in Turkey from 2009 to 2022.

Table 3: Summary statistics of the variables used in the study

	Mean	Maximum	Minimum	Standard Dev.
Capital structure	0.5626	4.3974	0.0057	0.3032
Market capitalization	2146446095	355256000000	935713.45	17310839690
ROA	0.0468	0.5272	−2.0509	0.1187
Current ratio	2.3569	120.7697	0.3.0317	5.6993
Size	19.3032	24.1554	13.0288	1.6844
Age	39.9855	87	3	14.3799

The capital structure, denoting the proportion of total debt to overall assets, has an approximate mean rate of 0.56, indicating that roughly, more than half of companies' assets are financed by debt. The maximum rate of 4.39 suggests that some companies have debt exceeding the value of their total assets. Market capitalization, computed by multiplying the specified share category by the most recent closing price, has a mean value of approximately 2.15 billion Turkish Liras, with a maximum of 355 billion and a minimum of 0.94 million Turkish Liras. ROA averages 0.046, signifying that companies roughly make a 4.6% return from their total assets. The maximum ROA is 0.52, slightly above half the value of total assets, while the minimum is −2.05, indicating negative earnings for some companies. The liquidity ratio, calculated as short-term assets over short-term debts, has a mean of 2.36, signifying the competence of firms to satisfy immediate financial commitments. The maximum current ratio is 120.77, while the minimum is 0.033. Size, represented by the natural log of aggregated assets, has a mean of 19.30318, a maximum of 24.15544, and a minimum of 13.02884. The average age of the studied companies is roughly 40 years, with the oldest at 87 years and the newest at 3 years.

Empirical Analysis and Interpretations

This section summarizes the key outcomes from conducting panel data regression across two models. The goal was to assess how financing decisions influence the financial performance and value of 138 companies in non-financial industries publicly traded on Borsa Istanbul from 2009 to 2022. The findings of Model (1) panel data analysis utilizing the Diriscoll-Kraay standard error method are shown in Table 4. In this model, ROA serves as a stand-in for business financial performance and is utilized as the dependent variable of the analysis, whereas capital structure, which represents financing decisions of the firms calculated by the total debt to overall assets ratio and used as the independent variable. Additionally, the study includes current ratio, company size, and age as control variables in both models. The coefficient, standard error, and *t*-statistics of each variable are listed in Table 4. The *F* statistic of 33.44 and a likelihood data point of 0.0000 indicate that the panel data model is robust and demonstrates a scientifically sound interpretation. With a $P>|t|$ statistics value of 0.000, the independent variable capital structure appears to bear a significantly adverse correlation with the accounting-based performance indicator ROA, which aligns with the discoveries in the analysis of Zeitun and Tian (2007), El-Sayed Ebaid (2009), Salim and Yadav (2012), Pouraghajan et al. (2012) and Le and Phan (2017). As for the variables used for control, current ratio with a $P>|t|$ statistics value of 0.222 shows no vital repercussion on the financial performance of the chosen sample. Regarding size, at a 10% significance level, the size of the selected firms shows a notably positive correlation with ROA, coherent with the outcomes of Zeitun and Tian (2007), Salim and Yadav (2012), and Aziz and Abbas (2019). Similarly, with a *t*-statistics value of 0.000, the control variable age also appears to exert a notably positive association with ROA, as in the study of Pouraghajan et al. (2012).

Table 4: Results of Model (1)—Regression with Driscoll-Kraay standard errors

Dependent variable: ROA			
Variable	**Coefficient**	**Standard Error**	***P*>|*t*| statistics**
Capital structure	−0.3222939	0.0370071	0.000
Current ratio	−0.0012184	0.0009503	0.222
Size	0.0208476	0.0114448	0.092
Age	0.0080518	0.0015011	0.000
Constant	0.4934251	0.1802981	0.017
Number of obs.	1932	F(4,13)	33.44
Number of groups	138	Prob> F	0.0000

The findings of Model (2) panel data analysis utilizing the Diriscoll-Kraay standard error method are shown in Table 5. In this model, firm value is expressed by market capitalization as the dependent variable of the analysis. Similar to the first model, capital structure which represents financing decisions of the firms calculated by overall debt to total assets proportion, serves as the independent variable of the analysis. Concerning control variables, liquidity, size and age of the firms are incorporated into the model. The coefficient, standard error, and t-statistics of each variable regarding Model (2) are listed in Table 5. The F statistics of 5.04 and a likelihood data point of 0.0000 imply that the panel data model as a whole is interpretable and robust statistically. With a $P>|t|$ statistics value of 0.013, the independent variable capital structure appears to have a significantly inverse correlation with the market capitalization which is the market based indicator of the company value. This result aligns with the findings of Titman (1984), Rajan and Zingales (1995), Booth et al. (2001), Huang and Song (2006), and Vo and Ellis (2017) who have used numerous proxies to explore the repercussions of financing decisions on companies' value and declared the same result. Moving to the control variables liquidity proxied by current ratio is found not to have any meaningful association with firm value. However, with a $P>|t|$ statistics value of 0.012, size appears to have a significantly positive relationship with market capitalization in regards to the selected firms consistent with the outcomes of the analysis by Hirdinis (2019) and Al-Slehat (2019). Similarly, with a $P>|t|$ statistics value of 0.003, the control variable age additionally identified as having a notably positive correlation with market capitalization.

Table 5: Results of Model (2)—Regression with Driscoll-Kraay standard errors

Dependent variable: market capitalization			
Variable	**Coefficient**	**Standard error**	***P*>|*t*| statistics**
Capital structure	−649000000	410000000	0.013
Current ratio	7623903	5697495	0.204
Size	1070000000	365000000	0.012
Age	133000000	36800000	0.003
Constant	−23400000000	8140000000	0.013
Number of obs.	1932	*F* (4, 13)	5.04
Number of groups	138	Prob > *F*	0.0000

Both of the models consistently reveal a significantly adverse correlation between debt, depicted by the leverage ratio, and financial performance and firm value proxies. This aligns with the Pecking Order conceptualization, advocating self-financing, then debt due to information asymmetry. Size and age, considered control variables, exhibit a notably positive correlation with financial performance and firm value across all models. Larger and older Turkish companies in the sample demonstrate improved financial performance and increased value. This is attributed to larger companies having diversified investment alternatives, better administration, and economies of scale. Older firms leverage their experience, access to resources, and reputation for economic advantages. The findings underscore the importance for financial managers and decision-makers to carefully manage debt levels while recognizing the affirmative impact of size and age on overall business performance and value.

Discussion and Conclusion

This research examines the impacts of financing decisions on the financial performance and value of 138 non-financial enterprises traded on Borsa Istanbul from 2009 to 2022. Financing decision, determined by total debt to total assets, reveals a notably inverse correlation with financial performance (ROA) and firm value (market capitalization). Control variables, size, and age exhibit a significantly affirmative correlation with the mentioned indicators. The findings align with the Theory of Pecking Order that greater profit-generating businesses have less debt in their capital structure. For the future, we suggest that financial managers and decision-makers adopt appropriate debt levels and cautiously consider the effect of overleveraging, such as not underrating the bankruptcy cost of reorganization or liquidation, which will decrease the financial metrics of the firms as a result. Moreover, sizeable and older companies are urged to leverage their advantages in experience, economies of scale, and reputation. Limitations include missing observations and potential bias in variable measurement proxies. It can be suggested for future research to involve expanding proxies, enlarging the dataset, and studying specific sectors for comparative analysis. The study contributes to understanding Turkish non-financial companies' capital structure preferences, providing valuable insights for financial executives and managers to enhance value and financial performance.

Bibliography

Abdulqader, R. (2022). *The Effect of Capital Structure on Profitability: A Study on Manufacturing Firms Traded in Istanbul Stock Exchange*, Karadeniz Teknik University. Master Thesis.

Abor, J. (2005). The effect of capital structure on profitability: an empirical analysis of listed firms in Ghana. *The Journal of Risk Finance*, *6*(5), 438–445.

Adesina, J. B., Nwidobie, B. M., & Adesina, O. (2015). Capital structure and financial performance in Nigeria. *International Journal of Business and Social Research*, *5*(2), 21–31.

Adetunji, A., Akinyemi, A., & Rasheed, O. (2016). Financial leverage and firms' value: A study of selected firms in Nigeria. *European Journal of Research and Reflection in Management Sciences*, *4*(1).

Ajibola, A., Wisdom, O., & Ol, Q. (2018). Capital structure and financial performance of listed manufacturing firms in Nigeria. *Journal of Research in International Business and Management*, *5*(01).

Albayrak, A. S., & Akbulut, R. (2008). Factors that affect profitability: The analysis on the firms registered in industrial and service sector of ISE. *Zonguldak Karaelmaz Üniversitesi Sosyal Bilimler Dergisi*, *4*(7), 55–82.

Al-Slehat, Z. A. F. (2019). Impact of financial leverage, size and assets structure on firm value: Evidence from industrial sector, Jordan. *International Business Research*, *13*(1), 109.

Antwi, S., Emire, E. F., Mills, A., & Zhao, X. (2012). Capital structure and firm value: Empirical evidence from Ghana. *International Journal of Business and Social Science*, 3(22).

Ayaz, M., Mohamed Zabri, S., & Ahmad, K. (2021). An empirical investigation on the impact of capital structure on firm performance: evidence from Malaysia. *Managerial Finance*, *47*(8), 1107–1127.

Aziz, S., & Abbas, U. (2019). Effect of debt financing on firm performance: A study on non-financial sector of Pakistan. *Open Journal of Economics and Commerce* *2*(1).

Baker, M., & Wurgler, J. (2002). Market timing and capital structure. *The Journal of Finance*, *57*(1), 1–32.

Baltagi, B. H. (2001). *Econometric Analysis of Panel Data* (3rd ed.).

Berger, A. N., & Bonaccorsi di Patti, E. (2006). Capital structure and firm performance: A new approach to testing agency theory and an application to the banking industry. *Journal of Banking & Finance*, *30*(4), 1065–1102.

Bhaduri, S. N. (2002). Determinants of capital structure choice: A study of the Indian corporate sector. *Applied Financial Economics*, *12*(9), 655–665.

Birgili, E., & Düzer, M. (2010). *Finansal Analizde Kullanılan Oranlar ve Firma Değeri İlişkisi: İMKB'de Bir Uygulama*. 46, 74–83.

Booth, L., Aivazian, V., Demirguc-Kunt, A., & Maksimovic, V. (2001). Capital structures in developing countries. *The Journal of Finance*, *56*(1), 87–130.

Boshnak, H. (2023). The impact of capital structure on firm performance: evidence from Saudi-listed firms. *International Journal of Disclosure and Governance*, *20*(1), 15–26.

Chadha, S., & Sharma, A. K. (2015). Capital structure and firm performance: Empirical evidence from India. *Vision: The Journal of Business Perspective*, *19*(4), 295–302.

Chinaemerem, O. C., & Anthony, O. (2012). Impact of capital structure on the financial performance of Nigerian firms. *Oman Chapter of Arabian Journal of Business and Management Review*, *1*(12), 43–61.

Desai, M. A. (2007). Corporate tax avoidance and firm value. *Review of Economics and Statistics*, *91*(3), 537–546.

Durand, D. (1952) Cost of debt and equity funds for business trends and problems of measurement. *Conference on Research in Business Finance, National Bureau of Economic Research, Inc.*, Cambridge, pp. 215–262.

El-Sayed Ebaid, I. (2009). The impact of capital-structure choice on firm performance: empirical evidence from Egypt. *The Journal of Risk Finance, 10*(5), 477–487.

Frank, M. Z., & Goyal, V. K. (2009). Capital structure decisions: Which factors are reliably important? *Financial Management, 38*(1), 1–37.

Gill, A., Biger, N., & Mathur, N. (2011). The effects of capital structure on profitability: Evidence from United States. *International Journal of Management, 8*(4).

Gujarati, D. N. (2003). *Basic Econometrics* (4th ed.), McGraw Hill.

Haron, R. (2014). Capital structure inconclusiveness: Evidence from Malaysia, Thailand and Singapore. *International Journal of Managerial Finance, 10*(1), 23–38.

Hirdinis, M. (2019). Capital structure and firm size on firm value moderated by profitability. *International Journal of Economics and Business Administration* 7(1).

Hsiao, C. (2007). Panel data analysis—Advantages and challenges. *TEST, 16*(1), 1–22.

Huang, G., & Song, F. M. (2006). The determinants of capital structure: Evidence from China. *China Economic Review, 17*(1), 14–36.

Jensen, M. C. (1986). Agency costs of free cash flow, corporate finance, and takeovers. *American Economic Review* 76(2).

Krishnan, V. S., & Moyer, R. C. (1997). Performance, capital structure and home country: An analysis of Asian corporations. *Global Finance Journal, 8*(1), 129–143.

Le, T. P. V., & Phan, T. B. N. (2017). Capital structure and firm performance: Empirical evidence from a small transition country. *Research in International Business and Finance, 42*, 710–726.

Longhi, & Nandi (2014). *A Practical Guide to Using Panel Data*. SAGE Publications.

Lopez, C. P. (2021). *Econometric Models with Panel Data: Applications with Stata*. Ceasar Perez.

Majumdar, S. K., & Chhibber, P. (1999). Capital structure and performance: Evidence from a transition economy on an aspect of corporate governance. *Source: Public Choice 98*(3).

McConnell, J. J., & Servaes, H. (1990). Additional evidence on equity ownership and corporate value. *Journal of Financial Economics*, *27*(2), 595–612.

Modigliani, F., & Miller, M. (1958) The cost of capital, corporation finance and the Theory of Investment. *American Economic Review*, *48*, 261–297.

Nassar, S. (2016). The impact of capital structure on financial performance of the firms: Evidence from Borsa Istanbul. *Journal of Business & Financial Affairs*, *5*(2).

Pathak, M., & Chandani, A. (2023). The nexus between capital structure and firm-specific factors: Evidence from Indian companies. *Journal of Economic and Administrative Sciences*, *39*(2), 470–487.

Pouraghajan, A., Malekian, E., Emamgholipour, M., Lotfollahpour, V., & Bagheri, M. M. (2012). The relationship between capital Structure and firm performance evaluation measures: Evidence from the Tehran stock exchange. *International Journal of Business and Commerce*, *1*(9).

Rajan, R. G., & Zingales, L. (1995). What do we know about capital structure? Some evidence from international data. *The Journal of Finance*, *50*(5), 1421–1460.

Rashid, A. (2022). *The effect of capital structure on firm financial performance: A study on the manufacturing sector in Turkey and Germany*. Pamukkale University, Master Thesis.

Salim, M., & Yadav, R. (2012). Capital structure and firm performance: Evidence from Malaysian listed companies. *Procedia—Social and Behavioral Sciences*, *65*, 156–166.

Sayılgan, G., Karabacak, H., & Küçükkocaoğlu, G. (2006). The firm-specific determinants of corporate capital structure: Evidence from Turkish panel data. *Investment Management and Financial Innovations*, *3*(3).

Solomon, E. (1963). Leverage and the cost of capital. *The Journal of Finance*, *18*(2), 273–279.

Tatoğlu, F. Y. (2020). *Panel Veri Ekonometrisi*. İstanbul: Beta Yayınevi.

Titman, S. (1984). The effect of capital structure on a firm's liquidation decision. *Journal of Financial Economics*, *13*(1), 137–151.

Uluyol, O., Lebe, F., & Akbas, Y. E. (2014). The relation between financial leverage and return on equity of the companies: A research on the companies traded on İstanbul stock exchange in the base of industries. *İşletme Araştırmaları Dergisi* 6(1), 70–89.

Vo, X. V., & Ellis, C. (2017). An empirical investigation of capital structure and firm value in Vietnam. *Finance Research Letters*, *22*, 90–94.

Wooldridge, M. J. (2003). *Introductory Econometrics* (2nd ed.). United States of America: Thomson South-Western.

Zeitun, R., & Tian, G. (2007). Capital structure and corporate performance: evidence from Jordan. *Australasian Accounting, Business and Finance Journal*, *1*(4), 40–61. <https://doi.org/10.14453/aabfj.v1i4.3>.

4. Battling the Pink Tax: How Awareness Campaigns Shape Fairness and Brand Perception

Eliza Starke, Angelina Egbers,* Lia Bo Josephs,* Alina Neumann,* Judith Quiring,* Jan Schilling,* and Manuel Stegemann**

ABSTRACT

Gender-related discrimination in all areas is an important societal topic and area of necessary preventive action. This study investigates the impact of awareness campaigns addressing the "Pink Tax," a form of gender-specific price discrimination, on individuals' brand perceptions. The construct refers to the phenomenon where men and women are charged different prices for similar products and services, with women often paying more for items. Building on Nudging Theory and Reactance Theory, this empirical study assesses the effects of awareness campaigns against the Pink Tax (vs. no campaign) on perceived price fairness and brand attitudes. We aim to determine whether the campaign will lead to women perceiving the price discrimination as unfair and consequently devaluing the brand, and to explore potential negative effects on male consumers. To elucidate this direct effect, we examine perceived reactance as the underlying mechanism. The findings suggest that the Pink Tax, exacerbated by heightened public discourse, may backfire, diminishing brand attractiveness.

Keywords: Pink tax, Gender-specific price discrimination, Gender equality research, Perceived price fairness, Brand attitude, Employer attractiveness

Introduction

Pricing decisions are widely recognized as a crucial factor for all types of firms. The concept of price fairness explores how consumers perceive the fairness of prices, often by comparing them with reference prices (Xia et al., 2004). The literature on price fairness is divided into two main research streams: the first examines factors that influence price fairness perceptions, and the second investigates the consequences of these perceptions (Malc et al., 2016). This study can be allocated to the former stream as it focuses on gender-specific

*Bielefeld University of Applied Sciences and Arts, Bielefeld, Germany
Emails: <eliza.starke@hsbi.de>, <angelina_fabiene.egbers@hsbi.de>, <lia_bo.josephs@hsbi.de>, <alina_marie_chiara.neumann@hsbi.de>, <judith.quiring1@hsbi.de>, <jan.schilling@hsbi.de>, <manuel.stegemann@hsbi.de>

price discrimination, its effect on price fairness perceptions, and the underlying mechanisms that drive these effects. These areas remain underexplored in empirical research so far. Prior studies have shown that consumer-based price differences, such as paying higher prices relative to others, tend to evoke stronger negative fairness judgments compared to variations due to the seller, timing, or pricing methods (Haws & Bearden, 2006). Hence, it seems highly likely that gender-based price differences should strongly impact fairness perceptions and attitudes towards those responsible for the differences.

Building on these insights into price fairness, our study examines a specific form of consumer-based price disparity: the Pink Tax, a type of gender-specific price discrimination where women are charged more than men for comparable products and services (Guittar et al., 2021). Despite significant progress in promoting gender equality, the Pink Tax remains a persistent issue, reinforcing ongoing economic disparities between men and women. These concerns are reflected in the consultation requests received by the German Federal Anti-Discrimination Agency (Ataman, 2022), whose 2022 annual report states that 21% of all inquiries were related to gender discrimination, with 20% specifically focused on goods and services. The report on gender-based price discrimination in Germany indicates that women, on average, pay more for similar products and services than men, which can pose a significant financial burden. Among 1,682 identified product variants, 3.7% exhibited price disparities; in 2.3% of cases, women faced higher prices, compared to 1.4% where men paid more for the male version of the same product (an der Heiden & Wersig, 2017). This price disparity is even more pronounced in the case of perfumes, where limited comparability creates a distinct category. Among 246 gender-differentiated perfume variants analyzed, only 31% were priced equally for both genders. In contrast, 61% of women's perfumes were more expensive, averaging 19.00 euros more than their male counterparts (an der Heiden & Wersig, 2017).

Existing literature demonstrates that, while these differences are not consistent across all types of products or services, women generally pay higher prices for items such as deodorants, haircuts, and dry-cleaning services (an der Heiden & Wersig, 2017). Beyond increasing the financial burden on women and exacerbating economic inequality, these pricing practices perpetuate gender stereotypes, reinforcing the notion of inherent differences between women and men (Duesterhaus et al., 2011). It is crucial not only to reduce gender-based pricing by manufacturers and retailers but also to increase consumer awareness of the Pink Tax. For instance, in 2019, the Hamburg

Consumer Center highlighted gender-based pricing disparities by showcasing identical moisturizers priced differently—6.90 euros for women and 4.90 euros for men—exposing the persistent Pink Tax in everyday products (Verbraucherzentrale Hamburg, 2024).

Mass media campaigns have been shown to significantly impact public behavior and awareness regarding issues such as health risks and safety concerns (Wakefield et al., 2010). Given the importance of addressing the Pink Tax and the lack of scientifically grounded awareness campaigns on this issue, this study aims to fill a critical research gap. Our research builds on two well-established theories in social sciences: Nudging Theory (Thaler & Sunstein, 2021) and Reactance Theory (Brehm, 1966; Brehm & Brehm, 1981). Using an online experiment, we aim to investigate the impact of Pink Tax awareness campaigns on consumer perceptions, specifically regarding perceived price fairness and brand attitudes, while exploring the underlying mechanisms involved. In particular, we present results from a study that examines the indirect effects fully mediated by perceived reactance, controlling for differences between men and women.

The anticipated outcomes include increased consumer awareness, a higher demand for fairly priced products, and a reduction in gender-based price segmentation. Recognizing the importance of consumer perceptions—particularly in terms of brand image, price fairness, loyalty, and satisfaction—businesses are encouraged to address gender-based discrimination to ensure long-term brand success (Bolton & Lemon, 1999). Perceived price fairness significantly affects brand image, so gender-based pricing could backfire by negatively affecting consumer attitudes (Malc et al., 2016). As brand image is in turn closely related to brand loyalty, these findings suggest that companies must carefully evaluate their pricing strategies to avoid alienating consumers, especially as transparency regarding gendered pricing increases. This study also aims to provide practical recommendations for policymakers and marketers on how awareness campaigns can promote economic equity and enhance brand reputation by positively influencing consumer attitudes toward fairly priced brands.

Pink Tax Awareness Campaigns

The phenomenon of gender-based price discrimination is widespread across diverse market sectors, prompting significant discussions about fairness and consumer perceptions (Ferrell et al., 2016). Research has shown that acceptance and perception of gender-based pricing are influenced by various factors, including biological differences and frequency of service utilization. For example, Hastie and Cosh (2013) found that consumer attitudes toward gender-specific pricing in health insurance premiums could be swayed by whether price differences were perceived as justified due to biological factors or seen as unfair. Ferrell et al. (2016) further examined this issue by analyzing student attitudes toward gender-specific price differences in services like haircuts and dry cleaning. Their findings indicated that males were more likely than females to anticipate such price discrepancies. Moreover, acceptance of gender-based price discrimination was higher when it was expected and when it could be justified by perceived differences in service quality.

Despite efforts to address gender-based price discrimination, awareness of the Pink Tax remains limited among consumers. Public awareness campaigns, similar to those successfully used in health and safety contexts, represent a promising strategy to enhance consumer understanding. Richard H. Thaler and Cass R. Sunstein's Nudging Theory (2021) suggests that subtle changes in the decision-making environment can promote positive behavioral changes. In this context, a Pink Tax awareness campaign can be viewed as an ethical nudge, influencing consumer behavior toward recognizing and rejecting gender-based price discrimination without the need for strict regulations or economic incentives. Such campaigns aim to foster transparency and contribute to societal well-being, ultimately promoting a more equitable and inclusive marketplace (Sunstein, 2014).

Campaigns that utilize attention-grabbing elements such as bold text and striking visuals have proven effective in influencing behaviors and perceptions on a variety of societal issues (Wakefield et al., 2010). For instance, anti-smoking campaigns that employ both positive and negative framing have been shown to impact smokers' attitudes and behaviors (Dono et al., 2020; Ghods et al., 2024). Campaigns aimed at reducing smoking rates and increasing seatbelt use have also achieved significant success, particularly when combined with enforcement measures and high-quality messaging (Akbari et al., 2021; Wakefield et al., 2003). This nudging approach is also reflected in the social science literature on prosocial behavior and sustainability. Specifically, for consumable products, sustainable product labeling with positive sustainability messages has been found to lead to better product evaluations (Borin & Krishnan, 2011). If green products emphasized the environmental benefits of being free from harmful ingredients and non-green products were required to disclose the negative environmental impacts of their ingredients, sustainable products would likely be perceived more favorably. In the food sector, organic labels can inform consumers about the sustainable origin of a product. Such labels positively influence purchase intentions and the willingness to pay a price premium (Bauer et al., 2013). The positive effect of organic labeling was confirmed in a field experiment that used point-of-purchase displays to make the entire range of organic products more visible to consumers, which subsequently made organic products less price-sensitive (Daunfeldt & Rudholm, 2014). The effectiveness of transparent labeling is also supported in the context of socially responsible companies, particularly when external Corporate Social Responsibility (CSR) endorsements are used. Moreover, perceived CSR motives act as mediators between external CSR labels and corporate credibility and brand attitude, respectively (Gosselt et al., 2019). These findings indicate that awareness and warning campaigns can significantly increase consumer awareness and positively influence behavior, especially regarding perceived price fairness and brand attitudes. Clearly presented information can substantially impact consumer evaluations of products.

Based on these theoretical perspectives and empirical evidence, we propose the following hypotheses:

H1a: Pink Tax awareness campaigns (vs. no campaign) increase the negative impact on perceived price fairness.

H1b: Pink Tax awareness campaigns (vs. no campaign) increase the negative impact on brand attitude.

The impact of transparent information presentation highlights the significance of consumer expectations in the perception of price fairness. Jack W. Brehm's Reactance Theory offers valuable insight into how consumers respond to perceived price unfairness. According to Brehm (1966) and Brehm and Brehm (1981), when individuals perceive that their freedom of choice is restricted, they experience psychological reactance—a motivational state that drives them to restore their freedom. This theory suggests that consumers who perceive gender-based price differences as unfair might resist such practices by avoiding products or services that engage in discriminatory pricing.

Unfair pricing could be regarded as a threat to the freedom of purchasing a desired good, but also be explained in the form of "stereotype reactance" (Kray et al., 2001, 2004). By explicitly rather than implicitly) activating stereotypes (e.g., "women are willing to pay more for beauty products like perfumes," "men care for prices of products more than women"), stereotype reactance is activated (Miron & Brehm, 2006). This reactance could thus contribute to negative brand attitudes and perceptions of price unfairness, particularly when consumers are aware of the discriminatory nature of these pricing strategies.

Building on Reactance Theory, this study also examines how reactance may mediate the relationship between Pink Tax awareness campaigns and consumer perceptions of price fairness and brand attitude:

H2a: Consumer reactance mediates the negative effect between Pink Tax awareness campaigns and perceived price fairness.
H2b: Consumer reactance mediates the negative effect between Pink Tax awareness campaigns and brand attitude.

Method

In the present study, we examine the impact of a Pink Tax awareness campaign on perceived price fairness and brand attitude for a gender-discriminated perfume that is priced higher for women than for men. This is done to test Hypotheses 1a and 1b. The Pink Tax was operationalized by presenting both groups with an image of two perfumes: one for men in blue and one for women in pink, both under the fictitious brand name Aurélys, with different prices. The men's perfume was priced at 43.17 euros, while the women's version was set at 57.54 euros, reflecting real market disparities commonly seen in gendered pricing. These prices were based on a uniform quantity of 30 milliliters. Additionally, we test Hypotheses 2a and 2b, which assume an indirect effect through perceived psychological reactance. Figure 2 illustrates the conceptual framework.

In line with a two-group posttest-only design, participants were randomly assigned to one of two conditions: (a) a control group with no awareness campaign ($n = 74$), or (b) an experimental group exposed to a Pink Tax awareness campaign ($n = 75$). After excluding participants who failed the integrated attention check, the final sample consisted of 149 completed questionnaires.

A description of the demographic profiles of the participants is shown in Table 6. The final sample of 149 respondents was sufficient for a power analysis calculated by G*power (power = 95%, small effect size, 5% alpha margin error).

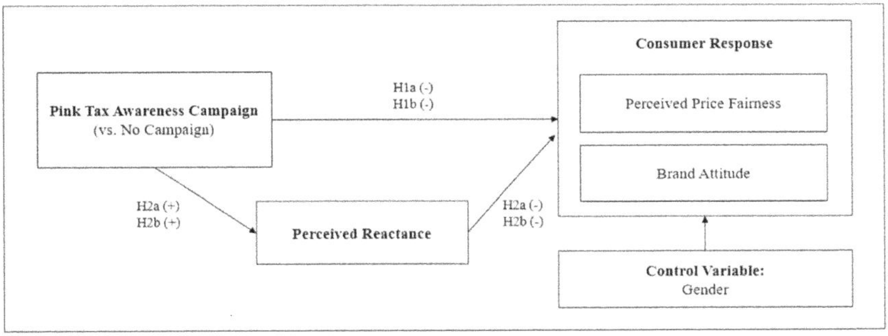

Figure 2: Conceptual framework.

Table 6: Sample distribution by gender, age, income, and educational level[a,b]

Gender	
Male	29.5
Female	69.8
Diverse	0.7
Age	
18–30 years	74.4
31–50 years	12.8
More than 50 years	12.8
Income (monthly)	
Less than 1,000 €	37.6
1,001–2,000 €	28.9
2,001–3,000 €	15.4
More than 3,001 €	18.2
Educational level	
High school	29.0
Vocational Education	13.0
Academic Degree	53.0
Others	5.0

[a]The study based on $n = 149$ participants.
[b]All numbers are in percentages.

Procedure

Prior to the main study, a pretest was conducted with twelve participants to identify potential difficulties in understanding the differences between the two perfumes. Based on feedback from the pretest, a clarification was added to explain that the perfumes contained distinctly masculine and feminine scents. This adjustment ensured that both the technical and content-related aspects of the questionnaire were comprehensible.

Data were collected via online questionnaire surveys. Participants for the main study were recruited through two primary methods. First, social media platforms such as WhatsApp and Instagram were used to distribute a hyperlink that provided access to the online survey. Second, the survey was published on the online platform "Survey Circle" to increase visibility and participant reach. At the beginning of the survey, participants were informed about the study's purpose, the expected duration, the anonymity of their responses, and the identities of the researchers. After providing their consent for the anonymized data to be used for scientific research, participants were randomly assigned to one of two groups. Both groups were then shown an image depicting two perfume variants representing the Pink Tax under the fictitious brand Aurélys, with the men's perfume priced lower than the women's. Participants were informed that the men's and women's perfumes differed in scent and were asked to imagine that they were familiar with and liked the scent of the relevant perfume. Following this, participants were asked to share their attitudes toward the Aurélys brand and their perceptions of price fairness. A subsequent attention check was included to ensure participants correctly recalled the price difference between the men's and women's perfumes. Afterward, participants were asked questions designed to measure psychological reactance. An additional attention check was embedded within the reactance measurement items to assess how carefully participants were reading and responding. Towards the end of the survey, participants provided demographic information, including gender, age, education level, occupation, and net income. The survey took approximately five minutes to complete and was accessible from May 29, 2024, to June 9, 2024. All stimuli are included in Appendix A.

Common method variance (CMV) can be an issue in surveys that rely on a single source and use the same type of measurement scales, such as Likert scales. Therefore, in this study, where multiple self-reported constructs were assessed, we implemented several measures to mitigate the risk of CMV. First, the independent variable was manipulated experimentally rather than being a survey-based construct. Second, we assured participants that their responses would remain anonymous to reduce the likelihood of socially desirable answering patterns (Podsakoff et al., 2003).

Measurement

The present study examines brand attitude and perceived price fairness as dependent variables, with perceived reactance serving as a mediator. All items were derived from previously validated and standardized questionnaires. Brand attitude was gauged using five items from the Brand Attitude Scale (BAS) (Aaker, 1997), employing a five-point Likert scale (1 = "strongly disagree," 2 = "somewhat disagree," 3 = "neither agree nor disagree," 4 = "somewhat agree," 5 = "strongly agree"). To assess perceived price fairness, five items from the Price Fairness Scale (Lutz, 1975) were utilized, employing the same five-point Likert scale. The construct of perceived reactance was operationalized using the Salzburger State Reactance Scale (SSR Scale; Sittenthaler et al., 2015). The initial step involved formulating a scenario that was pertinent to the study context. Subsequently, 10 items were devised to capture reactance levels in a manner tailored to the specific circumstances. These items were also evaluated using a five-point Likert scale (1 = "does not apply at all," 2 = "somewhat does not apply," 3 = "neither applies nor does not apply," 4 = "somewhat applies," 5 = "fully applicable"). For the items of the focal variables, we conducted reliability analyses, yielding the following Cronbach's alpha values: BAS ($\alpha = 0.906$), Price Fairness Scale ($\alpha = 0.779$), and SSR Scale ($\alpha = 0.859$), ranging from good to very good. A detailed description of the items can be found in Appendix B.

Results

To test H1, a one-way multivariate analysis of variance (MANOVA) was conducted, analyzing consumer responses as a function of the Pink Tax awareness campaign. The analysis revealed a marginally statistically significant difference in consumer responses based on the campaign demonstration ($F(2, 145) = 2.78, p < .10$; Wilk's $\Lambda = 0.96$, partial $\eta^2 = 0.04$). The results indicated significant mean differences in perceived price fairness ($F(1, 146) = 5.40$, $p < .05$) but no significant effect on brand attitude ($F(1, 146) = 2.66$, $p > .05$) (see Table 7). Pairwise comparisons were performed to further investigate the differences between groups. As shown in Table 8, participants exposed to the Pink Tax awareness campaign rated price fairness lower ($M = 2.07$, SD = 0.68) than those in the control group ($M = 2.34$, SD = 0.79). Therefore, H1a is supported, while H1b is not confirmed. Additionally, gender as a covariate has a significant effect ($p < .05$) on perceived price fairness, with women perceiving price fairness more negatively compared to men (see Table 8). The descriptive analysis also showed that the mean differences between the men who have not seen a campaign ($M_{\text{Price Fairness}} = 2.74$; $M_{\text{Brand Attitude}} = 3.32$) and those who have seen a campaign ($M_{\text{Price Fairness}} = 2.25$; $M_{\text{Brand Attitude}} = 2.85$) are greater than for the women who have not seen a campaign ($M_{\text{Price Fairness}} = 2.18$; $M_{\text{Brand Attitude}} = 2.98$) and those who have seen a campaign ($M_{\text{Price Fairness}} = 2.00$; $M_{\text{Brand Attitude}} = 2.79$).

Table 7: Multivariate analysis of variance

	Dependent variable	Type III sum of squared	df	Mean square	*F*	Sig.	Partial eta squared
Corrected model	Price fairness	8.09	2	4.04	7.89	< 0.001	0.10
	Brand attitude	4.60	2	2.30	2.718	0.07	0.04
Intercept	Price fairness	87.24	1	87.24	170.30	< 0.001	0.54
	Brand attitude	119.40	1	119.40	141.11	< 0.001	0.49
Gender	Price fairness	5.40	1	5.40	2.39	0.001	0.07
	Brand attitude	2.39	1			0.10	0.02
Campaign	Price fairness	2.76	1	2.76	5.40	0.02	0.04
	Brand attitude	2.25	1	2.25	2.66	0.11	0.02
Error	Price fairness	74.79	146	0.51			
	Brand attitude	123.54	146	0.85			
Total	Price fairness	807.56	149				
	Brand attitude	1408.64	149				
Corrected total	Price fairness	82.88	148				
	Brand attitude	128.14	148				

Table 8: Means in perceived price fairness and brand attitude across the different experimental groups

	Price fairness				Brand attitude			
	Control		Campaign		Control		Campaign	
	Mean	SD	Mean	SD	Mean	SD	Mean	SD
Total	2.34	0.79	2.07	0.68	3.05	0.99	2.81	0.86
Men	2.74	0.76	2.25	0.65	3.32	0.89	2.85	0.84
Women	2.18	0.76	2.00	0.68	2.98	0.99	2.79	0.87

Given the differences observed between the experimental groups regarding consumer responses, it is appropriate to examine the indirect effect of the Pink Tax awareness campaign on price fairness and brand attitude through perceived psychological reactance. To test H2a and H2b, we conducted a mediation analysis for each outcome using 5,000 bootstrap samples and employing PROCESS Model 4 (Hayes, 2022). The first step of our mediation regression analyses indicates that the Pink Tax awareness campaign has a significant effect on perceived reactance ($b = -0.26, p < 0.05$; 95% CI = –0.48 to –0.03). In the second step of our analysis, we found that perceived reactance significantly affects perceived price fairness ($b = -0.60, p < 0.05$; 95% CI = –0.74 to –0.46) and brand attitude ($b = -0.39, p < 0.05$; 95% CI = –0.60 to –0.18). Contrary to our theorizing, the direct effect of the awareness campaign on perceived price fairness and brand attitude is no longer significant after introducing the mediator ($p > 0.05$). Thus, the effect of the Pink Tax awareness campaign on these outcomes is fully mediated by perceived psychological reactance (see Table 9). Hypotheses H2a and H2b can be confirmed.

Table 9: Results of the mediation testing using PROCESS (Model 4)[a]

	Effect (SE)	*t*-Value	CI (95%)
Direct effects			
Campaign → Price Fairness	0.12 (0.10)	1.22	-0.07 to 0.31
Campaign → Brand Attitude	0.15 (0.15)	1.00	-0.14 to 0.44
Campaign → Perceived Reactance	-0.26 (0.11)*	-2.28	-0.48 to -0.03
Perceived Reactance → Price Fairness	-0.60 (0.07)***	-8.40	-0.74 to -0.46

(Continued)

Table 9: *(Continued)*

	Effect (SE)	*t*-Value	CI (95%)
Perceived Reactance → Brand Attitude	−0.39 (0.11)***	−3.64	−0.60 to −0.18
Indirect effects			
Campaign → Perceived Reactance → Price Fairness	0.15 (0.07)	–	0.02–0.30
Campaign → Perceived Reactance → Brand Attitude	0.10 (0.05)	–	0.01–0.23

[a]SE = standard error; CI = 95% bias-corrected confidence intervals; ***$p < 0.001$. **$p < 0.01$. *$p < 0.05$ (two-tailed).

General Discussion

In our study, we find evidence supporting our fundamental assertion that the Pink Tax awareness campaign reduces consumers' perceptions of price fairness and brand attitude towards a price-discriminated product. Moreover, this negative effect arises because of the heightened perceived psychological reactance that consumers experience when exposed to an awareness campaign featuring transparent information about the Pink Tax.

Theoretical Implications

Our findings contribute to the literature on consumer reactions to awareness campaigns against gender discrimination in several ways. First, we confirm the effectiveness of mass media campaigns in a new context related to the Pink Tax. Previous research has focused on the persuasiveness of warning campaigns (Wakefield et al., 2010), signaling logos (Borin & Krishnan, 2011; Daunfeldt & Rudholm, 2014), and the existence of the Pink Tax (Ferell et al., 2016). In contrast, our study highlights the potential risks and negative consequences of mass media dissemination of content addressing gender-discriminatory pricing. Making gender-specific discrimination transparent not only increases perceptions of price unfairness but also makes the brand seem less attractive. This finding aligns with existing research in the pricing literature, which demonstrates that dynamic pricing strategies can have negative effects on perceived price fairness (Haws & Bearden, 2006). The assessment of price fairness is subject to social comparison, so that especially women assess the price gap between men and women as negative (Malc et al., 2016). Additionally, our results emphasize the importance of reactance as a mediator between awareness campaigns and consumer reactions. This finding confirms Reactance Theory, showing that negative emotional responses to perceived injustices, such as the Pink Tax, significantly impact perceived price fairness and brand attitude (Brehm, 1966; Brehm & Brehm, 1981). This further explains the underlying mechanism of warning nudges, highlighting that an awareness campaign against discrimination is mediated through increased psychological reactance. Therefore, price perception is influenced not only by the actual pricing strategy of the company but also by both internal and external communication.

A noteworthy outcome of the descriptive analysis is the more pronounced response of males to the campaign in comparison to females. In the control group, men report higher levels of perceived price fairness and brand attitude than women. However, following exposure to the campaign, their evaluations converge with those of women. This may be attributed to differences in prior awareness: men may have been less aware of the existence of the Pink Tax before encountering the campaign, whereas women were likely already familiar with this form of gender-based pricing discrimination. Consequently, the campaign elicited a more substantial shift in men's perceptions, while women, having prior knowledge, exhibited relatively smaller changes in their responses.

Practical Implications

The study's findings may be relevant for various stakeholders, including companies, consumer organizations, and policymakers.

First, perceptions of price fairness influence multiple factors, such as purchase satisfaction (Haws & Bearden, 2006). However, they not only affect purchase intentions; they can also lead to negative behaviors that directly harm the seller (Malc et al., 2016). When perceived unfairness is high, customers may experience feelings of regret or disappointment, which can result in a range of negative behaviors, such as filing complaints, requesting refunds, spreading negative word-of-mouth communication, or, in some cases, terminating their relationship with the seller (Xia et al., 2004). Companies should set prices based on performance, aligning them with the actual effort involved (Bolton & Alba, 2006). Prices should also be transparent and gender-neutral.

Companies offering gender-specific products should be aware that price differences between genders can be problematic and may violate the General Equal Treatment Act (AGG) (an der Heiden & Wersig, 2017). For this reason, companies should avoid price discrimination to prevent being perceived as unfair.

It is also important to acknowledge that awareness campaigns are generally complex and are influenced by societal factors. Outrageous content, such as gender discrimination, can quickly spread through social media, leading to backlash against pricing discrimination. Campaigns addressing the Pink Tax, which are intensely debated within society, are partly driven by societal concerns themselves. By promoting fair pricing, companies can avoid potential disadvantages relative to competitors and prevent being viewed unfavorably. In the future, awareness campaigns could be an effective tool for increasing general awareness of gender-specific price differences and potentially fostering a rejection of gender-based price segmentation, which may encourage companies to reconsider their pricing strategies.

Furthermore, companies and consumer organizations should rethink and refine their communication strategies. Given the prominent role of reactance, campaigns should be tailored to engage consumers emotionally. By incorporating personal stories, providing concrete evidence, and using hashtags like "#FairPricing," while aligning with broader movements such as gender equality, these campaigns can significantly enhance their impact. Such approaches not only raise awareness but also strengthen customer loyalty in the long term. Consumer organizations can leverage insights from our study to improve their educational and awareness initiatives. By delivering targeted information that elicits reactance, they can shape public perception and apply pressure on companies to reevaluate their pricing practices.

For policymakers, these findings further underscore the need for regulating gender-discriminatory price differences. While the AGG prohibits gender-based pricing discrimination, the complexity of pricing practices remains a significant challenge (an der Heiden & Wersig, 2017). The Federal Anti-Discrimination Agency advocates for regular monitoring of products and services to identify gender-specific price disparities. Implementing such measures would help ensure the elimination of unfair pricing practices, promote price equity for all consumers, and strengthen the enforcement of the AGG.

Limitations and Future Research

This study has several limitations that highlight important directions for future research. First, the use of a convenience sample limits the representativeness of the findings, making it difficult to generalize them to the broader population. The small number of male participants ($n = 22$ per experimental group), due to randomization and sample cleaning, may further restrict the generalizability of the results for men, which should be taken into account when interpreting the findings. Future research should aim to improve sampling methods to achieve greater representativeness, potentially through field experiments, thereby enhancing the generalizability of the results. Increasing the number of male participants would also provide more balanced insights into gender-specific responses and enable a more comprehensive analysis. Furthermore, it is crucial to investigate how prior knowledge of the Pink Tax influences the effectiveness of awareness campaigns. Examining gender differences in awareness of the Pink Tax and their impact on perceived price fairness and brand attitude would also provide valuable insights for designing more targeted interventions. In addition, future studies should investigate other factors, such as cultural or regional differences, to gain a broader understanding of consumer perceptions of gender-based price discrimination across various product categories. While this study focused on a single product from a hypothetical company, future research should replicate the findings across different contexts and appeals to strengthen external validity.

Second, price fairness research is complicated by various implicit theories regarding what price fairness entails. Perceptions of price fairness are connected to related concepts such as price satisfaction and price levels (Malc et al., 2016). As a result, current approaches may not fully capture the complexities underlying price fairness perceptions. Future research should aim to clarify and standardize the concept by incorporating multiple dimensions, including subjective perceptions, contextual factors, and related constructs. Also, the effects on the perceived brand attitude may have been limited by the procedure of introducing a fictitious brand that the participants cannot be inclined to. Future research may attempt to investigate the effects of campaigns on attitudes towards actual brands.

Additionally, the scale used to measure perceived psychological reactance was adapted for this study's specific context, posing a limitation to the validity and reliability of the construct. Future research should focus on validating this adapted scale through confirmatory factor analysis to ensure its reliability in measuring reactance in similar contexts. Testing the scale across a wider range of scenarios would also help evaluate its generalizability and robustness in different situations.

Bibliography

Aaker, J. (1997). Dimensions of brand personality. *Journal of Marketing Research, 34*(3), 347–356. <https://doi.org/10.1177/002224379703400304>.

Akbari, M., Lankarani, K. B., Tabrizi, R., Heydari, S. T., Vali, M., Motevalian, S. A., & Sullman, M. J. (2021). The effectiveness of mass media campaigns in increasing the use of seat belts: a systematic review. *Traffic Injury Prevention, 22*(7), 495–500. <https://doi.org/10.1080/15389588.2021.1921168>.

An der Heiden, I., & Wersig, M. (2017). Preisdifferenzierung nach Geschlecht in Deutschland. *Antidiskriminierungsstelle des Bundes.* <https://www.antidiskriminierungsstelle.de/SharedDocs/forschungsprojekte/DE/Studie_Preisdifferenzierung_n_Geschlecht.html>.

Ataman, F. (2022). Jahresbericht 2022. *Antidiskriminierungsstelle des Bundes.* <https://www.antidiskriminierungsstelle.de/SharedDocs/downloads/DE/publikationen/Jahresberichte/2022.html>.

Bauer, H. H., Heinrich, D., & Schafer, D. B. (2013). The effects of organic labels on global, local, and private brands: More hype than substance? *Journal of Business Research, 66*(8), 1035–1043. <https://doi.org/10.1016/j.jbusres.2011.12.028>.

Bolton, R. N., & Lemon, K. N. (1999). A dynamic model of customers' usage of services: Usage as an antecedent and consequence of satisfaction. *Journal of Marketing Research, 36*(2), 171–186. <https://doi.org/10.1177/002224379903600203>.

Bolton, L. E., & Alba, J. W. (2006). Price fairness: good and service differences and the role of vendor costs. *Journal of Consumer Research, 33*(2), 258–265. <https://doi.org/10.1086/506306>.

Borin, N., Cerf, D. C., & Krishnan R. (2011). Consumer effects of environmental impact in product labeling. *Journal of Consumer Marketing, 28*(1), 76–86. <https://doi.org/10.1108/07363761111101976>.

Brehm, J. W. (1966). *A theory of psychological reactance.* Academic Press.

Brehm, S. S. & Brehm, J. W. (1981). *Psychological reactance: A theory of freedom and control*. Academic Press. <https://doi.org/10.1016/C2013-0-10423-0>.

Daunfeldt, S. O., & Rudholm, N. (2014). Does shelf-labeling of organic foods increase sales? Results from a natural experiment. *Journal of Retailing and Consumer Services, 21*(5), 804–811. <https://doi.org/10.1016/j.jretconser.2014.06.009>.

Dono, J., Miller, C., Ettridge, K., & Wilson, C. (2020). The role of social norms in the relationship between anti-smoking advertising campaigns and smoking cessation: a scoping review. *Health Education Research, 35*(3), 179–194. <https://doi.org/10.1093/her/cyaa008>.

Duesterhaus, M., Grauerholz, L., Weichsel, R., & Guittar, N. A. (2011). The cost of doing femininity: Gendered disparities in pricing of personal care products and services. *Gender Issues, 28*, 175–191. <https://doi.org/10.1007/s12147-011-9106-3>.

Ferrell, O. C., Kapelianis, D., Ferrell, L., & Rowland, L. (2018). Expectations and attitudes toward gender-based price discrimination. *Journal of Business Ethics, 152*(4), 1015–1032. <https://doi.org/10.1007/s10551-016-3300-x>.

Ghods, H., Aghayari, M., Golbazi Mahdipour, A., Arabi Zanjani, R., Aghayari, H., Soparnot, R., & Bonyadi Naeini, A. (2024). Maximizing the effectiveness of anti-smoking campaigns with targeted framing strategies: Evidence from behavioral and neurological studies. *Social Marketing Quarterly*. <https://doi.org/10.1177/152450042412606>

Guittar, S. G., Grauerholz, L., Kidder, E. N., Daye, S. D., & McLaughlin, M. (2022). Beyond the pink tax: gender-based pricing and differentiation of personal care products. *Gender Issues, 39(1)*, 1–23. <https://doi.org/10.1007/s12147-021-09280-9>.

Gosselt J. F., van Rompay T., & Haske L. (2019). Won't get fooled again: The effects of internal and external CSR eco-labeling. *Journal of Business Ethics*, 155(2), 413–424. <https://doi.org/10.1007/s10551-017-3512-8>.

Hastie, B., & Cosh, S. (2013). "What's wrong with that?" Legitimating and contesting gender inequality. *Journal of Language and Social Psychology, 32*(4), 369–389. <https://doi.org/10.1177/0261927X12473989>.

Haws, K. L., & Bearden, W. O. (2006). Dynamic pricing and consumer fairness perceptions. *Journal of Consumer Research, 33*(3), 304–311. <https://doi.org/10.1086/508435>.

Kray, L. J., Reb, J., Galinsky, A. D., & Thompson, L. (2004). Stereotype reactance at the bargaining table: The effect of stereotype activation and power on claiming and creating value. *Personality and Social Psychology Bulletin, 30*, 399–411.

Kray, L. J., Thompson, L., & Galinsky, A. (2001). Battle of the sexes: Gender stereotype confirmation and reactance in negotiations. *Journal of Personality and Social Psychology, 80*, 942–958.

Lutz, R. J. (1975). Changing brand attitudes through modification of cognitive structure. *Journal of Consumer Research, 1*(4), 49–59. <https://doi.org/10.1086/208607>.

Malc, D., Mumel, D., & Pisnik, A. (2016). Exploring price fairness perceptions and their influence on consumer behavior. *Journal of Business Research, 69*(9), 3693–3697. <https://doi.org/10.1016/j.jbusres.2016.03.031>.

Miron, A. M., & Brehm, J. W. (2006). Reaktanztheorie—40 Jahre später [Reactance Theory—40 Years Later]. *Zeitschrift für Sozialpsychologie, 37*(1), 9–18.

Podsakoff, P. M., MacKenzie, S. B., Lee, J.-Y., & Podsakoff, N. P. (2003). Common method biases in behavioral research: A critical review of the literature and recommended remedies. *Journal of Applied Psychology, 88*, 879–903. <https://doi.org/10.1037/0021-9010.88.5.879>.

Sittenthaler, S., Traut-Mattausch, E., Steindl, C., & Jonas, E. (2015). Salzburger state reactance scale (SSR scale). *Zeitschrift für Psychologie, 223*(4), 257–266. <https://doi.org/10.1027/2151-2604/a000227>.

Sunstein, C. R. (2014). Nudging: A very short guide. *Journal of Consumer Policy, 37*(4), 583–588. <https://doi.org/10.1007/s10603-014-9273-1>.

Thaler, R. H., & Sunstein, C. R. (2021). *Nudge: The final edition*. Yale University Press.

Verbraucherzentrale Hamburg (2024). Einkaufsfalle Supermarkt. Pink Tax: Frauen zahlen mehr. *Verbraucherzentrale Hamburg.* <https://www.vzhh.de/themen/lebensmittel-ernaehrung/einkaufsfalle-supermarkt/pink-tax-frauen-zahlen-mehr>.

Wakefield, M., Flay, B., Nichter, M., & Giovino, G. (2003). Effects of anti-smoking advertising on youth smoking: A review. *Journal of Health Communication, 8*(3), 229–247. <https://doi.org/10.1080/10810730305686>.

Wakefield, M. A., Loken, B., & Hornik, R. C. (2010). Use of mass media campaigns to change health behaviour. *Lancet, 376*(9748), 1261–1271. <https://doi.org/10.1016/s0140-6736(10)60809-4>.

Xia, L., Monroe, K. B., & Cox, J. L. (2004). The price is unfair! A conceptual framework of price fairness perceptions. *Journal of Marketing, 68*(4), 1–15. <https://doi.org/10.1509/jmkg.68.4.1.42733>.

Appendix A

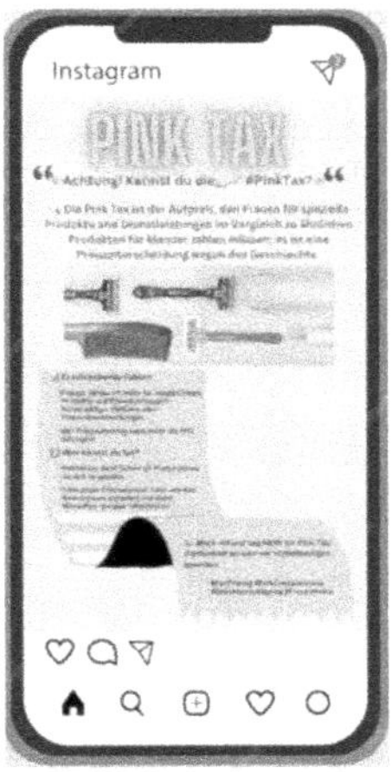

PINK TAX

"Watch out! Do you know the #PinkTax?"
The Pink Tax is the surcharge that women have to pay for special products and services compared to similar products for men; it is a price difference because of gender.

Shocking facts:

- Women often pay more for comparable products and services; personal care, perfumes or hairdressing services.
- The mark-up can be more than 50%!

What can you do?

- Inform yourself! Take a close look at prices and compare.
- Share your findings! Let's raise awareness and inform more people about it.

Join in and say NO to the Pink Tax! Together we can bring about change. #FairPricing #PinkTaxAwareness #Equality #WomenPower

Figure 3: Pink tax awareness campaign.

Aurélys - eau de parfum for men (30ml) 43.17€

Aurélys - eau de parfum for women (30ml) 57.45€

Figure 4: Pink tax offer.

Appendix B

Table 10: Measurements

Scale	English Item	German Items	Cronbach's alpha (α)
Price Fairness Scale	The pricing policy of the brand Aurélys seems fair to me.	Ich halte die Preispolitik der Marke Aurélys für fair.	$\alpha = 0.779$
	I consider the pricing policy of the brand Aurélys to be acceptable.	Ich betrachte die Preispolitik der Marke Aurélys als akzeptabel.	
	I consider the pricing policy of the brand Aurélys to be ethically justifiable.	Ich betrachte die Preispolitik der Marke Aurélys als ethisch vertretbar.	
	I would pay a fair price for Aurélys perfume.	Ich würde einen fairen Preis für das Parfüm von Aurélys bezahlen.	
	It is fair that two customers pay different prices for the same product from the brand Aurélys.	Es ist fair, dass zwei Kunden für das gleiche Produkt der Marke Aurélys unterschiedliche Preise bezahlen.	
Brand Attitude Scale (BAS)	I would consider purchasing the brand Aurélys in the future.	Ich würde erwägen, die Marke Aurélys in Zukunft zu kaufen.	$\alpha = 0.906$
	I would recommend the brand Aurélys to others.	Ich würde die Marke Aurélys anderen empfehlen.	
	I have a positive feeling toward the brand Aurélys.	Ich habe ein positives Gefühl gegenüber der Marke Aurélys.	
	I believe that Aurélys is a high-quality brand.	Ich glaube, dass Aurélys eine hochwertige Marke ist.	
	I have confidence in the brand Aurélys.	Ich habe Vertrauen in die Marke Aurélys.	
Salzburger State Reactance (SSR) Scale	Would you want to damage the reputation of the brand Aurélys by posting a negative review on the drugstore's online shop?	Würdest du den Ruf der Marke Aurélys öffentlich schädigen wollen, indem du im Online-Shop des Drogeriemarktes eine negative Bewertung veröffentlichst?	$\alpha = 0.859$
	Would you discourage other women from purchasing the brand Aurélys?	Würdest du anderen Frauen von der Marke Aurélys abraten?	
	Are you frustrated by the price difference?	Bist du über den Preisunterschied frustriert?	

Scale	English Item	German Items	Cronbach's alpha (α)
	Do you believe that the price difference also occurs in other areas?	Glaubst du, dass der Preisunterschied auch in anderen Bereichen vorkommt?	
	Do you feel offended/ bothered by the price difference?	Fühlst du dich beleidigt/gestört durch den Preisunterschied?	
	Does the price difference upset you?	Ärgert dich der Preisunterschied?	
	Do you perceive the price difference as limiting your freedom?	Empfindest du den Preisunterschied als freiheitseinschränkend?	
	Do you think it is likely that the brand Aurélys exploits women?	Hältst du es für wahrscheinlich, dass die Marke Aurélys Frauen ausnutzt?	
	Do you feel the desire to complain about the price difference?	Hast du den Wunsch, dich über den Preisunterschied zu beschweren?	
	Do you think the brand Aurélys might have biases against women?	Denkst du, dass die Marke Aurélys Vorurteile gegenüber Frauen haben könnte?	

5. Artificial Intelligence in Finance and Accounting of Small and Medium-Sized and Family-Owned Companies—Use Cases, Opportunities, and Risks

Tim Kampe and Andreas Uphaus**

ABSTRACT

Since the introduction of ChatGPT in 2022, artificial intelligence has become a real fashionable topic, also in the field of finance and accounting. In fact, the approach fulfills all the criteria of a management fashion or fad. Even in the academic debate, the presentation of Artificial Intelligence (AI) use cases in business practice often remains abstract and vague. Especially in small and medium-sized enterprise and family businesses, the use of AI could leverage considerable potential. This paper identifies specific use cases of AI in finance and accounting and evaluates their opportunities and risks on the basis of existing literature, current studies, explorative expert interviews, and generative AI models. A structured survey of experts is used to validate the findings and assess their specific potential applications, opportunities, and risks. As a result, those responsible in departments will be shown which specific options for action in the field of AI exist for their areas in the near future.

Keywords: Digitalization, Financial reporting, Fraud detection, Credit scoring, Automatic invoice booking, Mass data analysis

Introduction

Small and medium-sized enterprises (SMEs) have a significant share of the German economy, accounting for 99.4% of total companies, 55% of employees and 42% of gross value added (Destatis, 2024). The European Union also emphasizes the particular importance of SMEs (European Parliament, 2024). SMEs are typically defined as companies that fall below certain size criteria. According to EU Recommendation 2003/361, these are companies whose number of employees is less than 250 and whose turnover does not exceed EUR 50 million or whose balance sheet total does not exceed EUR

*Bielefeld School of Business, Hochschule Bielefeld—University of Applied Sciences and Arts, Bielefeld, Germany
Emails: <tim.kampe@hsbi.de>, <andreas.uphaus@hsbi.de>

43 million (European Commission, 2024). Family businesses, on the other hand, are companies that are controlled by a manageable number of natural individuals. This means that they are under the significant influence of one or few families, who do not necessarily have to hold the majority of voting rights or management functions (Berthold, 2010, p. 13; Chua et al., 1999, p. 35). Rather, there is a strong overlap between the family system and the business system in a profit-seeking organization (König et al., 2013, p. 421). Such family-controlled companies account for around 90% of all German companies, generate 55% of turnover, and provide around 57% of employment subject to social insurance contributions in Germany (Stiftung Familienunternehmen, 2024). The size of family businesses can significantly exceed the size according to the EU recommendation despite similar characteristics. In academic discussions, SMEs and family businesses are often grouped together under the German term "Mittelstand" (Kampe, 2017, pp. 95–98).

In SMEs and family businesses in particular, there are suboptimizations in the areas of finance and accounting due to a lack of adequate use of methods and instruments, inefficient digital processes, and limited human resources (Demelius et al., 2023, pp. 17–21; Mayr, 2021, p. 4). In this context, great hopes for optimization are placed in new approaches to artificial intelligence (AI) (Prümm et al., 2023, p. 6). AI is an area of informatics that deals with the development of systems that can imitate human intelligence. This includes the ability to learn from experience, recognize patterns and react flexibly to new situations. Within AI, generative AI as a subfield aims to generate new content such as texts, images, videos, or music (Brodersen et al., 2023, 1553). These systems use advanced machine learning models (deep learning), in particular, large language models (LLM). These models are trained to understand and generate human language. They can analyze texts, generate coherent responses, and perform various language-related tasks. One example of this is ChatGPT (Generative Pre-Trained Transformer) published by OpenAI, which has triggered a considerable wave of interest in generative AI with its introduction (Berge, 2023, p. 607; Schulze et al., 2023, p. 56).

In principle, an AI hype has also emerged in finance and accounting in recent years (Schulze et al., 2023). There is a lot of talk and writing about AI, but its actual use and implementation in finance and accounting is still very limited (Kreher et al., 2024, p. 14). The use of AI in companies could therefore be a management fashion (Abrahamson, 1996; Kieser, 1996) or a management fad (Miller et al., 2004). Following Abrahamson (1996, p. 257), a management fashion “is a relatively transitory collective belief, disseminated by management fashion setters, that a management technique leads rational management progress.” A management fashion is not necessarily negative or temporary, although management fashion theory can explain why some concepts experience a temporary hype before possibly establishing themselves permanently in companies on a smaller scale (Kieser, 1996, p. 34).

Although the potential and use cases in finance and accounting are sometimes discussed very comprehensively, they are usually rather generalized and with little concrete application reference (Boritz & Stratopoulos, 2023). Furthermore, the vast majority of SMEs and family firms do not yet use artificial intelligence in finance and accounting (Kreher et al., 2024, p. 14). The aim of the paper is therefore twofold: the first step is to examine whether AI is a management fashion in companies. In a second step, possible concrete and meaningful applications in SMEs and family firms, as well as their opportunities and risks, will be determined. Finance and accounting are analyzed separately in order to more clearly identify differences and similarities, as well as the different types of use cases. Finance is understood in the narrower sense as treasury with all tasks in the area of cash and liquidity management, financial risk management, and corporate financing, while accounting is understood in the narrower sense as external accounting and book-keeping, cost accounting, and controlling. Basic opportunities and risks of the use of AI in finance and accounting for SMEs are developed and evaluated. Recommendations for priorities for the use of AI in SMEs are derived from the evaluation.

Method

The article basically follows a mixed-methods approach. In a first approach (1), with reference to Kieser (1996), it will be clarified whether the application of AI in companies can be described as a management fad. Building on this, an extended approach to the field is chosen by evaluating existing literature and existing studies and flanking them with explorative expert interviews (2). AI analysis is used to (further) identify the most common use cases as well as opportunities and risks, and (3) the results are validated with a structured expert survey (4) and assessed in terms of their feasibility.

(1) Review of management fad

In a first step, stylized facts based on the findings of Kieser (1996) are used to check whether the use of AI in general, and thus in particular in the areas of finance and accounting, is a management fashion. If this is the case, it would explain why there are many examples of the use of AI in processes, but few structured and extensive actual implementations in finance and accounting.

(2) Literature research, studies, and exploratory expert interviews

The survey of use cases (examples and implementations, hereinafter also referred to as use cases) as well as opportunities and risks is carried out in a first step on the basis of a comprehensive literature review (Milana & Ashta, 2021; Pargmann et al., 2023) and the evaluation of existing studies on digitalization in finance and accounting (Demelius et al., 2023; Kreher et al., 2024; Prümm et al., 2023). The auditing firm KPMG has been conducting a regular online survey on the status of digitalization in accounting since 2017 (Kreher et al., 2017). More than 2,500 companies in Germany, Austria, and Switzerland were recently surveyed for this purpose (Kreher et al., 2022, p. 9). Between 350 companies (Kreher et al., 2021, p. 5) and most recently 232 companies (Kreher et al., 2024, p. 9) regularly took part. The companies came from all size classes and industries (Kreher et al., 2024, p. 10). The auditing firm PWC is already in its eighth year of conducting a similarly designed study with around 100 participating companies (Prümm et al., 2023, p. 3). The auditing firm Deloitte Austria last conducted a study on automation in accounting and its impact on the skills of accounting employees among 268 Austrian companies of all sizes and sectors in 2023 (Demelius et al., 2023, p. 8). This was the fourth repetition of a study that was first conducted in 2016 (Vlk et al., 2016).

In a further step, the previously acquired literature and study findings were validated and supplemented in a total of eight exploratory expert interviews with auditors and those responsible for finance and accounting from companies in the Ostwestfalen-Lippe region in Germany (Döring, 2023, pp. 371–372; Strübing, 2018, pp. 106–108). These interviews were recorded and transcribed (Strübing, 2018, pp. 117–119). Categories were formed on the basis of the literature and the interviews, and the transcriptions were coded accordingly (Mayring, 2022, pp. 49–103). The aim was to gain up-to-date and exploratory access to the field on the one hand and to be able to illustrate the theoretical explanations with concrete statements on the other.

(3) AI analysis
As further possible use cases as well as opportunities, and risks are likely in addition to the previous findings, several generative AI systems (GenAI) are surveyed on these aspects in a third step in order to optimally supplement the known aspects.

The questions about the use cases are asked separately for the areas of finance and accounting, as different cases are to be expected. Opportunities and risks/challenges, on the other hand, are considered together for both areas, as they are fundamentally very similar.

The six most widely used, respectively available systems and language models were selected as GenAI systems (Bager, 2024): ChatGPT 4o from OpenAI, Gemini from Google, Microsoft Copilot, Llama 3.1 405b from Meta, Claude from Anthropic, as well as the university-specific HSBIKI. Although some systems are based on a similar language model (ChatGPT, Copilot, and HSBIKI on GPT-4(o)), it is likely that different results will be achieved.

The following questions are asked:

(a) What are the most important concrete *use cases* or applications for AI in the area of *finance*, and specifically in treasury?
(b) Are there any other use cases in this area?
(c) What are the most important specific *use cases* for AI in the area of *accounting*, and specifically in accounting?
(d) Are there any other use cases in this area?
(e) What *opportunities* exist for the use of AI in finance and accounting?
(f) What are the *risks* and challenges for the use of using AI in finance and accounting?

Questions (a) and (c) are regarded as primary (p) results. As further possibilities are expected, questions (b) and (d) are supplemented and considered as secondary (s) results.

All questions are only asked once. If the questions had been repeated, slightly different results would have been observed. The results are summarized manually in key points according to context, and the frequency of mentions is counted. Overarching fields of application, which can be relevant in several areas and are mentioned by the AIs in both finance and accounting, are considered separately in order to be able to summarize them again in the further course. For the use cases, primary and secondary mentions are counted individually and then totaled across all systems. Only results with three or more mentions were included in the further analyses in order to establish a common sense, so to speak, and to prevent the results from becoming too fragmented.

(4) Structured expert survey
Based on the results of (1)–(3), a structured expert survey is created and conducted. The survey includes the expectations of experts on AI in the areas of treasury and accounting. The survey of key experts appears to be essential, as only they can adequately assess the significance of AI based on their activities and market knowledge.

The survey is conducted separately for finance and accounting, as these are generally different areas of responsibility or departments. The experts were explicitly selected from larger SMEs and family-run companies. Larger SMEs were chosen because the scope of the AI application depends on the size of the company and the available capacity (Ludwig et al., 2024, p. 111; Prümm et al., 2023, p. 31). Family businesses are chosen in order to virtually exclude requirements from the capital market. The experts should be department heads, internal specialists, or CFOs, that is, very high-ranking. At least five experts, each should be interviewed for finance and accounting. The companies should be as representative as possible of different sectors.

The survey is structured on the basis of a corresponding questionnaire, which is created and administered at umfrageonline.com. The content of the questionnaire is structured with the following questions:

(a) How important can the use of AI become in the following finance/accounting application fields?
(b) How important can the use of AI become in the following overarching application areas for finance/accounting?
(c) How do you rate the following opportunities for the use of AI in finance/accounting in the future?
(d) How do you assess the following risks/challenges when using AI in finance/accounting in the future?

For each question, the results from steps (1) to (3) are given as possible answers. The assessment should be made on a scale of 1–10: for use cases from extremely unimportant to extremely important, for opportunities and risks/challenges from extremely low to extremely high. All 10 levels are verbally coded in such a way that approximately equal perceived distances between levels can be assumed. Thus, 10 levels are selected in order to achieve a quasi-interval scale level for an ordinal scale.

In addition, each question offers the opportunity to name further aspects.

Despite the small number of responses and quasi-interval scaling, the arithmetic mean of the responses is calculated and compared as a position parameter and the empirical standard deviation as a dispersion parameter as "orientation measures." In this way, an attempt is made to determine initial comprehensive empirical evidence for the actual estimated use of AI and its framework conditions in the areas of finance and accounting.

Findings

As mentioned at the beginning, a certain amount of AI hype has also arisen in finance and accounting due to the hopes associated with the emergence of new AI technologies (Schulze et al., 2023). In fact, according to Kieser (1996), AI can be described as a management fashion. The use of AI in finance and accounting currently remains correspondingly vague. Nevertheless, various use cases can be found, some of which are associated with considerable opportunities, but also risks.

Artificial Intelligence as a Management Fashion?

Strategic management has always been characterized by certain ideas and concepts, which Kirsch (1997, p. 637ff.) generally describes as the "ecology of knowledge." Through intensive discussion and use by managers, management consultants, and academics, some of these concepts regularly achieve such prominence that they can also be described as management fashions. Ringlstetter and Schuster (2003) cite concepts such as "Business Process Reengineering," "Shareholder Value," "Balanced Scorecard" or "Corporate Citizenship" and "Corporate Social Responsibility" as examples of this. In the following, we will examine whether the concept of artificial intelligence can also be described as a management fashion. With reference to Kieser (1996), various indicators can be reconstructed to identify such fashions:

A first indication of a management fashion can be the existence of a management bestseller that presents the guiding ideas of the concept clearly and makes them available in practice (Kieser, 1996, p. 23). Although it is not easy to identify such a bestseller in the AI discussion at present, a glance at the virtual bookshelf of a large Internet bookseller shows that a significant proportion of the numerous monographs currently available on the subject of AI have "practice" in the prefix or suffix of the title. The top three titles in a query on Amazon.de (as at August 31, 2024; >80,000 hits for the search term "artificial intelligence") are "Artificial intelligence: superior to humans—how AI saves and threatens us | The neuroscientist, psychiatrist and SPIEGEL bestselling author of 'Digital Dementia,'" "Artificial intelligence for dummies" and "Artificial intelligence: how it works and what it means for us. The bestseller from Norway—now available in German." Nevertheless, Kieser (1996), p. 35, points out that the existence of a bestseller is a sufficient but not a necessary condition for the existence of a management fashion.

A management fashion is also characterized by the fact that the topic is taken up by management magazines, consulting firms, and further education institutions, processed and disseminated in corporate practice. This applies in particular to the topic of AI, which is currently attracting a great deal of attention in the (specialist) press. Large consulting and auditing firms in particular have recognized the potential of the topic and offer corresponding services, which are publicized in the market via studies and other publications (e.g., Demelius et al., 2023; Kreher et al., 2024; and above all the services mentioned in Prümm et al., 2023, pp. 33–35). In the area of training and further education, the offer is also very diverse and ranges from the one-day seminar "The ChatGPT revolution: operation, fields of application, business models; practical use of artificial intelligence—without prior technical knowledge" (Haufe Akademie, 2024) to certificate programs (DHBW, 2024; HPI, 2023) and entire bachelor's and master's degree courses (Frick, 2024).

In academic discourse, a management fashion is generally accompanied by increased discussion in academic journals, at meetings and conferences, and ultimately manifests itself in the founding of societies and journals dedicated to this concept (Kieser, 1996, p. 28; Ringlstetter & Schuster, 2003, p. 170). This development becomes clearest when one looks at the number of legal and business publications on the topic of "artificial intelligence" in German scientific databases (WISO, Beck online, SpringerLink) (Figure 5), which have risen sharply in recent times.

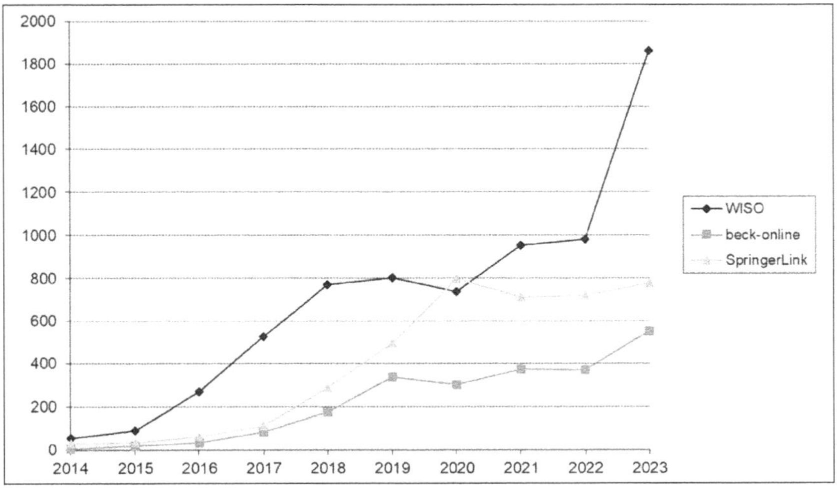

Figure 5: Number of legal and business publications on the topic of "artificial intelligence" listed in German-language databases (*Source*: Own survey in August 2024).

In summary, it can be said that the concept of artificial intelligence can be described as a management fashion, as the necessary prerequisites according to Kieser (1996) are cumulatively fulfilled as described above. This is not necessarily negative (Kieser, 1996, p. 34), but it is a possible explanation for the fact that, despite intensive discussion in academic discourse and in practice, the actual penetration in finance and accounting is low. This also becomes clear when looking at the implementation in the finance and accounting departments of German companies, as shown below.

Status of AI Penetration in Finance and Accounting in Literature and Existing Studies

Kreher et al. (2021, 2022, 2024) show in their regular survey of German companies for the accounting firm KPMG that digitization is progressing in accounting in general, especially in core processes. Basic systems are becoming increasingly homogenized, master data quality is being improved, and paperless end-to-end processes are being established. More than half of the companies surveyed have already implemented this across the board or at least in some areas, while the majority of the remaining companies are in the process of implementing it or are planning to do so (Kreher et al.,

2024, p. 14). However, the use of artificial intelligence has not yet achieved a breakthrough (Kreher et al., 2024, p. 14): only 15% of the companies surveyed use learning systems (machine learning, neural networks, ChatGPT) across the board or in initial pilot projects. This even represents a decrease of two percentage points compared to the previous study, as this figure was previously 17% (Kreher et al., 2022, p. 22). Predictive analytics, automated invoice posting, and the creation of (internal) financial reports are cited as examples of the use of AI in accounting (Kreher et al., 2024, pp. 14, 16). AI-based liquidity planning is mentioned as a use case in the area of finance (Kreher et al., 2022, p. 23).

The aforementioned figures on the use of AI in accounting are generally supported by the study by Prümm et al. (2023, p. 31) for the accounting firm PWC. According to the study, 17% of respondents are already using AI-based solutions, and 27% are planning to do so. However, significantly more than half of the companies surveyed (56%) say that they are not currently considering the use of AI in accounting (Prümm et al., 2023, p. 31). The main reason given by 82% of companies for not using AI is a lack of resources to deal with the technology. Other reasons cited for not using AI include high development costs (55%), a lack of certification (52%), a lack of trust in the technology (41%) and a lack of quality (34%) (Prümm et al., 2023, p. 31). Prümm et al. (2023, p. 31) cite document entry, pre-accounting, consistency checks, and data extraction from unstructured data as examples of the use of AI in accounting.

The penetration of AI in the finance and accounting departments of Austrian companies appears to be higher. In the study by Demelius et al. (2023, p. 20) for Deloitte Austria, 40% of the companies surveyed stated that they were already working on AI projects. For 22% of those surveyed, the emergence of ChatGPT was the main reason for getting to grips with the technology for the first time. Demelius et al. (2023, p. 20) cite the analysis and creation of texts as the main use cases in finance and accounting. These are, in particular, summaries of complex texts, the creation of checklists and documentation, reviewing and revising previously created documents, and the creation of code for business users. Nevertheless, Demelius et al. (2023, p. 20) also state that the majority of use cases for AI tend to be in areas of the company other than finance and accounting. The main challenges and reasons cited against AI in finance and accounting are a lack of expertise within the company (50%), a lack of use cases (44%), and excessive risks (42%). Demelius et al. (2023, p. 21) then cite data protection, hallucination, and a lack of transparency in the sense of a lack of reproducibility of results as examples of these risks.

The current situation in the finance and accounting departments of SMEs and family firms can be summarized in the words of one interviewee in the exploratory expert interviews, a partner in a medium-sized auditing firm in Bielefeld: "We have this a bit on the radar. But artificial intelligence is not yet an issue for us internally and our clients are not yet ready. Yes, and now we'll just wait and see [...]."

Further use cases for the use of AI in accounting can be found in the literature. In his experimental article, Hacker (2023, pp. 118–119) cites in particular the automation of routine tasks, the improvement of efficiency, and better insights into financial data when using AI. According to Hacker (2023, p. 118), the automation of routine tasks primarily concerns data entry, the creation of reports, and the reconciliation of financial reports. The improvement in efficiency can then be seen above all in the area of financial reporting, where routine questions from stakeholders can be answered by AI or financial reports can be created automatically (Hacker, 2023, p. 118). In the area of financial data, AI can be used above all to analyze large amounts of data, to identify trends or even future developments (predictive analytics) (Hacker, 2023, pp. 118–119). Hacker (2023, p. 120) cites the fact that AI cannot (yet) make human discretionary decisions and that AI tends to "hallucinate," that is the results have logical or factual errors, as criticisms or risks of AI. Privacy and data security are also one of the biggest problems (Hacker, 2023, p. 120). In principle, the use of AI is also subject to possible operating errors, and the results can sometimes only be validated to a limited extent due to missing or incorrect source references (Hacker, 2023, p. 120).

In the field of finance, Bahrammizaee (2010, p. 1166) has already highlighted credit evaluation, credit risk analysis, bond rating, financial risk assessment, portfolio management, and financial prediction and planning, exchange rate predictions, among others, as key areas of application in a very comprehensive literature review. A variety of AI methods are considered, including various forms of Artificial Neural Networks (ANN), support vector machines, regressions, and decision trees. Berdiyeva et al (2021, pp. 66–67) also focus on the opportunities of AI in accounting and finance as part of a meta-analysis, in particular productivity, reducing errors, increasing efficiency, and cost savings. Azman et al. (2021, pp. 225–227) also analyze SMEs in particular and mention optimizations in automated book-keeping, such as invoice pattern recognition and automated journal entry, reducing errors, cost reduction, and their optimization with various AI methods. In addition to many technical details, Milana & Ashta (2021, pp. 194–196) also discuss fraud detection, forecasting, cash flow prediction, pattern recognition, robo advisors, decision making assistance, credit scoring, and simulation.

Use cases, opportunities, and risks of AI in finance and accounting according to the assessment of AI itself.

The results of the AI analysis described above are summarized in the table (Figure 6). The primary (p) and secondary (s) mentions per system, as well as the total sum of all mentions and systems per characteristic, are shown.

In total, there are 10 specific use cases with at least three mentions and seven specific use cases for accounting. Four use cases were classified as "general," as these were mentioned for both finance and accounting. In total, an additional seven use cases for finance, seven for accounting, and two for both as well as 11 opportunities and seven risks/challenges were proposed as very comprehensible possible answers with only one or two mentions.

It is noticeable in the complete data that Gemini (53 possible answers) and ChatGPT 4o (47) clearly gave the most answers—followed by Claude (41), Copilot (31), and HSBIKI (29), while Llama only generated 18 possible answers.

Validation of the Results in a Structured Expert Survey

Seven experts from the accounting sector and 10 experts from the finance sector from medium-sized family businesses were interviewed.

Questions (a) and (b) on the respective future significance use cases in finance and accounting led to the result, as shown in Figure 7.

Overall, the average mean value is 7.34, that is, important. This means that AI is probably considered to be relatively important in practice. Individual aspects such as the automation of processes and forecasts in finance, and automated document recognition, invoice verification, and automation in accounting are even considered to be extremely important.

It can also be observed that as the importance decreases, the uncertainty as to whether the use cases are relevant increases, as the standard deviation

	Gemini 21.08.2024 (p/s)	HSBIKI 21.08.2024 (p/s)	Copilot 21.08.2024 (p/s)	ChatGPT 4o 21.08.2024 (p/s)	Llama 3.1 405b 22.08.2024 (p/s)	Claude 3.5 Sonnet 22.08.2024 (p/s)	total
1. Use Cases Finance and Treasury							
Lending/worthiness	1/1	0/1	0/1	0/1		1/1	**7**
Cash flow forecasting	1/0	1/0	0/1	1/1		1/0	**6**
Risk management	1/0	1/0		1/0	1/0	1/0	**5**
Automation processes	1/0	1/0	1/0	1/0		1/0	**5**
Portfolio optimization	0/1	0/1	1/0	0/1		1/0	**5**
Prediction of market movements	0/1	0/1	1/0	0/1			**4**
Trading strategies			0/1	1/1	0/1		**4**
Robo-Advisor	1/0				1/0	1/0	**3**
Stress tests	0/1		0/1	0/1			**3**
Supply chain finance	0/1			0/1		0/1	**3**
2. Use cases Accounting							
Accounting automation	1/0	1/0	0/1	1/0	1/0	1/0	**6**
Forecasts	1/1	1/1		1/0		1/0	**6**
Automatic document recognition	1/0	0/1	1/0	1/0		1/0	**5**
Tax planning/advance sales tax return	1/1			1/0	1/0		**5**
Account assignment: Classification of transactic	1/0		1/0			1/1	**4**
Analysis of cost structures		1/0	0/1	0/1			**3**
Travel expenses	1/0			1/1			**3**
3.General							
Financial report analysis (News)	0/1	1/0	0/1	1/1	1/1		**8**
Fraud detection	1/0	1/0	0/1	1/1	1/0	1/0	**7**
Compliance monitoring	0/1	0/1	0/1	1/0		1/1	**6**
Customer service	1/0	0/1	1/0				**3**
4. Chances							
Increased efficiency	1	1	1	1	1		**5**
Improved accuracy	1	1		1	1	1	**5**
Automated decision making		1	1	1		1	**4**
Lower costs	1		1	1			**3**
Personalized solutions	1		1	1			**3**
Automation of routine tasks	1			1		1	**3**
Better risk assessment	1	1	1				**3**
Improved compliance	1				1	1	**3**
5. Risks/challenges							
Lack of transparency	1	1	1	1	1	1	**6**
Data quality/bias	1	1	1	1		1	**5**
Data security	1		1	1	1	1	**5**
Regulation	1	1	1	1		1	**5**
Investment costs	1		1	1		1	**4**
Privacy		1		1	1	1	**4**
Job losses	1		1	1			**3**
Ethical concerns	1				1	1	**3**
Know-how	1	1				1	**3**
Discrimination		1	1	1			**3**

Figure 6: Results of the survey of six large language models on the use cases of AI in finance and accounting (*Source*: Own survey in August 2024).

Use Cases in Finance	Mean	SD	Use Cases in Accounting	Mean	SD
Automation processes	8.90	1.30	Automatic document recognition	9.29	0.45
Forecast of cash flows/liquidity planning	8.80	1.17	Invoice verification/error detection	9.29	0.45
Risk management	7.80	0.87	Accounting automation	8.71	0.88
Stress tests	7.50	1.20	Account assignment: Classification of transactions	8.57	1.40
Working capital management	7.20	1.54	Credit risks	7.86	1.73
Bank fee analysis	7.10	0.94	Reconciliation and clearing	7.86	1.81
Lending/credit worthiness	6.80	2.18	Prediction of payment defaults	7.71	1.75
Trading strategies	6.50	1.63	Analysis of cost structures	7.57	2.13
Prediction of market movements	6.40	2.54	Forecasts	7.29	1.83
Portfolio optimization	6.00	1.79	Real-time audits	6.43	1.84
Robo-Advisor	6.00	2.05	Tax planning/advance sales tax return	6.29	2.31
Supply Chain Finance	5.90	1.81	Travel expenses	6.00	2.51

Figure 7: Overview of the identified use cases in finance and accounting with average and standard deviation (*Source*: Own survey in August 2024).

increases. All of the following aspects were related to the finance and accounting groups together, as these are general AI characteristics, and the individual results did not show any significant deviations (Figure 8).

	Mean	SD
Fraud detection	9.06	0.87
Compliance monitoring	8.29	0.96
Financial report analysis (news)	7.47	1.72
Customer service	7.41	1.88

Figure 8: General use cases in finance and accounting with average and standard deviation (*Source*: Own survey in August 2024).

Fraud monitoring and compliance dominate the general areas of application mentioned in both Finance and Accounting and are rated as extremely important.

In addition, the experts mentioned a few other areas of application, which are mainly related to process efficiencies. Process efficiencies through automation were also highlighted as further opportunities. A possible lack of transparency was repeatedly emphasized as the greatest additional risk. In detail, the opportunities and risks are assessed as shown in Figure 9.

The average opportunities are rated at 7.6, that is, approximately "high." Efficiency, automation, and compliance are once again at the forefront. The risks are less important at 6.1, that is, only "rather high." Data quality, lack of transparency, and security dominate here.

Opportunities	Mean	SD
Automation of routine tasks	8.71	1.36
Increased efficiency	8.65	1.23
Improved compliance	7.71	1.74
Improved accuracy	7.59	1.29
Better risk assessment	7.59	1.24
Lower costs	7.53	1.88
Automated decision making	7.06	1.55
Personalized solutions	6.13	1.69

Risks	Mean	SD
Data quality/bias	7.71	1.81
Lack of transparency	7.06	2.07
Data availability	6.94	1.86
Data security	6.88	1.60
Privacy	6.76	1.80
Know how	6.76	1.86
Investment costs	6.47	1.68
Regulation	6.12	1.41
Job losses	5.41	1.78
Ethical concerns	4.13	1.76
Discrimination	4.00	2.30

Figure 9: Opportunities and risks in the use of artificial intelligence in finance and accounting with average and standard deviation (*Source*: Own survey in August 2024).

Discussion and Conclusions

Overall, a relatively uniform picture emerges for the use of AI in the areas of finance and accounting in SMEs and family-owned companies: Firstly, it can be stated that there are clear indications that the potential use of AI in finance and accounting is obviously a management fashion and that the concrete development remains to be seen with caution. Process automation to increase efficiency in various areas, such as the invoice receipt process, is seen as a key area of application. Compliance and risk management (e.g., also with credit risk checks and stress tests) is seen as another fundamental area of application. Furthermore, use in the area of planning and forecasting (in finance, for example, for liquidity and market prices, in accounting for payment defaults and taxes) is obviously promising. In addition, specific processes such as working capital management, capital market trading, and bank fees in finance and cost analyses, or travel expenses in accounting were highlighted. Potential is also seen in fraud detection and reporting. Once again, the greatest opportunities lie in process efficiency, costs, analysis, and compliance, while the greatest risks lie in qualitatively appropriate data availability, transparency, security, and costs. The opportunities are rated significantly higher than the risks.

The limitations of the study are that it was primarily larger medium-sized family businesses that were surveyed, which are not representative of the SME sector at all, but where pilot projects could be carried out and then also used by smaller companies due to slightly higher resources. Furthermore, only a small number of companies were surveyed, meaning that the results are only partially representative, but they do point in a clear direction due to the experts with relatively similar assessments.

In this respect, despite limitations, a relatively clear and still optimistic picture of the use of AI in finance and accounting can be seen. The result appears plausible in terms of content, but it remains to be seen to what extent the fields of application will be integrated into the standard system landscape or whether AI was more of a hype. The new possibilities offered by GenAI and potential technical advances could also lead to new potential. In this respect, the development should be further researched.

Overall, the situation still appears optimistic, but not euphoric. Many hopes seem to be pinned on efficiency gains and automation in particular, that is, the optimization of basic problems in these areas. This may indicate that the hype cycle is already slightly above the peak of exaggerated expectations.

Bibliography

Abrahamson, E. (1996). Management fashion. *The Academy of Management Review, 21*(1), 254–285.

Azman, N. A., Mohamed, A., & Jamil, A. M. (2021). Artificial intelligence in automated bookkeeping: a value-added function for small and medium enterprise. *International Journal on Informatics Visualization, 5*(3), 224–230.

Bager, J. (2024). Finde Antworten! Acht Suchmaschinen mit KI im Kreuzverhör. *c't—Magazin für Computertechnik*, (13), 94–99.

Bahrammizaee, A. (2010). A comparative survey of artificial intelligence applications in finance: artificial neural networks, expert system and hybrid intelligent systems. *Neural Computing and Applications*, *19*, 1165–1195.

Berdiyeva, O., Islam, M. U., & Saeedi, M. (2021). Artificial intelligence in accounting and finance: Meta-analysis. *NUST Business Review, 3*(01), 56–79.

Berge, T. (2023). IT and more: Generative Künstliche Intelligenz: Nutzungsmöglichkeiten für die Wirtschaftsprüfung. *Die Wirtschaftsprüfung, 76*(11), 607–609.

Berthold, F. (2010). *Familienunternehmen im Spannungsfeld zwischen Wachstum und Finanzierung.* Eul, Köln

Boritz, J. E., & Stratopoulos, T. C. (2023). AI and the accounting profession: Views from industry and academia. *Journal of Information Systems*, *37*(3), 1–9. <https://doi.org/10.2308/ISYS-2023-054>.

Brodersen, J. S., & Mattig, D. (2023). Generative AI—Ein praktischer Leitfaden für Gesellschafts- und Steuerrechtler. *Der Betrieb* 70(27–28), 1553–1556.

Chua, J. H., Chrisman, J. J., & Sharma, P. (1999). Defining the family business by behavior. *Entrepreneurship: Theory & Practice*, *23*(4), 19–39.

Demelius, K., Viveros, N., Herrmann, M., & Wolfsberger, J. (2023). Automatisierung und Digitalisierung im Rechnungswesen 2023. *Eine Studie von Deloitte Österreich*. Wien: Deloitte. <https://www2.deloitte.com/content/dam/Deloitte/at/Documents/presse/at-digitalisierung-im-rechnungs wesen-2023.pdf>.

Destatis (2024, 30th May). Kleine und mittlere Unternehmen. <https://www.destatis.de/DE/Themen/ Branchen-Unternehmen/Unternehmen/Kleine-Unternehmen-Mittlere-Unternehmen/_inhalt.html>.

DHBW—Duale Hochschule Baden-Württemberg (2024, 31st August). *Künstliche Intelligenz—Zertifikatsprogramm*. <https://www.wissenschaftliche-weiterbildung.dhbw.de/kuenstliche-intelligenz>.

Döring, N. (2023). Forschungsmethoden und Evaluation in den Sozial- und Humanwissenschaften. 6., vollst. überarb. u. erw. Aufl., Berlin: Springer.

European Commission (2024, 30th May), SME definition. <https://single-market-economy.ec.europa.eu/smes/sme-fundamentals/sme-definition_en>.

European Parliament (2024, 30th May). Kleine und mittlere Unternehmen. <https://www.europarl.europa.eu/factsheets/de/sheet/63/kleine-und-mittlere-unternehmen>.

Frick, L. (2024, 11th May). Künstliche Intelligenz an der Uni: An diesen Hochschulen können Sie KI studieren. <https://www.wiwo.de/erfolg/hochschule/kuenstliche-intelligenz-an-der-uni-an-diesen-hochschulen-koennen-sie-ki-studieren/29793038.html>.

Hacker, B. (2023). Wird ChatGPT das Rechnungswesen revolutionieren? Der Nutzen von Künstlicher Intelligenz (KI) im Rechnungswesen. IRZ *Zeitschrift für Internationale Rechnungslegung*, *18*(3), 117–121.

Haufe Akademie (2024, 31st August). *Künstliche Intelligenz*. <https://www.haufe-kademie.de/hierarchy/ki>.

HPI—Hasso Plattner Institut (2023, 12th June). Kurs im Selbststudium—ChatGPT: Was bedeutet generative KI für unsere Gesellschaft? <https://open.hpi.de/courses/kizukunft2023>.

Hüsch, A., Distelrath, D., & Hüsch, T. (2023). *Einsatzmöglichkeiten von GPT in Finance, Compliance und Audit: Vorteile, Herausforderungen, Praxisbeispiele*. Wiesbaden: Springer. <https://doi.org/10.1007/ 978-3-658-41419-1>.

Kampe, T. (2024), Auswirkungen des Bilanzrichtlinie-Umsetzungsgesetzes (BilRUG) auf die Bilanzierung mittelständischer Unternehmen. In: Steckler, B. (Ed.), *20 Jahre Wirtschaftsrecht im Verbundstudium*, 93–119.

Kieser, A. (1996), Moden & Mythen des Organisierens. *Die Betriebswirtschaft, 56*(1), 21–39.

Kirsch, W. (1997). *Strategisches Management: Die Geplante Evolution von Unternehmen*. München und Herrsching: B. Kirsch.

König, A., Kammerlander, N., & Enders, A. (2013). The family innovator's dilemma: How family influence affects the adoption of discontinuous technologies by incumbent firms. *Academy of Management Review, 38*(3), 418–441.

Kreher, M., Eichner, V., Sellhorn, T., Hess, T., Köster, A., & Weiß, K. (2021). *Digitalisierung im Rechnungswesen 2021. Studie*. Berlin: KPMG. <https://hub.kpmg.de/studie-de-digitalisierung-im-rechnungswesen-2021>.

Kreher, M., Sellhorn, T., & Hess, T. (2017). *Digitalisierung im Rechnungswesen: Studie zum Status quo deutscher Unternehmen*. Berlin: KPMG.

Kreher, M., Winkler, M., Sellhorn, T., Hess, T., & Köster, A. (2022). *Digitalization in accounting: 2022/2023 edition. Study*. Berlin: KPMG. <https://hub.kpmg.de/digitalisation-in-accounting-2022>.

Kreher, M., Winkler, M., Sellhorn, T., Hess, T., Sehn, V., & Meythaler, A. (2024). *Digitalisierung im Rechnungswesen. Studienausgabe 2023/2024*. Berlin: KPMG. <https://hub.kpmg.de/de/digitalisierung-im-rechnungswesen>.

Ludwig, T., Azabal, N., Fries, M., & Nießner, J. (2024). KI-Kompetenzen in der Praxis: Eine Analyse deutscher KMUs. *HMD Praxis der Wirtschaftsinformatik, 61*, 100–113.

Mayr, S. (2021). Digitalisierung des Rechnungswesens und des Controllings in KMU—Umsetzung mithilfe von Steuer- und Unternehmensberatungen. *Controlling—Zeitschrift für erfolgsorientierte Unternehmenssteuerung, 33*(4), 4–9.

Mayring, P. (2022). *Qualitative Inhaltsanalyse: Grundlagen und Techniken*. 13., überarb., Aufl., Beltz, Weinheim.

Milana, C., & Ashta, A. (2021). Artificial intelligence techniques in finance and financial markets: A survey of the literature. *SC – Strategic Change, 30*(3), 189–209.

Miller, D., Hartwick, J., & Le Breton-Miller, I. (2004). How to detect a management fad—and distinguish it from a classic. *Business Horizons, 47*(4), 7–16.

Pargmann, J., Riebenbauer, E., Flick-Holtsch, D., & Berding, F. (2023). Digitalisation in accounting: A systematic literature review of activities and implications for competences. *Empirical Research in Vocational Education and Training, 15*(1). <https://doi.org/10.1186/s40461-023-00141-1>.

Prümm, D., Loitz, R., & Dittmar, H.-P. (2023). *Digitalisierung im Finanz- und Rechnungswesen 2023—und was sie für die Zukunft der Abschlussprüfung bedeutet: Befragungen zum Status quo und zur digitalen Weiterentwicklung.* Frankfurt am Main: PricewaterhouseCoopers. <https://pages.pwc.de/digitalisierung-im-finanz-und-rewe-2023>.

Ringlstetter, M., & Schuster, M. (2003). Corporate Citizenship—Eine aktuelle Mode der Strategischen Unternehmensführung. In: Ringlstetter, M. J., Henzler, H. A., & Mirow, M. (Eds.), *Perspektiven der strategischen Unternehmensführung: Theorien—Konzepte—Anwendungen*, pp. 169–198.

Schulze, M., Broßmann, F., & Wallraff, B. (2023). KI in controlling und finance: Einsatzmöglichkeiten und Risiken. *Controller Magazin, 48*(6), 56–61.

Stiftung Familienunternehmen (2024, 30th May). *Daten, Fakten, Zahlen zu Familienunternehmen*. <https://www.familienunternehmen.de/de/news/daten-fakten-zahlen-zu-familienunternehmen>.

Strübing, J. (2018). *Qualitative Sozialforschung: Eine komprimierte Einführung. 2., überarb. u. erw. Aufl.* Berlin und Boston: De Gruyter Oldenbourg.

Vlk, G., Demelius, K., & Karigl, B. (2016). Automatisierung und Digitalisierung im Rechnungswesen. *Eine Studie von Deloitte Österreich.* Wien: Deloitte. <https://www2.deloitte.com/content/dam/Deloitte/at/Documents/about-deloitte/at-studie-automatisierung-und-digitalisierung-im-rechnungswesen.pdf>.

6. Lessons Learned? The Challenges of Generative AI and LLM Implementation Projects Within the Corporate Office World

Dorothee Wilm and Alexander Förster**

ABSTRACT
Only about 15 years ago, so-called Web 2.0 technologies—wikis, forums and blogs—had their heyday. Every other company implemented at least one of these technologies—mostly an internal company wiki—hoping to foster an innovation-propelling company culture and knowledge-sharing work practices. Anyhow, measured against the high expectations, most of these IT-implementation projects failed. The wikis ran dry quickly, employees did not share their knowledge as hoped, soon other and new technologies knocked on the door (i.e., SharePoint, all sorts of apps) and the operational daily business went on.

Today, Large Language Models (LLM) tools like Microsoft Copilot are the latest IT craze within the corporate office world. Many companies purchase licenses and push the new tool into their organization. The anticipated performance effects are huge, yet somehow vague. Not only the early adopters and test users within these companies but also Microsoft itself is searching for suitable daily use cases. Apparently, the current time is of critical importance for the adoption of this new technology and therefore the realization of the anticipated performance effects.

Based on an analysis of studies on Web 2.0 implementation projects and recent reports on Copilot implementations as well as the scientific line of discourse regarding LLM and AI-implementation more generally, the paper addresses the question whether the current LLM implementation-projects in corporate offices face the same challenges that have caused the failings 15 years ago implementing Web 2.0 technologies and could therefore benefit from the lessons learned back then.

***Keywords*:** LLM, AI, Web 2.0, IT-implementation project, Corporate office, Lessons learned, Technology adoption, HOT fit-model

*Bielefeld School of Business, Hochschule Bielefeld—University of Applied Sciences and Arts, Bielefeld, Germany
Emails: <dorothee.wilm@hsbi.de>, <alexander.foerster@hsbi.de>

Introduction: The History and Future of Office Technologies

When Microsoft launched Copilot in March 2023,[1] the promises and hopes coming along with it were tremendous: The software would no less than reshape how people work by providing a business chat experience and task handling across applications. It was promised that Copilot could summarize virtual meetings as they happen and that any person would be able to master that "computational wizardy" of for example, Excel because with Copilot at your side, you simply describe the calculation you want it to perform and do not need to know the functions yourself (Dastin, 2023; Spataro, 2023; Warren, 2023).

The Copilot launch and the following first implementation projects happen at a time when companies, entrepreneurs, politicians, and academia still try to grasp the economic possibilities and societal consequences of Artificial Intelligence (AI) and Large Language Models (LLM) (i.e., Ångström et al., 2023; Iansiti & Lakhani, 2021; Meckel & Steinacker, 2024). As until today large portions of employees have *not yet* used generative AI in their workplace (i.e., Schlude et al., 2023)[2] one could proclaim a huge market potential, but must state that the integration of generative AI and LLM systems such as Copilot is still more hype than reality. Nevertheless, if one considers the history of office technologies, it is obvious that computers automated work which was previously done by typists (Vella & Shariah, 2024) and that today generative AI technologies have the potential to automate the clerical activities performed in offices around the world much further (Asatiani et al., 2021).

---

1 <https://www.linkedin.com/events/thefutureofwork-reinventingprod7038508574142074880/>.

2 In a 2023 study on the spread and acceptance of generative AI in Germany and within German workplaces, the Bavarian research institute for digital transformation (bidt—Bayrisches Forschungsinstitut für Digitale Transformation) asked 3,020 Internet users, including 1,008 employed persons, about their usage and attitudes towards generative AI tools. They found that two-third of the employees have not yet used generative AI in their workplace (Schlude et al., 2023).

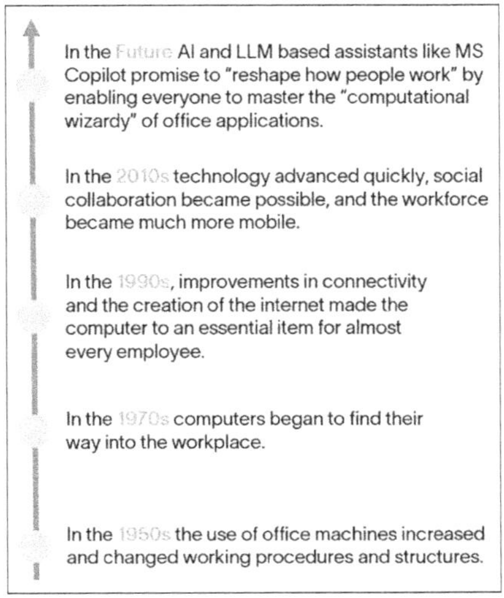

Figure 10: A brief history of office technologies.[3]

The hype about how AI and LLM technology reshape office work awakens memories made not long ago: Only about 15 years ago, so-called Web 2.0 technologies—wikis, forums, and blogs—had their heyday. Every other company implemented at least one of these technologies—mostly an internal corporate wiki—hoping to foster an innovation-propelling company culture and knowledge-sharing work practices (Lykourentzou et al., 2012). Very similar to the excitement accompanying the Copilot launch, in a 2004 Business Week article, it is said that "wikis [are] transforming the way people work at a company." (Hof, 2004). Wikis were praised as instruments eliminating countless meetings, conference calls, and back-and-forth emails and step up productivity as "working on a wiki has cut daily phone calls to one a week [...]." (Hof, 2004). Wiki usage in corporate environments grew exponentially between 2004 and 2006, along with other Web 2.0 technologies like blogs, podcasts, and RSS (Gibson, 2006). However, history shows that despite the allegedly early successes and measured against the high expectations, most

---

3 <https://www.condecosoftware.com/modern-workplace/history-of-the-workplace/>.

of these Web 2.0 implementation projects failed. The wikis run dry quickly (Arazi & Croitoru, 2010), employees did not share their knowledge as hoped, and soon other and new technologies knocked on the door (i.e., SharePoint), and the operational daily business went on. The problems were manifold and are discussed in reports and studies on the lessons learned of the Web 2.0 implementation projects (e.g., Arazi & Croitoru, 2010; Baxter & Connolly, 2014; Gibson, 2006; Hildreth, 2007).

Today, considering the huge, yet somehow vague, anticipated performance effects of generative AI and LLM systems in corporate offices, one needs to be afraid that history could repeat itself. First implementation reports reveal that not only the early adopters and test users within these companies, but also Microsoft itself, is searching for suitable daily use cases.[4] Likewise, Ångström and colleagues argue that "(…) the promises of AI often stand in stark contrast with the many failing AI initiatives that companies experience when embarking on the quest to become data-driven and AI savvy" and emphasize that until now, many AI implementations are unsuccessful (Ångström et al., 2023).

Against this background, the paper at hand addresses the question if AI and LLM implementation projects today face the same or similar problems as Web 2.0 implementation projects 15 years ago. If that is the case, project managers and software developers could benefit from studying the lessons learned back then. Alternatively, one could assume that LLM and AI are technologically so fundamentally different that respective implementation projects have no history to learn from. The authors aim to answer this question by analyzing and comparing Web 2.0 technologies and their implementation projects to LLM and AI technologies and their respective implementation as depicted in early adopters' user and implementation reports and in the scientific line of discourse regarding LLM and AI implementation. Given that Gartner predicts that global spending in AI software will rise from $124 billion in 2022 to $297 billion in 2027 (Columbus, 2024), the authors assume, that the present time is very critical for the future payoff of these investments and that it is crucial to analyze, understand and thereby improve the implementation process of AI and LLM tools.

---

4 <https://practical365.com/microsoft-365-copilot-launches/>.

Methodology

The research question of this paper and the following line of argument contribute to the research field on technology adoption and acceptance. As this field of research spans information science, sociology, economics, and psychology, it is rather wide. Xu and Lu provide a comprehensive overview and summary of the most relevant theories and models of technology adoption and acceptance (Xu & Lu, 2022). The authors criticize the classical models for either focusing on too few explanatory factors, underestimating the characteristics of modern technologies or not differentiating clearly between technology adoption within an infinite pool of users (e.g., Rogers diffusion of innovation model; e.g., Rogers, 2003) vs. within a closed organization and therefore suggest a model themselves (Xu & Lu, 2022). For the paper at hand, the encompassing *HOT-fit model* proposed by Xu and Lu will serve as a framework to address its research question.

The model by Xu and Lu, as well as a large share of the research on technology adoption and acceptance, is based on a general socio-technical perspective on organizations (e.g., Bendel & Latniak, 2020; Davis et al., 2014; Hirsch-Kreinsen, 2018; Pasmore, 2019). Proponents of this theoretical position argue that technology, work, and organization are inseparable as the acting and decision making of the organizational members is framed by the formal and informal organizational structures on the one hand and the technological structures and features on the other hand (e.g., Orlikowski & Scott, 2008). Concurrently, the organization as well as the technology is being enacted, formed, and changed by the acts and decisions of the organizational members. These complex mutual relations of interdependence need to be taken into consideration if one wants to understand and explain the implementation of a new technology into an organization.

Accordingly, the HOT-fit model of technology adoption and acceptance in organizations by Xu and Lu constitutes the analytical framework for the comparative analysis of Web 2.0 technology and implementation projects with AI and LLM technology and corresponding first implementation experiences. Three types of sources form the analytical basis of the comparative analysis: First, reports and (meta-) studies, discussing the lessons learned from Web 2.0 implementation projects are analyzed to systematically derive the learnings that can be taken away from these experiences. The second type of sources are copilot early adopter user reports by Microsoft partners and independent users. Since these reports are rare and partly carry a commercial bias, the scientific line of discourse on LLM and AI implementation projects (which is not focused on corporate offices) is taken into consideration as a third type of source to complement the analytical basis of the comparative analysis.

The first paragraph of the following paper introduces the HOT-fit model of technology adoption in organizations, as it constitutes the analytical framework of the comparative analysis. The analysis that follows a three-stage structure. First, the similarities and differences between Web 2.0 technology and AI, as well as LLM technology, are identified. In the second step, the learnings related to the human-technology relationship are analyzed and compared. In the third step, the focus shifts to the learnings concerning the organization-technology relationship, which are also compared. The article concludes with recommendations for future LLM and AI technology implementation projects and an outlook on future research in this area.

A Human-Organization-Technology Model of Technology Adoption in Organizations

The realization that technology imposed on an organization is unlikely to be used as intended and that the success or failure of technology adoption depends not only on the technology itself—its features and customization—but also significantly on social, cultural, and organizational factors, has been repeatedly acknowledged by practitioners over the past decades. This understanding has also become a common notion in academic discourse concerning technology adoption in organizations (e.g., Ångström et al., 2023; Assatiani et al., 2021; Boag et al., 2024; Cabitza et al., 2020; Hopf et al., 2023; Tse et al., 2020; Xu & Lu, 2022).

The paper at hand chooses the *HOT fit model* by Xu and Lu (Xu & Lu, 2022) as a theoretical and methodological frame to address the research questions stated above. The model names human, organization, and technology as the significant dimensions in technology adoption (Xu & Lu, 2022). The graphical outline of the model (Figure 10) illustrates the mutual inter-relations. The model depicts that personal characteristics of humans (e.g., personality, knowledge, abilities, skills, and experiences) influence how they use, develop, and tweak technologies within their daily fulfillment of tasks. These tasks and work routines are at the same time enabled and constrained by technologies and their characteristics (i.e., Adele & Brangier, 2013). The accessibility, convenience, usefulness, and reliability of technological applications (summarized as system quality), for example, structure how employees accomplish what they need to do, and even to some extent what experiences they make and which skills they acquire (Xu & Lu, 2022).

Like this human-technology relation, the second side of the triangle depicts how technology characteristics and organization's internal and external characteristics influence each other (Xu & Lu, 2022). The internal and external characteristics of an organization encompass how work is formally and informally organized and structured. Xu and Lu explain that job definitions, hierarchical positions, responsibilities and powers, policies, business goals and strategies, rules, procedures, as well as cultural factors all belong to "organization" (Xu & Lu, 2022). With respect to the relation of organizational characteristics and technology, the model explains that while organizations (try to) customize technologies to their needs, technologies, vice versa, enforce organizational investments and adoptions—of technical, structural, or cultural kind. Similarly, the third side of the triangle describes the human-organization fit. It explains that organizational structures, strategies, and policies influence attitudes and behavior of the embedded humans and that this very behavior of the employees, vice versa, drives the formation and change of organizational structures, processes, and culture (e.g., Xu & Lu, 2022) (Figure 11).

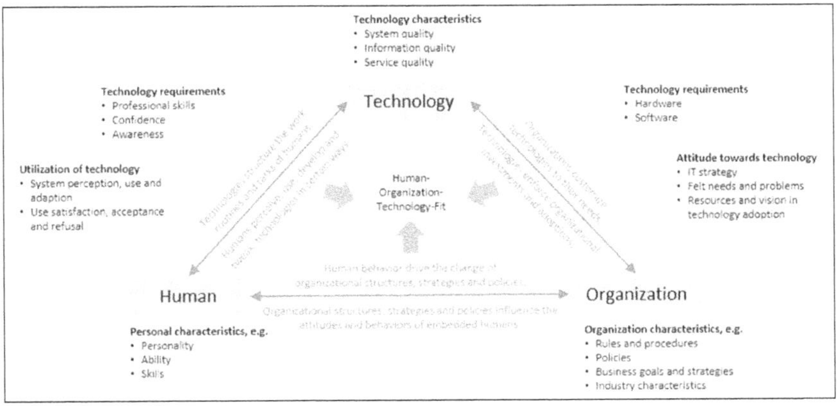

Figure 11: The HOT fit model by Xu and Lu.

Building on this general socio-technical understanding of the mutual relation of humans, organization, and technology, Xu and Lu argue that technology adoption will be more successful, the better the fit of personal, organizational, and technological characteristics is (Xu & Lu, 2022). It is noteworthy that *fit* refers to an objective and/or subjective (respectively perceived) fit. In this model, the inter-relationships of the three dimensions are of peculiar interest. Accordingly, the bi-party fits determine the final Human-Organization-Technology fit (HOT fit) (Xu & Lu, 2022). In the paper at hand, the attention will be primarily directed to the technological characteristics of the Web 2.0 as well as AI and LLM technology and the respective inter-relationships with the human and organizational dimension of the triangle. Nevertheless, the model reminds us not to neglect the human–organization relationship as an influencing factor for the adoption of these technologies.

Differences and Similarities in the Technological Characteristics of Web 2.0 and AI/LLM-Projects

Common to the websites in the early days of the Web was that they mainly consisted of so-called *static pages*, which were designed primarily for information presentation and did not feature much user interaction.[5] With the new millennium and the emergence of Web 2.0 applications this was about to change as the widely accepted core feature of these systems is that users are invited to not only consume websites but are also allowed to engage in different kinds of interaction with it.

Typical representatives of Web 2.0 systems are

- blogs (e.g., the popular *comunio* blog on football news),
- forums (e.g., *Reddit*, which is often considered the largest online community),
- wikis (e.g., the public and popular *Wikipedia*),

[5] This interaction of the user with the website was limited to free navigation on the site by following links according to the hypermedia concept, which was one of the main innovations on the Web, therefore, that is, the name HTTP—hypertext transport protocol. The only other way of interaction possible was filling out and sending forms such as feedback forms, which were technically realized by sending an e-mail to the website owner ("Web 2.0," 2024).

- media sharing platforms (e.g., *YouTube*),
- messaging networks (e.g., *WeChat*, *Facebook Messenger* or *MS Teams*),
- and social networks (e.g., *Facebook*, *Instagram* or *LinkedIn*).

Thus, the widely accepted core feature of the Web 2.0 is that users are invited to not only consume websites but are also allowed to engage in different kinds of interaction with a website, which then turns to be merely a *platform*. Consequently, if they decide to move on from the passive read mode, the users change their role from being consumers to prosumers, as a blending of producer and consumer. Web 2.0 systems have in common that they provide mainly user generated content as opposed to editorial content. The users of these systems can engage in a many-to-many (or few-to-many) communication paradigm, whilst classic static websites follow a one-to-many information multiplication approach. Today, many systems follow a blended approach such as media outlets featuring editorial articles with an attached discussion forum (e.g., tagesschau.de) or Facebook and X (formerly Twitter) enriching the personal timeline with editorial content and ads.

In the corporate and enterprise domain, research shows that wikis are by far the most widely adopted Web 2.0 technology, while blogs, forums and media sharing are rather prevalent in the public domain (Lykourentzou et al., 2012). Therefore, the line of argument focuses on wikis in the remainder as the most common example for the use of Web 2.0 technology in organizations. Wikis can be defined as "[...] a website that enables the creation and publishing of interlinked web pages through the collaborative efforts of a group of web users. This collaborative content creation is achieved in a remote manner, through a web browser and by using either the syntax of a simple mark-up language or through a What you see is what you get (WYSIWYG) text editor" (Lykourentzou et al., 2012). Lykourentzou and colleagues list the key features that can be found in most wiki platforms:

Based on these features wikis offered an added value for different scenarios at the workplace (Lykourentzou et al., 2012). The first and most prevalent use case is the management and preservation of corporate knowledge. This includes knowledge codification, management, and publishing. It is assumed that wikis, due to their open and democratic nature, facilitate the collaboration among loosely connected units of the organization. Another main aspect connected to the knowledge management use case is the "prevention of loss of knowledge in the case of retiring experts" (Hildreth, 2007). Besides knowledge management, wikis are also used as tools to support project planning and project organization. In that case wikis are set up to manage and spread information within confined projects. A third distinct use case of wikis within corporations is the interaction with third parties like customers, suppliers, and service organizations (Lykourentzou et al., 2012) (Figure 12).

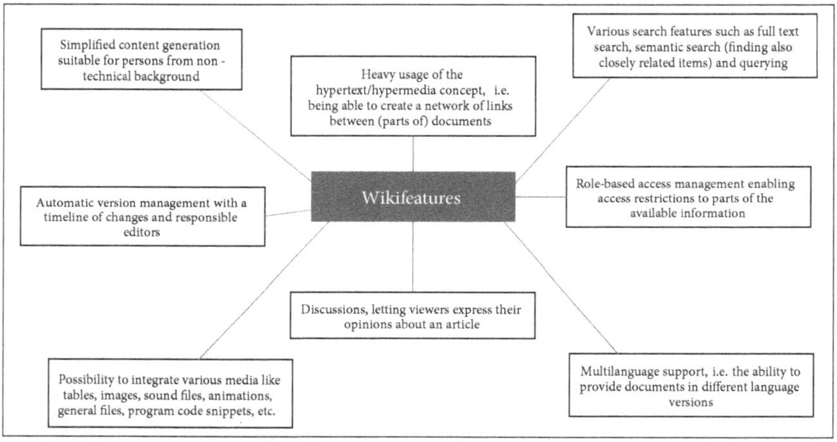

Figure 12: Key features of wiki systems, based on Lykourentzou et al. (2012).

In the following years, with the decay of the Web 2.0 hype, and although the underlying technology was widely available to everyone and easy and cost-efficient to implement, the industry focused on new ways to support collaboration within companies. Especially four technological innovations paved the way for todays' AI and LLM in corporate office-hype: concurrent document editing, apps, cloud storage, and real-time messaging. Although real-time messengers existed as desktop applications almost from the first of the Internet (e.g., IRC—Internet Relay Chat introduced 1986), they became ubiquitous in the private domain as smartphone apps. Since companies obviously do not want corporate information to be shared over third-party technology privately installed by the employees like WhatsApp, etc., they started to provide their employees with their own corporate solutions such as *Microsoft Teams*.

Starting as a chat, audio, and video conferencing software originally based on Microsoft Lync and Skype (purchased by Microsoft in 2011), Teams was soon designated to become an overall collaboration platform. In its basic form it provides chat, messaging, audio, and video conferencing, and a share file storage similar to OneDrive and SharePoint, but better integrated, as well as basics like authorization, access management, management of groups and teams etc. Additionally, there is a complete Teams app store providing all sorts of different plugins and extensions, for example, for polls, discussions, common calendars, and integration conduits to many external systems. Today, Microsoft Teams is dominating the collaboration-software market with about 300 million users per day (Binbir, 2023).[6] The market dominance was heavily pushed by the corona pandemic (Spataro, 2020). Its permanence builds the foundation of the promises and hopes connected to MS Copilot.

In the late 2010s, LLM became increasingly popular with the introduction of Google's BERT and OpenAI's GPT-1, both in 2018. LLMs use huge artificial neural networks to language understanding, processing, and generation. Based on a huge amount of texts publicly available in the Internet, these models have a general language understanding capability for most popular languages. Today's models can be used through textual prompting in natural language. LLMs generate their output basically by predicting the next most likely word following the current word. As they can generate various outputs from textual explanations to program code, tables etc., LLMs also have a generative AI component.

LLMs are trained based on information publicly available on the Internet by scraping websites. It is important to note that the actual way the outputs are generated is enclosed in millions of weights and factors within the neural network and are non-transparent to the outside user. Thus, classic reasoning about the functionality of a computer program or an algorithm is not possible with AI systems and outputs are always fuzzy in the sense of being based on chances and likeliness; they even may be outright wrong although seemingly logical (Ångström et al., 2023; Bojaryn, 2024; Cabitza et al., 2020).

---

6 See also: <https://de.statista.com/statistik/daten/studie/1189929/umfrage/anzahl-der-taeglich-aktiven-nutzer-von-microsoft-teams-weltweit/>.

Within corporate offices, two fundamentally different scenarios of usage can be distinguished:

- *Using cloud-based LLMs*: In an enterprise setting, either publicly available cloud LLMs like Google's Gemini, Meta's LLaMA, IBM's Granite, OpenAI's (Chat-)GPT or Microsoft's Copilot can be used. In this scenario, the companies' specific data the model is supposed to reason on has to be provided to the LLMs with the prompt. With this approach, the companies' potentially secret data gets transferred to an external partner.
- *Implement LLMs on the company's own systems*: Companies can implement general LLMs with a general language understanding on their own systems and fine-tune these systems with their own data. This way, a company's classified data would at least stay within the company. However, this scenario comes at a high cost since the data used to fine-tune the model needs to be extensively preprocessed and consistently structured. Additionally, the hardware and operations cost to fine-tune LLMs are still immense. This scenario entails numerous available tools which can be summarized as data analytics management tools (Wayner, 2023).

The focus of the paper at hand is on Microsoft Copilot, as it is the most popular and most widely discussed AI tool in the business world. *Copilot* is the brand under which Microsoft consolidates a whole bunch of existing and new solutions around the general topic of AI to provide a consistent and streamlined marketing message. Since it was only rolled out in February 2023, at first called Bing Chat, it combines a whole bouquet of different services under the same name, and its composition and use cases are still constantly changing, the following assessment is based on current online resources. One should distinguish between:

- *Copilot as a cloud LLM*: Available to everyone and free of charge is the website copilot.microsoft.com, which features a general LLM trained on publicly available information from the Internet and based on GPT-4. The same service comes with some integrations, for example, in the Windows Desktop, in Microsoft's Browser Edge, in Microsoft's search engine Bing and as mobile app. The scenario falls into the "cloud-based LLM" category and is not at the center of the papers interest.

- *Copilot Pro*: This product is targeted to consumers and provides integration of the before mentioned features into Microsoft's office suite and additional features specific to the respective office tool such as formula generation in Excel, summaries in Word, image generation in PowerPoint etc. As this product is not addressed to corporate users it is not relevant for the paper hand.
- *Copilot for Microsoft 365*: This product is targeted at professional users and "lets them use Copilot to get answers and suggestions based on company data" (PCMag) by using, for example, the documents in the company's OneDrive, Teams, etc. Opposed to Copilot as cloud LLM and important for businesses, it "keeps interactions private to the organization and doesn't use your input to train the versions of Copilot that other people use" (PCMag). For our analysis, this is the most relevant product.
- *Copilot for Sales, Copilot for Service, GitHub Copilot* and *Copilot Studio*: Other Microsoft services now running under the name Copilot and relevant for businesses are "Copilot for Sales," "Copilot for Service" and "GitHub Copilot," but their uses cases are so specific that we are not going into further details with them. Finally, there is Copilot Studio, which provides a development environment and "lets you program custom versions of Copilot that incorporate custom data to deliver predictable responses within conversations" (PCMag).

Copilot for Microsoft 365 tries to bridge the gap between the two different scenarios shown above: It is essentially a cloud service where a pre-trained LLM is readily available, but it also automatically incorporates all your data already available in other Microsoft tools and services like emails from Outlook, Documents from OneDrive, and SharePoint etc. This results in some practical use cases as it can automate and streamline many clerical tasks (Vella & Shariah 2024). Copilot can summarize content from the Internet, summarize Teams conversations, transcribe meetings, and automatically summarize resulting action items. It can create replies based on received emails, taking the context into consideration. Copilot is also able to brainstorm a topic and create ideas for, that is, an agenda for a meeting, a framework for a report, or starting research for a strategy. Finally, it can act as a personal mentor as the chatbot can generally assist with many topics (Vella & Shariah, 2024).

Looking at the technological characteristics of Web 2.0 tools, especially corporate wikis on the one hand and AI and LLM tools, especially MS Copilot on the other, it is very clear that these are very different technologies. Nevertheless, two similarities also become clear. Firstly, for both technologies, the dynamic content generated by the users is of central importance for the qualitative added value of working with the system. If the information entered into a wiki is of poor quality and the content is not well linked, then the promise of wikis cannot be fulfilled. Although Copilot does not present user-generated content in the same way, the system processes content that was previously created by users. And the database on which the system provides its services is just as dynamic and quality sensitive as that of a company wiki.

Another similarity between the two technologies lies in the (supposedly) low demands on the skills and competencies of the users of the respective system. Wikis promised that, for the first time, anyone could create and share their own content online. Similarly, MS Copilot promises that anyone can use the tool thanks to natural language processing and can even use it to access other, more complicated applications. The following sections will examine the extent to which these similarities are reflected in similar challenges in implementation projects.

Learnings Regarding the Human–Technology Relationship in Web 2.0 and AI/LLM Implementation Projects

Analyzing and comparing the different studies on the experiences that have been made with the implementation of Web 2.0 applications in corporate settings reveals that a major lesson from the Web 2.0 implementation projects is the heterogeneity of personal characteristics. Employees, respectively the supposed users of the new technology, differed enormously regarding their confidence in sharing their content and editing that of others, regarding their willingness to give up ownership of personal knowledge and regarding their openness towards and optimism about the usefulness of the new technology (Baxter & Connolly, 2014; Gibson, 2006; Lykourentzou et al., 2012).

Looking at Copilot early adopter reports and studies on the implementation of AI and LLM applications more generally, it is striking that one major challenge is the skill requirements coming along with the new technology. This challenge has two different variations. Firstly, companies that want to deploy a generative AI or LLM system require respective data scientists and domain experts to conduct the project. These human resources, especially data scientists and domain experts who are able to understand each other's perspective and interests, are rare and often quite expensive (Ångström et al., 2023; Ross, 2018). Secondly, besides the importance of AI-relevant competencies of data scientists and domain experts, the lack of adequately trained employees is regarded as problematic (Ångström et al., 2023). This is interesting, because the technology promises great and easy user experience and Microsoft emphasizes that the end-users do not need any tech-knowledge about the service. Nevertheless, first experiences in practice report that the use of copilot requires certain skills—first prompting—which the majority of employees still misses (Muth, 2023). Moreover, the lack of understanding of AI technology among employees is considered to foster high and maybe unrealistic expectations. Whereas Strohm and colleagues refer to high expectation of AIs potential added value as a facilitating factor for AI implementation (Strohm et al., 2020), others point to the risk of disappointment of the exaggerated expectations which could cause frustration and refusal of the technology (Ångström et al., 2023; Hopf et al., 2023).

This risk is real, as the experiences with Web 2.0 implementation reveal. Analyzing the reports makes it clear that the disappointment of the expectations related to the new technology was a serious problem these projects faced (Baxter & Connolly, 2014; Hildreth, 2007). Besides the motivational and competence-related problems, technical weaknesses, especially with regard to the search function, diminished the knowledge management possibilities of the technology. In theory, semantic search and querying encompass the ability to localize information even if the query or search text is fuzzy, words are misspelled, or synonyms are used. While semantic search vastly improves the possibility to find and retrieve information in a wiki, it is a rather complex technology that requires high technological implementation efforts and skills, and is not readily available for self-implementation to SMUs. While companies highly advanced in search technology, like Google and

Microsoft, exceled in this area, SMU could not easily copy this technology and may only overcome this problem by relying on cloud services provided by the big tech companies, thus allowing them full access to the company's private information (Baxter & Connolly, 2014).

With regard to Web 2.0 implementations Baxter and Connolly point out that, employees tend to stick to their known routines and technologies, diagnosing a "lack of motivation among employees to engage with wikis" (Baxter & Connolly, 2014). Whereas motivation is a complicated phenomenon, theorized and discussed in numerous motivation theories (e.g., Locke & Latham 1990; Maslow, 1943), willingness to change is a common attribute differentiated in change management textbooks (e.g., Klimmer, 2020). It is depicted as a personal characteristic that is closely accompanied and interlinked to the ability to change—referring to the presence of skills needed to embrace the change (Stoffers & Mordant-Dols, 2015). Against this background, it is not surprising that the Web 2.0 implementation studies report that the level of familiarity with Web 2.0 applications was also quite heterogeneous and a critical success factor (Lykourentzou et al., 2012).

Very similar to that, it is consistently highlighted how important the ability and willingness of the employees to work routinely with AI-based processes is. The inertia of routines is considered a serious hurdle that needs to be overcome in AI and LLM implementation (Ångström et al., 2023). Potential causes of this inertia are manifold: lack of data awareness and a data-driven mindset, preference for gut- or experience-led decision-making, concerns regarding the liability and trustworthiness, skepticism because of the opacity of the tool, as well as fears of job loss, loss of expertise, and autonomy (Angtsroem et al., 2023; Schlude et al., 2023). Whereas Strohm and colleagues mention the large variance in acceptance and trust of the adopters (Strohm et al., 2020), Cabitza and colleagues highlight the hiatus of human trust as the most serious hindrance to the full realization of the potential of AI (Cabitza et al., 2020). That is because, as they write, even the most accurate systems are affected when they are not trusted by users as a result of 'prejudice against the machine' (Cabitza et al., 2020; Muth, 2023). Moreover, several authors assume that the willingness to adopt the new technology is also influenced by the success or failure of AI to make a reliable positive impact on decisions, irrespective of its intrinsic accuracy (Cabitza et al., 2020; Strohm et al., 2020).

With regard to the scenario of an LLM implemented on the company's system, Cabitza and colleagues name different reasons for the absence of reliable positive value for generative AI and LLM users: inadequate interface, that the good advice comes too late or among too many false advices, automation bias, and automation complacency (Cabitza et al., 2020). Effects like those mentioned are the object of investigation of research on ML and Human-Computer-Interaction (HCI) (e.g., Cappelli et al., 2024). One example of the surprising findings is given by Perry and colleagues, who conducted an empirical study on the performance of programmers with and without an AI assistant (Perry et al., 2023). They found that participants with access to an AI assistant wrote insecure solutions more often and were at the same time more likely to believe that they wrote secure code than those without access to an AI assistant (Perry et al., 2023). Although not yet in the center of the HCI research interest, it can be assumed that these findings can be applied to the use and interaction with AI-assistants like Copilot for MS 365 as well.

Nevertheless, consulting the recent reports on Copliot implementation by practitioners, it is striking that the main reason for the uncertainty about the added value for Copilot users in corporate offices are technological weaknesses of the service. The tool fails to perform simple tasks like summarizing a blog (Meffert, 2024), tends to hallucinate (Bojaryn, 2024), and exhibits limitations in terms of contextual understanding and sensitivity to prompts (Ming, 2024). Problems that constrain users to prompt very carefully and double-check any output. An effort that prunes the promised performance gains drastically.

In summary, it can be said that the technological characteristics of MS Copilot pose a number of specific challenges. Concerns about job losses and the loss of expertise and autonomy certainly have a different quality than with Web 2.0 implementations. Equally unique are the skepticism associated with the tool and the trust issues of (potential) users due to the opacity of how the tool works.

However, in addition to these differences, there are also some similarities in the challenges of Web 2.0 implementations and co-pilot implementations. For example, both technologies place certain requirements on the skills and competencies of employees, and in both cases, these requirements tend to be underestimated as the systems are accompanied by the promise of very easy usability. What both cases also have in common is that there is a major risk that potential users will be disappointed if their expectations are too high or incorrect. Ultimately, the risk is that the disappointed expectations result in frustration and possibly a rejection of the technology.

Learnings Regarding the Organization–Technology Relationship in Web 2.0 and AI/LLM Implementation Projects

The studies on Web 2.0 implementation projects outline different lessons that can be learned with regard to the organization–technology relationship. First, Hildreth points out that the implementation of Web 2.0 applications imposes certain requirements to the organization. Although available as a hosted service, due to security concerns most companies decided to realize the Web 2.0 application in-house by buying the software (Hildreth, 2007). Besides the (not too big) initial investments for the software, the organization then needed to establish some IT support and integrate the Web 2.0 applications with existing systems (Hildreth, 2007). Especially the last point is highlighted as a critical success factor.

In the same way, the soft- and hardware investments necessary when implementing a generative AI or LLM solution are one challenge that is reported (Ångström et al., 2023; Zabala, 2023). Whereas the Copilot for MS 365 costs 28,10€/month[7] per user in addition to the regular MS-Office license, the costs of projects where a generative AI or LLM is developed and trained by the company itself can be enormous (Hopf et al., 2023). In addition to these evident investments, it should not be underestimated that the implementation of generative AI and LLM systems requires ongoing IT management and support (Ångström et al., 2023; Tse et al., 2020). One reason for these long-term investments is that the systems need to be integrated not only into the existing but also into any future IT infrastructure of the company (Boag et al., 2024). Another reason for the required ongoing evaluation and adoption is the continuously changing restrictions and regulations. If a company does not want to risk breaking these laws and regulations, it must evaluate and eventually adopt its systems regularly (Zabala, 2023).

Against this background of technological requirements from the organization, the challenge of data management is highlighted as especially critical in scientific articles and practice reports alike (e.g., Cabitza et al., 2020;

---

[7] <https://www.microsoft.com/de-de/microsoft-365/copilot?market=de#tabs-pill-bar-oc498c_tab2 (November 2024)>.

Finnegan, 2023). When it comes to generative AI and LLM implemented and self-trained on company systems, it is obvious that data availability, data quality, and data consistency across the company are of major importance for the success of such a project (Ångström et al., 2023; Boag et al., 2024; Cabitza et al., 2020; Tse et al., 2020). Without a unified language, structured data assets, and proper coordination across the company, it becomes nearly impossible to implement AI. It is reported that AI/LLM-projects often focus on the development of the algorithm and lose sight of the indispensable data management prerequisites (Ångström et al., 2023; Hopf et al., 2023). Moreover, it appears to be critical that the efforts needed in data management do not limit themselves to the implementation phase, but will be necessary constantly in the future (Hopf et al., 2023).

One could assume that these challenges not hold true for the implementation and usage of Copilot for MS 365 within a corporate office setting, as the system's LLM is not trained on company data. However, as it does digest company data input (documents in the company OneDrive, all interactions in Teams, emails, calendars, etc.), the quality of the output heavily depends on the availability, quality, and consistency of this data input (Finnegan, 2023). Simply speaking, all data, which is not part of the Microsoft-sphere (e.g., WhatsApp chats, documents on local file systems, information contained in any other company system), is not available for Copilot to perform its tasks. The availability of data for Copilot depends on the discipline across the company to only and consistently use MS Teams and related Microsoft products. But even if the data is available in the Microsoft sphere, its quality is again a challenge. As early adopters report, Copilot for MS 365 digs deep into the shady sediments of the company's knowledge base and exhumes decaying data (Finnegan, 2023; Meffert, 2024; Ming, 2024). Finnegan, moreover, points to the security risks coming along with the challenge of data quality. He writes: "Just as the MS365 Copilot can help employees access information relevant to their roles, it could equally return sensitive and confidential files that haven't been properly categorized and protected–anything from customer or research-and-development information to HR and payroll data." (Finnegan, 2023). In addition to the quality challenges regarding the company data input, there are concerns about the quality of the data on which the LLM of Copilot—ChatGPT—was trained, as that has been masses of publicly available data.

These data-related challenges reveal an underlying basal tradeoff between the accuracy of the generative AI and LLM system and its performance on the one hand and the ongoing data management efforts and time restrictions of the daily operational business on the other hand. Cabitza and colleagues cite the colloquial expression “garbage in, garbage out” to refer to the fact that no algorithm, no matter how smart or intelligent it is, can produce value if its input lacks value in the first place (Cabitza et al., 2020). The authors ad for consideration that if inadequate input is used to allegedly optimize work performance and yet remains undetected, not only is the data input not appropriately improved and the system’s output is not discarded, but also it is instead erroneously considered truthful and fit for purpose (Cabitza et al., 2020). The risk is that garbage output is being viewed as the proper advice of an accurate tool. As has been discussed with regard to the human-AI/LLM interaction above, this sort of automation complacency is quite natural for individuals working with an AI. Here it is to emphasize that this is not just a personal characteristic of single employees. It is likewise a characteristic of the shared company culture. A company trying to avoid these pitfalls would need to invest much attention, time, and discipline to improve the data awareness and quality consistently across the company. Time and effort which are constantly under pressure from the daily operational business.

A very similar and fundamental tradeoff situation was experienced in Web 2.0 implementation projects. A central theme in all studies can be subsumed as the *governance-paradox*. The tradeoff exists between the features of the technology, the routines and culture its usage requires, which enable the promised and hoped for positive performance effects on the one hand, and the multiple potential problems and risks that are attached to the technology on the other hand. Three risks result from the open, democratic, easy-to-use character of Web 2.0 technology: (a) the risk of unsuitable content being distributed, (b) the risk of poor quality and organization of the stored information, and generally (c) the risk of losing authority and control. Paradoxically, every solution considered to cope with these risks-set up role-based access rights, forbid anonymous contributions, install so-called wiki gardeners curating all contributions, or the enforcement of a certain predefined wiki structure-negate the benefits of Web 2.0 technology. Thus, organizations need to find a balance between the technological benefits and the risks that come along with them.

Moreover, it can be summarized that Web 2.0 implementation reports highlight the importance of an appropriate formal and informal organization, which includes (a) the vision and mission of the company, (b) the shared priority and value of knowledge sharing, (c) the behavior and value system of managers, (d) management support of the implementation project, and (e) existing formal and informal knowledge codification practices (Baxter & Connolly, 2014; Gibson, 2006; Lykourentzou et al., 2012). These facets or modes of the organization are *appropriate* if they match the characteristics of the Web 2.0 technology as summarized above. That means, they need to promote confidence in contributing and editing, demonstrate the usefulness of the new technology, encourage upskilling to build the required skill sets, and welcome the variation of established routines.

Unsurprisingly, Copilot projects also identify corporate culture as a factor critical to success. Strohm and colleagues, as well as Zabala highlight the presence of an organization-wide innovation strategy as a facilitating factor (Strohm et al., 2020; Zabala, 2023) and point out the importance of managers acting as role models (Zabala, 2023). All of what we have discussed about the ability and willingness of employees to work and adopt the new technology earlier applies to managers as well. However, their decisions and actions are defining the shared culture even more than any organizational member does, intended or not. That is why the (collective) behavior of managers is considered part of the organization-technology relationship.

Besides the interrelated bundle of technological requirements from the organization and the corporate-culture implications, the literature on generative AI and LLM implementations as well as the practice reports mention that it is necessary to establish new roles (Boag et al., 2024; Vaast, 2021) as well as to reorganize workflows to enable the technology to perform best (Boag et al., 2024; Ross, 2018). Process Reengineering towards AI-efficient workflows means most often to disassemble the process into smaller components so that the AI can perform the steps of the process in which it outperforms its human colleague. As the intention (maximization of performance efficiency) and approach (labor division) of this Process-Reengineering attempt remind us of the scientific management approach Frederik Taylor once promoted during the Industrial Revolution, and is therefore (critically) discussed under the headline of "Digital Taylorism" (Nyckel, 2020).

Comparing the experiences of the Web 2.0 implementation projects with the first copilot implementation projects, it can be seen that the main similarities are the investments required and the great importance of corporate culture for the success of the technology implementation. What is new and different about the implementation of Copilot is the associated requirements for organizational structural changes. Finally, it is very interesting to note that the implementation of new technologies seems to be regularly associated with a fundamental trade-off.

Conclusions and Recommendations for LLM Implementation

Companies, entrepreneurs, politicians, and scholars agree that the latest technological developments—the development and increasing spread of LLM and generative AI technologies—have a new and radical quality. It is reasonable to assume that these new technologies will fundamentally change the way work is performed (e.g., Haenlein & Kaplan, 2019; Meckel & Steinacker, 2024). While both research and public debate have been focusing on the substitution effects in the area of industrial work for some time, office work is now gradually becoming the focus of attention. Applications such as MS Copilot and other AI and LLM office technologies are said to have the potential not only to automate simple, repetitive administrative tasks, but also to make creative and evaluative tasks such as drafting a strategy paper, programming code, or evaluating various designs much more efficient. Considering the history of office technologies, this appears to be an inevitable continuation of the development.

However, the history of office technology implementation projects also clearly shows that the adoption and acceptance of new technologies in corporate offices is challenging. The present study demonstrates that the challenges of a technology implementation project depend, among other things, on the characteristics of the technology. As the comparison of Web 2.0 technology (wiki) and the corresponding implementation experience with AI and LLM technology (MS Copilot) and initial usage and implementation experiences in this regard clearly shows that there are numerous commonalities, but also—technology-specific—differences. Table 11 concisely summarizes the key results.

Table 11: Commonalities and differences of Web 2.0 and AI/LLM implementation projects

	Specific to Web 2.0 implementation	Commonalities of Web 2.0 and AI/LLM implementation	Specific to AI/LLM implementation
Technological characteristics	Communication m:n User as Producer and Consumer Use Cases: Knowledge Management, project management	(Second hand, background) User-generated, dynamic content is decisive for the quality of the service provided Promise: Low skill level required	Bidirectional interaction between the user and Copilot Use Case: Copilot as a personal assistant for almost any task
Human–technology relationship	Heterogeneity of personal characteristics, for example, confidence to edit and publish	Heterogeneity of personal characteristics, e.g., skill set, awareness Actual skill requirements mismatch with the promise of low skill-level requirements No reliable positive impact on daily work tasks and routines; poor quality of the service added. Disappointment of the expectations related to the new technology	Skill requirements: data scientists; adequately trained employees; data-driven mindset Skepticism because of the opacity of the tool; trustworthiness and liability concerns Fears of job loss, loss of expertise and autonomy
Organization–technology relationship	Soft- and hardware investments and ongoing expenses for IT management and support Corporate culture: organization-wide innovation strategy; Managers need to promote confidence, demonstrate usefulness, and welcome organizational change Tradeoff-situation: The features of the technology, the routines and culture it requires to unfold its full performance efficiency vs. the ongoing efforts and potential problems and risks that are attached to the technology		Adaptation of the organizational structure (Digital Taylorism) Data management prerequisites

In view of these results of the comparative study, a number of recommendations can be proposed for future AI and LLM implementation projects. First, it is of key importance to not let the tool—its shining promises and potential performance effects—fool you. The tool might be simple, but its usage as well as implementation, maintenance, and support will require certain skills and abilities. Future implementation projects should learn systematically about these requirements in pilot projects. If the requirements are understood, the respective skills need to be built patiently.

Second, future implementation projects need to take the heterogeneity of humans more into account. It appears to be a crucial success factor to develop individual change stories as well as to evaluate and listen to group-specific fears and concerns carefully. That the corporate culture is of key importance for the success of a technology adoption is not surprising. Anyhow, the results make clear that AI and LLM implementation projects face respective challenges again, and that the lessons from the failed Wiki projects have not been learned. Therefore, it is suggested here to assess the corporate culture and readiness of a company *before* the implementation project is kicked off. If the assessment reveals that the company culture is not ready yet, it needs patient improvement. This might sound like bad advice since there is a risk of missing out on the promised performance gains. Although this cannot be entirely dismissed, it must be stated that the risk of a failed implementation project is even higher since the company culture is of fundamental importance.

Moreover, one should not be fooled by the hype. Future tools might promise great performance effects like the Wiki and Copilot proponents did and do, but—as it must be stated with regard to the Web 2.0 technology 10 years ago and regarding Copilot today—the technological maturity might not be sufficient. The lesson to be learned here is that the technological maturity of any tool should be evaluated and verified carefully. To gain realistic expectations is very important, as one can learn from experiences that unrealistic expectations backfire. Moreover, it is important that the cost-benefit analysis does not underestimate the long-term costs of the implementation.

Finally, it appears to be crucial to realize, understand, and then continuously reflect together upon the underlying tradeoff of technology use and performance. As this tradeoff situation cannot be solved with a one-time-yes-or-no decision, it is important that the organization establish a process and organizational format to regularly discuss how it can balance it. Doing so will improve the organization's dynamic capability.

Bibliography

Adelé, S., & Brangier, E. (2013). Evolutions in human technology relationship model: rejection, acceptance and technosymbiosis. *International Journal on WWW/Internet*, *11*(3), 46–60.

Ångström, R. C., Björn, M., Dahlander, L., Mähring, M., & Wallin, M. W. (2023). Getting AI implementation right: Insights from a global survey. *California Management Review*, *66*(1), 5–22. <https://doi.org/10.1177/00081256231190430>.

Arazy, O., & Croitoru, A. (2010). The sustainability of corporate wikis: A time-series analysis of activity patterns. *ACM Transactions on Management Information Systems*, *1*(1), 1–24. <https://doi.org/10.1145/1877725.1877731>.

Asatiani, A., Malo, P., Nagbøl, P., Penttinen, E., Rinta-Kahila, T., & Salovaara, A. (2021). Sociotechnical envelopment of artificial intelligence: An approach to organizational deployment of inscrutable artificial intelligence systems. *Journal of the Association for Information Systems*, *22*(2), 325–352. <https://doi.org/10.17705/1jais.00664>.

Baxter, G., & Connolly, T. (2014). Implementing Web 2.0 tools in organisations: Feasibility of a systematic approach. *The Learning Organization*, *21*(1), 6–25. <https://doi.org/10.1108/TLO-11-2012-0069>.

Bendel, A., & Latniak, E. (2020). Soziotechnisch—agil—lean: Konzepte und Vorgehensweise für Arbeits- und Organisationsgestaltung in Digitalisierungsprozessen. *Gruppe Interaktion Organisation Zeitschrift für Angewandte Organisationspsychologie*, *51*, 285–297. <https://doi.org/10.1007/s11612-020-00528-8>.

Binbir, S. (2023, July 28): Workspace, UNIKI, Slack und Co.: 5 Alternativen zu Microsoft Teams. Computerwoche. <https://www.computerwoche.de/article/2820669/5-alternativen-zu-microsoft-teams.html>.

Boag, W., Hasan, A., & Kim, J. Y. (2024). The algorithm journey map: A tangible approach to implementing AI solutions in healthcare. *NPJ Digital Media*, 7. <https://doi.org/10.1038/s41746-024-01061-4>.

Bojaryn, J. (2024, February 7). *Copilot für Microsoft Office im Test: Ist das KI-Tool wirklich eine Hilfe?* <https://www.rnd.de/digital/copilot-von-microsoft-buero-ki-fuer-alle-wie-gut-ist-das-tool-7Q6S2VDF7RGWZFX35QEWIF3KZI.html>.

Cabitza, F., Campagner, A., & Balsano, C. (2020). Bridging the "last mile" gap between AI implementation and operation: "data awareness" that matters. *Annals of Translational Medicine*, *8*(7). <https://doi.org/10.21037/atm.2020.03.63>.

Cappelli, P., Tambe, P., & Yakubovich, V. (2024). Will Large Language Models Really Change How Work Is Done? *MIT Sloan Management Review*, *65*(3), 48–53.

Columbus, L. (2024, January 22). *Gartner Predicts AI Software Will Grow to $297 Billion By 2027.* <https://www.linkedin.com/pulse/gartner-predicts-ai-software-grow-297-billion-2027-louis-columbus-okpfc/>.

Dastin, J. (2023, March 16). *Microsoft unveils AI office Copilot in fast-moving race with Google. Reuters*. <https://www.reuters.com/technology/microsoft-unveils-ai-its-office-suite-increased-competition-with-google-2023-03-16/>.

Davis, M., Challenger, R., Jayewardene, D., & Clegg, C. (2014). Advancing socio-technical systems thinking: A call for bravery. *Applied Ergonomics*, *45*(2), 171–180. <https://doi.org/10.1016/j.apergo.2013.02.009>.

Davis et al., (2014). *Advancing socio-technical systems thinking: A call for bravery.*

Finnegan, M. (2023, October 24). As M365 copilot launch looms, businesses likely to move cautiously. *Computerworld*. <https://www.computerworld.com/article/1638183/as-m365-copilot-launch-looms-businesses-likely-to-move-cautiously.html>.

Gibson, S. (2006, November 20). Veni, vidi, wiki. *eWeek*.

Haenlein M., & Kaplan A. (2019). A brief history of artificial intelligence: On the past, present, and future of artificial intelligence. *California Management Review*, *61*(4), 5–14. <https://doi.org/10.1177/0008125619864925>.

Hildreth, S. (2007, June 4). Web 2.0 Goes Corporate. *Computerworld*.

Hirsch-Kreinsen, H. (2018). Das Konzept des Soziotechnischen Systems—Revisited. *AIS-Studien*. *11*(2), 11–28. <https://doi.org/10.21241/ssoar.64859>.

Hof, R. (2004, June 7). Something Wiki this way comes. They're Web sites anyone can edit-and they could transform corporate America. *BusinessWeek*.

Hopf, K., Müller, O., Shollo, A., & Thiess, T. (2023). Organizational Implementation of AI: Craft and mechanical work. California Management Review, *66*(1), 23–47. <https://doi.org/10.1177/00081256231197445>.

Klimmer, M. (2020). *Unternehmensorganisation. Eine kompakte und praxisnahe Einführung mit Online-Training inklusive*. 5., akt. Aufl., NWB Verlag. <ISBN 978-3-482-54975-5>.

Iansiti, M., & Lakhani, K. (2021). Competing in the age of AI. How machine intelligence changes the rules of business. *HBR Special Issue*, 12–19.

Locke, E., & Latham, G. (1990). *A theory of goal setting & task performance.* Prentice-Hall, Inc.

Lykourentzou, I., Dagka, F., Papadaki, K., Lepouras, G., & Vassilakis, C. (2011). Wikis in enterprise settings: A survey. *Enterprise Information Systems*, *6*(1), 1–53. <https://doi.org/10.1080/17517575.2011.580008>.

Maslow, A. (1943). A theory of human motivation. *Psychological Review, 50*(4), 370–396. <https://doi.org/10.1037/h0054346>.

Meckel, M., & Steinacker, L. (2024). Alles überall auf einmal. Wie Künstliche Intelligenz unsere Welt verändert und was wir dabei gewinnen können. 2. Aufl., Rowohlt.

Meffert, K. (2024, Juli 10). Das vollständige Versagen von Microsoft Copilot. *Dr. DSGVO Blog.* <https://dr-dsgvo.de/copilot/>.

Ming, C. (2024). A Reality check of the benefits of LLM in business. *ACM*. <https://doi.org/10.48550/arXiv.2406.10249>.

Muth, M. (2023, November 29). Microsofts copilot: Was bringt die künstliche Intelligenz den Unternehmen? *Sueddeutsche*. <https://www.sueddeutsche.de/wirtschaft/kuenstliche-intelligenz-copilot-microsoft-1.6311182>.

Nyckel, E.-M. (2020). "Digital Taylorism"? *Data Practices and Governance in the Enterprise Software Salesforce* (Weizenbaum Series 9). <https://doi.org/10.34669/WI.WS/9>.

Orlikowski, W., & Scott, S. (2008). 10 Sociomateriality: Challenging the separation of technology, work and organization. *The Academy of Management Annals*, *2*(1), 433–474. <http://dx.doi.org/10.1080/19416520802211644>.

Pasmore, W., Winby, S., Mohrman, S., & Vanasse, R. (2019). Reflections: Sociotechnical systems design and organization change. *Journal of Change Management*, *19*(2), 67–85. <https://doi.org/10.1080/14697017.2018.1553761>.

Perry, N., Srivastava, M., Kumar, D., & Boneh, D. (2023). Do users write more insecure code with AI assistants? *Proceedings of the 2023 ACM SIGSAC Conference on Computer and Communications Security*, 2785–2799.

Rogers, E. M. (2003). *Diffusion of innovations.* 5. Aufl., Free Press.

Ross, J. (2018).The fundamental flaw in AI implementation. *MIT Sloan Management Review.* 59(2), 10–11.

Schlude, A., Schwind, M., Mendel, U., Stürz, R. A., Harles, D., & Fischer, M. (2023, November 17). Verbreitung und Akzeptanz generativer KI in Deutschland und an deutschen Arbeitsplätzen. *Bidt DE.* <https://www.bidt.digital/publikation/verbreitung-und-akzeptanz-generativer-ki-in-deutschland-und-an-deutschen-arbeitsplaetzen/>.

Spataro, J. (2020, March 19). *Microsoft Teams at 3: Everything you need to connect with your teammates and be more productive.* <https://www.microsoft.com/en-us/microsoft-365/blog/2020/03/19/microsoft-teams-3-everything-you-need-connect-teammates-be-more-productive/>.

Spataro, J. (2023, March 16). *Introducing Microsoft 365 Copilot – your copilot for work.* <https://blogs.microsoft.com/blog/2023/03/16/introducing-microsoft-365-copilot-your-copilot-for-work/>.

Strohm, L., Hehakaya, C., Ranschaert, E. R., et al. (2020). Implementation of artificial intelligence (AI) applications in radiology: Hindering and facilitating factors. *European Radiology, 30,* 5525–5532. <https://doi.org/10.1007/s00330-020-06946-y>.

Stoffers, J. & Mordant-Dols, A. (2015). *Transformational Leadership and Professionals' Willingness to Change: A Multiple Case Study in Project Management Organisations.* <https://doi.org/10.5923/j.hrmr.20150502.03>.

Tse, T., Esposito, M., Goh, D., & Mizuno, T. (2020, June 8). The dumb reason your AI project will fail. *Harvard Business Review.* <https://hbr.org/2020/06/the-dumb-reason-your-ai-project-will-fail>.

Vaast, E., & Pinsonneault, A. (2021). When digital technologies enable and threaten occupational identity: The delicate balancing act of data scientists. *MIS Quarterly.* 45, 1087–1112. <https://doi.org/10.25300/MISQ/2021/16024>.

Vella, S., & Shariah, S. (2024). All you need is knowledge, experience and tools: A Framework for integrating digital labour with white collar work. *2024 4th Interdisciplinary Conference on Electrics and Computer (INTCEC),* Chicago, IL, USA, pp. 1–7. <https://doi.org/10.1109/INTCEC61833.2024.10602875>.

Warren, T. (2023, March 16). Microsoft announces copilot: the AI-powered future of office documents. *The Verge.* <https://www.theverge.com/2023/3/16/23642833/microsoft-365-ai-copilot-word-outlook-teams>.

Wayner, P. (2023, November 24). Top 8: Die besten Predictive Analytics Tools. *Computerwoche*. <https://www.computerwoche.de/article/2797839/die-besten-predictive-analytics-tools.html>.

Xu, J., & Lu, W. (2022). Developing a human-organization-technology fit model for information technology adoption in organizations. *Technology in Society*, 70, 102010. <https://doi.org/10.1016/j.techsoc.2022.102010>.

Zabala, F. (2023). Grow your business with AI. A *First Principles Approach for Scaling Artificial Intelligence in the Enterprise*. Springer Nature.

Links

Web 2.0 (2024, September 9). In *Wikipedia*. <https://en.wikipedia.org/wiki/Web_2.0#Characteristics>.

<https://www.linkedin.com/events/thefutureofwork-reinventingprod7038508574142074880/>.

<https://www.condecosoftware.com/modern-workplace/history-of-the-workplace/>.

<https://practical365.com/microsoft-365-copilot-launches/>.

<https://de.statista.com/statistik/daten/studie/1189929/umfrage/anzahl-der-taeglich-aktiven-nutzer-von-microsoft-teams-weltweit/>.

<https://www.microsoft.com/de-de/microsoft-365/copilot?market=de#tabs-pill-bar-oc498c_tab2>.

7. Unraveling Regenerative Finance: Economic Insights into Blockchain's Disruptive Potential

Margareta Teodorescu and Ela Sibel Bayrak Meydanoğlu***

ABSTRACT
This paper explores the emerging concept of regenerative finance (ReFi), which extends the principles of blockchain technology to foster economic systems that are not only efficient and transparent but also environmentally sustainable and socially inclusive. Leveraging the fundamental aspects of smart contracts, ReFi aims to revolutionize traditional financial models by integrating environmental, social, and governance (ESG) criteria into financial practices. The study provides an examination of how ReFi could potentially reduce transaction costs, increase financial inclusion, and promote sustainable economic practices. Through a structured analysis of different financial instruments, we assess the potential for ReFi to facilitate a transition towards a more sustainable and equitable financial ecosystem. We analyze how ReFi can contribute to achieving global sustainability goals while maintaining financial stability and growth, and outline the challenges and opportunities of implementing ReFi, such as scalability, regulatory adaptation, and market acceptance. This analysis aims to delineate the pathways through which blockchain technology can underpin the growth of financial systems that not only prosper economically but also regenerate the natural environment and foster sustainable community development.

Keywords: Blockchain, Regenerative finance, Climate neutrality, Financial technology, Decentralized platforms, Sustainable financial ecosystem

Introduction

Undoubtedly, the global economic system has, over the past years, undergone an unprecedented transformation driven by the imperative need to address climate change and ecological degradation. The rapid escalation of greenhouse gas emissions and the accelerating degradation of natural ecosystems due to human activities have led to a significant decline in biodiversity (Zhai et al., 2023). This decline poses significant risks to economic development, social

*Koblenz University of Applied Sciences, Faculty of Business and Management, Koblenz, Germany.
**Turkish-German University, Faculty of Economics and Business Administration, Department of Business Administration, Istanbul, Turkey.
Emails: <teodorescu@hs-koblenz.de>, <meydanoglu@tau.edu.tr>

stability, and overall quality of life. Therefore, it is imperative to urgently act and address these environmental issues in order to avoid an imminent ecological disaster and secure a lasting and environmentally balanced future for everyone. What is urgently needed is a fundamental transition to a sustainable economic model capable of effectively addressing and managing the current global environmental emergency. While this is a highly complex, multifaceted challenge with no single solution, a unified global effort is essential to achieve genuine environmental stability (Shih et al., 2023).

Traditional economic models, characterized by linear and extractive practices, are increasingly being recognized as unsustainable due to their detrimental impact on the environment and their inability to ensure long-term social equity and prevent accelerating inequality. In an extractive economy, assets achieve their value primarily from their potential of being traded or exchanged at the optimal moment—be it through physical means, like mining coal during periods of high demand, or through legal mechanisms, such as acquiring property rights during periods of high supply. These shifts create arbitrage opportunities for natural resources and factors of production. The fundamental principle of value creation in extractive economies is exploiting these opportunities for maximum short-term profit. This approach is central to extractive economics and disregards the resulting social costs and the associated negative externalities (Schletz et al., 2023).

Extractive economics sharply differs from regenerative economics, which is centered around finding and establishing an economic system that is both sustainable and equitable and is focused on restoring natural resources, fostering community well-being, and promoting long-term value creation. While extractive economics operates under the assumption of limitless growth, ecological and regenerative economics acknowledge that economic growth is inherently limited by the planet's ecological boundaries and must be balanced by the restoration of natural capital (Daly, 1991, 1997). The fundamental distinction between extractive and regenerative economies lies in their fundamental principles: vitality, viability, and evolutionary capacity. *Vitality* is defined as being that capacity that makes a system to generate and sustain abundance, diversity, and overall health. *Viability* denotes the system's capability to endure and adjust effectively to evolving conditions, all while preserving its core objective and foundational values. *Evolutionary capacity*, on the other hand, describes a system's ability and potential to learn, innovate, and evolve, thereby ensuring its continuous performance enhancement and adaptation to ongoing changes and new challenges. Collectively, these principles establish positive feedback mechanisms that foster resilience, adaptability, and an ongoing process of development and optimization, ultimately supporting and sustaining life (Benne & Mang, 2015; du Plessis, 2012; Mang & Reed, 2012).

As the global economic system undergoes an unprecedented transformation driven by the necessity of addressing climate change and ecological degradation, the concept of regenerative finance (ReFi) has, over recent years, emerged as a potential game-changer for addressing environmental challenges, particularly in the context of climate change, ecological degradation, and sustainability. Acknowledging that the current economic model is primarily extractive, growth-driven, and relying heavily on finite natural resources while disregarding planetary boundaries, the need for a systemic shift in how value is created and distributed in economic systems is more pressing than ever. This has led to the development of alternative frameworks that focus on sustainability, resilience, and regeneration (Daly, 2008; Schletz et al., 2023). Among these emerging paradigms, ReFi has gained significant importance, being able to offer a holistic approach to align financial systems with the health of natural ecosystems as well as social well-being (Mang & Reed, 2012).

Regenerative Finance merges Decentralized Finance (DeFi) technologies with the core principles of regeneration, allowing for an alternative approach by employing digital technologies such as Internet of Things (IoT), machine learning (ML), and blockchain, to facilitate transparent and equitable economic models that are compatible with ecological thinking. The Regenerative Finance movement aims to enhance information sharing and establish an overarching system of rules. At the same time, this emerging movement is focusing on leveraging these technologies to create the financial tools needed to realize economic concepts, including those such as "economies of permanence" and "regenerative economy" (Hartley & Rennie, 2022; Schletz et al., 2023).

In the context of ReFi, the blockchain technology offers significant disruptive potential, enabling transparency and traceability that are crucial for environmental finance. Previous research and empirical studies highlight the importance of blockchain in improving the integrity and efficiency of regenerative finance projects, due to blockchain's ability to record all types of transaction data in a traceable and immutable way, enhancing trust and accountability in the system and eliminating the need for a central authority (Baumann, 2018; Chen, 2018; Culotta et al., 2022; Dorfleitner et al., 2021; Frake et al., 2020). Therefore, this study is centered around the role and the impact of blockchain in the context of regenerative finance and delves into how blockchain's inherent transparency, decentralization, and immutability can disrupt traditional financial systems, driving a shift from extractive economic models to ones that restore and regenerate natural ecosystems (Hartley & Rennie, 2022).

Several types of regenerative finance initiatives are emerging across various sectors, each aiming to restore ecosystems, improve community well-being, and contribute to sustainable development. As the existing body of literature does not equally consider all these types, the present study aims to close this gap and is therefore centered around two primary types:

(a) *Blockchain-enhanced carbon markets:* These projects aim to address systemic inefficiencies in carbon trading, such as either bringing carbon credits or otherwise supporting the trading of these credits.
(b) *Projects that incentivize regenerative practices:* These initiatives promote regenerative ecosystem projects by providing incentives. Although they may utilize carbon or other ecological credit systems, their primary focus is on creating and funding new regenerative efforts, rather than bringing pre-existing credits on the blockchain.

Both models leverage blockchain's ability to ensure accountability, create immutable records, and facilitate decentralized governance (Hartley & Rennie, 2022).

Using a case-based approach proposed in the seminal papers by Eisenhardt (1989) and Ketokivi and Choi (2014), this study delves into how blockchain's inherent transparency, decentralization, and immutability can disrupt traditional financial systems, driving a shift from extractive economic models to ones that restore and regenerate natural ecosystems. Through a comprehensive analysis of selected cases, this paper highlights the mechanisms, implementation strategies, challenges, and impacts of blockchain integration into climate action finance. The findings show the similarities as well as the differences between the two types of regenerative initiatives. Furthermore, the study leads to theoretical propositions to guide future research and policy, emphasizing the creation and development of sustainable, resilient economic and financial systems capable of supporting regenerative guiding principles and promoting ecological regeneration.

The rest of the paper is organized as follows. After the Introduction in Section 1, the subsequent section describes a short literature review of the topic of the study. The methodology and the essential analytical principles that guide the research investigation follows in Section 3. The next section presents both the within-case and the across-case analysis, while Section 5 presents the results and discussion of the topic. The last section concludes the paper.

Literature Review

Regenerative Economics and the Foundations of ReFi

The foundational theories of ReFi stem from the concepts of regenerative and ecological economics. Daly (1991) introduced the idea of a steady-state economy, namely an economic model that respects the physical limits of the planet, advocating for resource use in a way that allows natural systems to regenerate. This foundational theory directly contrasts with neoclassical economics, which seeks unlimited growth, often at the expense of ecological health (Daly, 1991, 1997). Fullerton (2015) expanded on these principles, proposing a framework that emphasizes systemic health, resilience, and the need to redesign economic systems that align with natural cycles and community well-being.

According to Fullerton (2015), the history of economic theory is not over with Keynes or Hayek, Minsky or Friedman, as their disciples cannot argue endlessly into the future. Since climate change can be considered as being the largest market failure in the history of capitalism, regenerative capitalism is called to contribute to the fundamental shift in thinking towards a more sustainable and nature-oriented way of economic thinking. Acknowledging that living systems are inherently sustainable and regenerative in the long run, it is important to investigate whether applying nature's principles of health, prosperity, and development could also foster sustainably thriving economic systems (Fullerton, 2015).

In his work "Regenerative Capitalism—How Universal Principles and Patterns Will Shape Our New Economy," Fullerton (2015) described eight principles that could underpin a new economic system that ensures collective prosperity on a flourishing planet. And the "Regenerative story," as Fullerton (Fullerton, 2015, p. 8) calls it, is based on a one-of-a-kind, fundamental idea:

> *"The universal patterns and principles the cosmos uses to build stable, healthy, and sustainable systems throughout the real world can and must be used as a model for economic-system design."*

Nevertheless, the concept of regenerative economy or, respectively, of economy of permanence is not new. Initially proposed in 1945 by Kumarappa (1945), the concept promotes and fosters human prosperity, development, and well-being. It refers to the maintenance of consistent inputs and sustainable outputs, ensuring that critical resources are not depleted and that no harm is caused to other components of the broader societal and environmental systems that it relies on Kumarappa (1945).

The regenerative paradigm emphasizes that development should actively enhance the capacity of all natural, cultural, and economic systems in a given location to grow and sustain their health and long-term viability. This is what Sanford (2011) refers to as the "quintessential top line." The foundation of this belief rests on the co-creative, life-sustaining relationship between humans and the environments they inhabit. Many scholars argue that it is through a deep connection to their surroundings that humans develop a sense of responsibility to the living world, discovering both identity and purpose (Cameron, 2002; du Plessis, 2012; Sack, 1977).

Blockchain Technology as an Enabler of ReFi

Sustainable finance, including green finance and green fintech, has emerged as a response to the need for economic activities that align with sustainability goals (Shih et al., 2023). However, green finance is often criticized for its focus on damage mitigation rather than creating positive impacts. Regenerative finance extends beyond sustainability to actively restore ecosystems, leveraging financial mechanisms to create net-positive outcomes for both the environment and society.

Blockchain technology is well-suited to the goals of ReFi due to its properties of transparency, immutability, and decentralization. These features address key weaknesses in traditional environmental finance, such as lack of transparency, double-counting of carbon credits, and difficulty in verifying the authenticity of ecological claims (Schletz et al., 2023). Blockchain can support decentralized governance, allowing local communities to participate in decision-making processes, thus improving the inclusivity and fairness of financial systems (Ostrom, 2010).

Tokenization, a fundamental blockchain feature, allows ecological assets—such as carbon credits or ecological services—to be represented digitally, enabling easy transfer, trading, and financialization. This process introduces a new paradigm where ecological value can be quantified, monetized, and exchanged, creating direct incentives for stakeholders to engage in climate-positive actions. Moreover, DeFi mechanisms can reduce barriers to entry, allowing more stakeholders, including marginalized communities, to access regenerative finance opportunities (Berg et al., 2019).

Methodology

This study employs qualitative case study methodology to explore the potential of blockchain-enabled ReFi projects. Case studies are particularly effective for examining new, complex phenomena, such as the implementation of blockchain-based applications to regenerative finance projects, where existing theoretical frameworks are still evolving (Eisenhardt, 1989). The approach includes both within-case and cross-case analysis to explore similarities, differences, and emerging patterns.

Eisenhardt (1989) highlights the iterative nature of case study research, allowing for theory development that is grounded in empirical observations. This is critical for ReFi, where rapid technological advancements and innovative applications are reshaping traditional finance. (Ketokivi & Choi, 2014) further discuss the diversity within case research methodologies, emphasizing the value of methodological diversity in capturing the full complexity of emergent models (Ketokivi & Choi, 2014).

The main objective of this study is that of analyzing what are the differences and similarities between the practices of implementing blockchain technologies in ReFi projects, by using the case study method. Using a theory-building approach, we present in this paper several case studies for ReFi projects from two types, whereas the cases were selected based on their relevance to the two categories under investigation: carbon markets and incentivizing regenerative practices. Data sources include project whitepapers, academic literature, and media reports. By integrating data from various sources, the study aims to develop a robust understanding of the mechanisms, outcomes, and potential of blockchain in promoting regenerative finance.

Analysis

Within-Case Analysis

In this section, we present a detailed examination of selected projects from each type of ReFi initiative to provide comprehensive insights into the modalities of implementing the blockchain technology in ReFi initiatives.

(A) Carbon Markets

(a) *KlimaDAO*
KlimaDAO (<https://www.klimadao.finance/>) is a decentralized autonomous organization that aims to address inefficiencies in the carbon market by purchasing and retiring carbon credits, thereby creating a price floor. This pricing floor creates a stable demand for carbon credits, providing financial sustainability for carbon reduction initiatives (Hartley & Rennie, 2022). The project's use of blockchain enables transparent governance through decentralized participation, allowing stakeholders to vote on key decisions, such as which credits to purchase and how to retire them.

Implementation and Impact: KlimaDAO operates on the Polygon blockchain, taking advantage of the platform's low transaction fees to enable efficient and frequent credit transactions. KlimaDAO has successfully aggregated a significant number of carbon credits, thereby impacting the overall market price and ensuring that carbon remains a valuable, tradable commodity. This approach encourages industries to reduce emissions since the higher price of carbon credits makes it economically viable to invest in emissions reduction technologies.

(b) *Toucan Protocol*
The Toucan Protocol (<https://toucan.earth/>) focuses on bridging the gap between legacy carbon credits and blockchain ecosystems

by tokenizing these credits. The tokenization process involves bringing real-world carbon credits onto the chain, creating Base Carbon Tonne (BCT) tokens that represent verified carbon offsets (Schletz et al., 2023). Toucan uses a Web3 approach to enable transparent and efficient trading of carbon credits, eliminating intermediaries and reducing costs.

Implementation and Impact: By creating a bridge between existing carbon registries and blockchain networks, Toucan increases liquidity in carbon markets. This increased liquidity enables a broader range of participants, including businesses, NGOs, and individuals, to engage in carbon offsetting.

(c) *MOSS*

MOSS focuses on the Amazon rainforest, issuing carbon credits tied to conservation efforts in one of the world's most critical ecosystems. By tokenizing these credits, MOSS connects international investors directly with conservation activities, ensuring transparency and accountability in the allocation of funds (Shih et al., 2023).

Implementation and Impact: MOSS leverages blockchain to monitor how funds are used, ensuring that funds reach intended conservation projects without unnecessary intermediaries. MOSS has collaborated with numerous conservation NGOs to verify the outcomes, ensuring that the tokenized credits are credible. While the project has generated millions of dollars in funding for rainforest preservation, it has also raised global awareness of the Amazon's role in carbon sequestration and biodiversity.

(d) *Thallo*

Thallo (<https://www.thallo.io/>) is a blockchain-based marketplace that facilitates direct transactions between carbon credit buyers and sellers. The platform provides on-chain verification to eliminate the double-counting of credits and ensures transparency throughout the carbon trading process (Schletz et al., 2023).

Implementation and Impact: Thallo addresses inefficiencies in traditional carbon markets by allowing for seamless and transparent peer-to-peer trading. By employing smart contracts, Thallo automates the settlement process, ensuring rapid and secure transactions. The decentralized nature of the platform allows users to engage in carbon trading without relying on centralized authorities, reducing transaction costs and increasing market transparency and accessibility.

(B) Incentivizing Regenerative Practices

(a) *Regen Network*

Regen Network (<https://www.registry.regen.network/>) aims to financially reward farmers and landowners for practices that contribute to ecological health, such as carbon sequestration, soil regeneration, and improved water retention. Blockchain technology is used to verify these practices, ensuring that rewards are linked to measurable ecological outcomes (Hartley & Rennie, 2022).

Implementation and Impact: Regen Network uses satellite imagery and on-the-ground sensors to monitor regenerative activities. This data is then recorded on the blockchain, providing an immutable proof of action before tokens are issued as rewards. The project also emphasizes community involvement, allowing local stakeholders to have a say in how regenerative efforts are managed. The Regen Network's model has been adopted by hundreds of farmers, leading to demonstrable improvements in soil carbon levels and water quality in various regions.

(b) *BasinDAO*

BasinDAO focuses on incentivizing local communities to implement water conservation and soil regeneration projects. The DAO structure allows community members to propose and vote on initiatives that aim to improve watershed health, with successful projects receiving tokenized rewards (Hartley & Rennie, 2022).

Implementation and Impact: BasinDAO has implemented projects aimed at reducing agricultural runoff and improving water quality in several watersheds. The use of blockchain enables transparent voting and allocation of funds, ensuring that resources are directed towards the most impactful projects. By focusing on water conservation, BasinDAO has created a replicable model that can be applied in different geographical areas, addressing one of the most pressing environmental issues faced by agriculture today.

(c) *Nori*

Nori operates as a marketplace for carbon removal credits, rewarding farmers and ranchers for practices that store carbon in soil. Blockchain technology is used to verify these practices, ensuring that carbon removal is accurately measured and publicly recorded (Schletz et al., 2023).

Implementation and Impact: Nori's marketplace uses blockchain to ensure transparency in carbon removal transactions. Farmers who adopt regenerative practices, such as no-till farming, can earn Nori tokens, which are then sold to buyers seeking to offset their emissions. This approach provides a financial incentive for farmers to adopt sustainable practices, making carbon sequestration a viable source of income. Nori has demonstrated success in building a robust ecosystem involving agricultural experts, carbon scientists, and buyers, creating a holistic and effective approach to carbon removal.

(d) *Katalyst.earth*
Katalyst.earth is a crowdfunding platform that supports regenerative projects, such as reforestation and soil carbon sequestration. Blockchain technology is used to verify the impact of projects, provide transparency to donors, and ensure that funds are allocated effectively (Hartley & Rennie, 2022).

Implementation and Impact: Katalyst.earth has facilitated numerous small-scale projects that would have struggled to secure funding through traditional means. By providing a transparent platform for crowdfunding, the project has attracted a wide range of contributors, from individual donors to institutional investors. Blockchain ensures that funds are traceable, and donors can see the results of their contributions, creating a strong incentive for continued engagement.

Cross-Case Analysis

Analyzing the projects within each of the two distinct project types, several key similarities and differences become evident. These findings not only highlight shared characteristics across the projects but also underscore unique aspects that distinguish one project type from the other.

(a) *Blockchain-enhanced carbon markets*
Projects such as KlimaDAO and the Toucan Protocol both focus on enhancing liquidity and transparency within carbon markets. However, their strategies differ significantly. KlimaDAO's approach is to create a floor price by buying up carbon credits, while Toucan Protocol and Thallo focus on making credits more accessible through tokenization and direct trading mechanisms. While all projects leverage blockchain to address issues such as double-counting, their methods for ensuring market stability and accessibility differ, reflecting different theories of market intervention.

(b) *Projects that incentivize regenerative practice*
Projects such as Regen Network, Nori, and BasinDAO all focus on rewarding positive ecological actions through blockchain-verified practices. However, their focus differs. Regen Network and Nori prioritize soil health and carbon sequestration, while BasinDAO focuses on water conservation. Despite these differences, they all share a decentralized governance structure that empowers local stakeholders to directly influence projects, ensuring that solutions are community-driven and context-specific.

By now, comparing the two types of projects, carbon markets and incentivizing regenerative practices, we find the following similarities and differences:

- *Similarities*: Both categories leverage blockchain's transparency and accountability to create financial incentives aligned with climate-positive outcomes. The emphasis on tokenization allows ecological assets to be traded and monetized, creating direct economic incentives for environmental stewardship.
- *Differences*: The fundamental difference between these two types of projects lies in their approach. Carbon market projects primarily focus on optimizing the financial mechanisms around existing ecological credits, such as carbon sequestration, by making these credits more liquid and accessible. In contrast, projects incentivizing regenerative practices create new ecological value through direct intervention. This suggests that carbon markets are more focused on commoditizing and financially optimizing ecological assets, while regenerative practice projects seek to expand the underlying ecological base.

Results and Discussion

Proposition 1: Blockchain as a Transparency Enabler

The ability of blockchain to increase transparency and reliability in carbon markets is a critical factor in addressing long-standing issues such as double-counting and fraud. By tokenizing carbon credits, projects such as the Toucan Protocol and MOSS have demonstrated how blockchain can transform traditional carbon markets, making them more efficient, trustworthy, and accessible. This transparency is essential for restoring stakeholder trust and ensuring that carbon credits have real environmental value (Schletz et al., 2023).

Proposition 2: The Effectiveness of Tokenization in Aligning Incentives

Tokenization, as employed by ReFi initiatives, provides a versatile mechanism for both monetizing existing ecological assets and generating new value through regenerative practices. This model allows stakeholders to derive financial benefits from their contributions to sustainability, aligning economic incentives with ecological health. Tokenized incentives have proven effective in projects ranging from carbon trading to community-driven reforestation, suggesting that tokenization is a powerful tool for scaling environmental finance.

Proposition 3: Broader Social and Ecological Impact of Regenerative Practices

Projects that incentivize regenerative practices, such as Regen Network and BasinDAO, have a greater impact on local communities compared to those focusing solely on carbon markets. These projects provide co-benefits, such as improved biodiversity, enhanced soil fertility, and better water retention, which directly contribute to community resilience and well-being. The localized focus of these projects enables tangible, positive ecological and social outcomes that go beyond the trading of carbon credits (Fullerton & Lovins, 2023).

Proposition 4: Cross-Sector Collaboration and Governance

Decentralized governance models that encourage stakeholder participation are crucial for the success of ReFi projects. The involvement of local communities, governments, and NGOs helps create a sense of ownership and accountability that is essential for the success of community-driven regenerative projects. Cross-sector collaboration ensures that initiatives are well-supported, contextually relevant, and able to scale effectively (Hartley & Rennie, 2022).

Proposition 5: Regulatory Challenges and the Need for Standards

One of the main challenges facing ReFi projects, particularly those in carbon markets, is the lack of consistent regulatory standards. The development of global standards and coordinated regulatory frameworks is essential for blockchain-based carbon credits to be widely accepted and integrated into existing environmental policies. Without such standards, ReFi projects may struggle to gain the legitimacy needed to scale effectively (Shih et al., 2023).

Conclusion

This study has highlighted the transformative potential of blockchain technology in advancing regenerative finance, particularly through its application in carbon markets and projects that incentivize regenerative practices. The analysis shows that blockchain's transparency, efficiency, and decentralized governance offer significant advantages for both enhancing existing carbon markets and directly supporting new ecological initiatives. However, the full potential of ReFi will only be realized if challenges such as regulatory barriers, scalability, and integration with traditional financial systems are addressed.

The theoretical propositions derived from this analysis provide a framework for guiding future research and policymaking. Future research should focus on exploring the scalability of ReFi projects in diverse contexts, integrating blockchain-based regenerative initiatives into existing financial systems, and developing of comprehensive regulatory framework to support the widespread adoption of regenerative finance.

Bibliography

Baumann, T. (2018). Blockchain for planetary stewardship. Using the disruptive force of distributed ledger technology to fight climate disruption. *Blockchain Research Institute*. <https://www.blockchainresearchinstitute.org/project/blockchain-for-planetary-stewardship/> (Retrieved September 25, 2024)

Benne, B., & Mang, P. (2015). Working regeneratively across scales – Insights from nature applied to the built environment. *Journal of Cleaner Production, 109*, 42–52. <https://doi.org/10.1016/j.jclepro.2015.02.037>.

Berg, F., Kölbel, J. F., & Rigobon, R. (2019). Aggregate confusion: The divergence of ESG ratings. *Review of Finance*. <https://ssrn.com/abstract=3438533> (Retrieved September 18, 2024).

Cameron, J. (2002). *Working with polarities: An inclusive approach to sense of place and environmental advocacy*. <http://sites.uws.edu.au/research/SERG/Polarities_jcameron.htm> (Retrieved September 28 2024).

Chen, D. (2018). Utility of the blockchain for climate mitigation. *The Journal of the British Blockchain Association*, *1*(1), 1–9. <https://10.31585/jbba-1-1-(6)2018>.

Culotta, C., Brüning, S., Schulte, A., Gesmann-Nuissl, D., Märkel, C., & Beck, R. (2022). Nachhaltigkeit im Kontext der Blockchain-Technologie, *WIK-Consult und Fraunhofer-Institut für Materialfluss und Logistik IML*. <https://www.bmwk.de/Redaktion/DE/Publikationen/Digitale-Welt/blockchain-nachhaltigkeit.pdf?__blob=publicationFile&v=4> (Retrieved September 20, 2024).

Daly, H. (1991). *Steady-State Economics* (2nd ed. with New Essays). Island Press.

Daly, H. E. (1997). *Beyond Growth: The Economics of Sustainable Development*. Boston: Beacon Press.

Daly, H. E. (2008). Ecological economics and sustainable development, selected essays of herman daly, *Advances in Ecological Economic Series*. Edward Elgar Publishing.

Dorfleitner, G., Muck, F., & Scheckenbach, I. (2021). Blockchain applications for climate protection: A global empirical investigation. *Renewable and Sustainable Energy Reviews*, *149*, 111378. <https://doi.org/10.1016/j.rser.2021.111378>.

du Plessis, C. (2012). Towards a regenerative paradigm for the built environment. *Building Research and Information*, *40*(1), 7–22. <https://doi/org/10.1080/09613218.2012.628548>.

Eisenhardt, K. M. (1989). Building theories from case study research. *The Academy of Management Review*, *14*(4), 532–550. <https://doi.org/10.2307/258557>.

Franke, L. A., Schletz, M., & Salomo, S. (2020). Designing a blockchain model for the Paris Agreement's carbon market mechanism. *Sustainability*, *12*(3), 1068. <https://10.3390/su12031068>.

Fullerton, J. (2015). Regenerative capitalism: How universal principles and patterns will shape our new economy. *Capital Institute – The Future of Finance*.

Fullerton, J., & Lovins, H. (2023), Transforming finance and the regenerative economy. *Capital Institute, Frontiers in Blockchain*, *6*, 1165133

Hartley, S., & Rennie, E. (2022). Regenerative Finance "ReFi": Blockchain for Climate Action, Report for Intel, *ARC Centre for Automated Decision-Making and Society: Melbourne*. <https://apo.org.au/sites/default/files/resource-files/2022-11/apo-nid321467_0.pdf> (Retrieved September 24, 2024).

Ketokivi, M., & Choi, T. (2014). Renaissance of case research as a scientific method, *Journal of Operations Management*. <https://doi:org/10.1016/j.jom.2014.03.004>.

KlimaDAO. <https://www.klimadao.finance/> (Retrieved November 10, 2024)

Kumarappa, J. C. (1945). *Economy of permanence: A quest for a social order based on non-violence*. <https://www.mkgandhi.org> (Retrieved September 29, 2024).

Mang, P., & Reed, B. (2012). Designing from place: A regenerative framework and methodology, *Building Research and Information*, *40*(1), 23–38. <https://doi:10.1080/09613218.2012.621341>.

Nakamoto, S. (2008). *Bitcoin: A Peer-to-Peer Electronic Cash System*. <https://bitcoin.org/bitcoin.pdf> (Retrieved September 14, 2024).

Ostrom, E. (2010), Polycentric systems for coping with collective action and global environmental change Philipp Degens, *Global Environmental Change, 20*(4): 550–557. <https://www.researchgate.net/publication/365907730_Ostrom_Elinor_2010#fullTextFileContent> (Retrieved September 23, 2024).

Regen Network. <https://www.registry.regen.network/> (Retrieved on November 12, 2024)

Sack, R. D. (1977). *Homo Geographicus: A Framework for Action, Awareness, and Moral Concern*. Baltimore: Johns Hopkins University Press.

Sanford, C. (2011). *The Responsible Business: Reimagining Sustainability and Success*. San Francisco: Josey-Bass.

Schletz, M., Constant, A., Hsu, A., Beck, R., & Wainstein, M. (2023). Blockchain and regenerative finance: Charting a path toward regeneration. *Frontiers in Blockchain*, *6*, 1165133. <https://doi:10.3389/fbloc.2023.1165133>.

Shih C., Gwizdalski, A., & Deng, X. (2023). Building a sustainable future: Exploring green finance, regenerative finance, and green financial technology. *World Scientific Annual Review of Fintech* (Forthcoming), Nanyang

Business School Research Paper No. 23-18, Nanyang Technological University. <https://nbs.ntu.edu.sg/> (Retrieved September 30, 2024).

Thallo. <https://www.thallo.io/> (Retrieved November 10, 2024).

Toucan Protocol. <https://toucan.earth/> (Retrieved November 10, 2024).

Zhai, L., Ji, L., Caccetta, P., & Xie, Y. (2023), Editorial for special issue on "Remote sensing in identifying degraded natural ecosystems and assessing the impact of ecological restorations," *Ecological Engineering*, *191*, 106960. <https://doi.org/10.1016/j.ecoleng.2023.106960>.

8. Investment Franchising: Is It a Viable Solution for Small Investors Facing Governance Problems in Emerging Markets?

Hüseyin Hayri Nuroğlu

ABSTRACT

Franchising governance can vary significantly, ranging from market-driven to hierarchical structures. While both franchisors and franchisees often exhibit entrepreneurial characteristics, excessive hierarchical rigidity can diminish these traits, posing a common governance challenge in franchising networks. Conversely, a purely market-oriented approach may compromise control and standardization within the network. Numerous theoretical frameworks have been proposed to address franchising governance issues. Literature suggests that investment franchises, as a hybrid model, can enhance franchisor support and mitigate conflicts within networks. This paper aims to explore the intricacies of franchising governance by analyzing the impact of ownership rights structures on the relationship between franchisors and franchisees. Through secondary data analysis and reporting, valuable insights are gained. Furthermore, a comparative analysis between conventional and investment franchising models is presented, highlighting their respective strengths and weaknesses in fostering effective governance and increasing the visibility of investment options.

Keywords: Franchising governance, Shareholder franchising, Distribution of decision rights, Ownership

Introduction

Business network governance, especially in franchising, is an emerging field of study (Dant & Kaufmann, 2003; Gorovaia, & Windsperger, 2018; Windsperger & Dant, 2006). The field's understanding of franchising governance has been shaped by a focus on ownership and control at the individual outlet level. This perspective has often overlooked the importance of ownership and governance structures at the broader organizational level. This perspective suggests that franchisors have complete freedom to determine the structure of their franchise channels without considering other factors

Department of Business Administration, Turkish-German University, Istanbul, Turkey
Email: <h.nuroglu@tau.edu.tr>

that might affect their strategy. Consequently, academic research in this area has often neglected the impact of external investors and lenders on contemporary franchise systems.

Two mainstream perspectives are prominent in explaining why firms choose franchising to expand. First, capital scarcity theory claims that small and new companies can easily collect capital through franchising (Oxenfeldt & Thompson, 1968). Second, agency theory claims that firms prefer to franchise to prevent shirking and free riding problems (Rubin, 1978).

Existing research primarily focuses on franchisees that are established and owned by small or large businesses. There is a lack of studies exploring how ownership can grow and consolidate at both the franchisor and franchisee levels. Different types of organizations can own franchise networks, and hybrid investment modes are emerging. These differences in ownership structure affect how the organizations are managed, their financial situation, and their level of risk.

Franchising offers an important opportunity to investigate governance issues because its arrangements are special contractual agreements between autonomous franchisees and franchisors that own the network. Franchisees also make significant financial commitments to the franchise system through limited-term contracts. Franchisees' substantial investments in transaction-specific assets bind them to the franchisor.

In essence, a franchisee may view themselves as an independent contractor and an entrepreneur (Kidwell et al., 2007), but they are also closely associated with the brand's identity. Ownership of a franchising chain is not only related to by whom decisions will be taken, but it is also the issue of transferring the owner's local knowledge. It is claimed that a franchisor's local experience reduces the failure rates (Kalnins & Mayer 2004). The transfer of the local knowledge can be better absorbed into network by a local owner than an appointed manager.

Franchising offers an "additional financial source for franchisors" (Park & Jang, 2018). An emerging mode for franchisors and investors is investment franchising. It might require less capital and effort to join a network. Nevertheless, it might offer less profit chance. As a different franchising network involvement mode, investment franchising needs more attention.

This study aims to enlarge the understanding of franchising governance by incorporating the influence of the ownership and financial structures of both parties in a franchising firm. Through literature research on investment franchising, this research aims to contribute to the existing knowledge on corporate governance, business, and franchising networks. This research also examines the differences between the recently emerging governance model and traditional ownership, considering the viewpoints of both the franchisor and the franchisee.

Governance in Franchising

The roots of franchising go back to the Middle Ages, when the word "franchise" meant rights such as freedom from taxes, duties, or feudal rule (Lafontaine & Blair, 2009). Today, a franchise agreement is typically understood as a contractual arrangement between two separate legal entities. One entity, the franchisee, pays a fee to the other entity, the franchisor. In exchange, the franchisee obtains the right to sell the franchisor's products, utilize their trademarks and business model, and operate within a specific geographic area for a designated period.

Governance serves as the foundation of businesses, and due to the sensitive nature of governance matters such as ownership, and decision-making authority, the governance design of a franchising network has always been crucial. Since the inception of the franchising model, several factors have influenced the development of franchising governance. Globalization, contemporary management trends, and advancements in management tools such as artificial intelligence are some examples of these factors. Moreover, franchising contracts are "necessarily and intentionally incomplete" because of "linguistic ambiguity, or from the absence of provisions specifying the performances required under certain, perhaps unanticipated, conditions" (Hadfield, 1989). As a result, an optimal franchising governance structure has always been an important topic to be studied.

The governance structure of a franchising firm is composed of two elements: decision rights and ownership rights (Windsperger & Yurdakul, 2007). Successful franchise governance depends on the appropriate allocation of decision rights between franchisor and franchisee (Mumdziev & Windsperger, 2011). The distribution of decision rights is designed according to the ownership distribution of the organization. Windsperger (2002) argues that ownership should be granted to those who have the ultimate decision-making authority, and this authority should be given to individuals with intangible knowledge assets (know-how).

In the franchising sector, there are various franchise types depending on factors like industry, size, and operational model. As an entrepreneur, managing a franchise chain requires serious effort and time, besides a remarkable amount of investment. Even though the franchising sector is growing globally and is expected to grow by almost 10 % by 2032 (Business Research Insights, 2024), the turnover rate in the sector is quite high. A 2010–2013 Franchise Industry Report by FranchiseGrade.com surveyed 1,695 franchisors and found an average turnover rate of approximately 28% within the franchise industry (Bradley, 2015). Another report by Franchise Facts and Figures claims the franchise turnover rate as 10.23% over five years for the whole franchise sector (Lefler, 2016).

A franchise turnover rate below 5% suggests stability and satisfaction among franchisees. While a double-digit turnover rate stated above may indicate problems. Even though franchising offers a solid model that offers a proven performance (Soliman, 2022), it contains high risks as well. McDermott et al. (2023) offer 12 factors in a ranking order that influence purchasing a franchise business. They claim that "advisory council, culture, due diligence, hard work, open mind, passion, return on investment, self-assessment, support, system, talk to existing & previous franchisees, and value" have an impact on the investment decision. It might be difficult to evaluate all these factors efficiently for small investors. Small investors might face significant financial challenges, as established brands with a long history often require substantial investments. This may lead them to consider newer, less experienced franchise networks that require less capital. However, the turnover rate is quite high among new franchisors.

Beyond the stated investment risks above, small investors in single-unit franchises may face challenges related to franchisor governance. While franchisees are considered entrepreneurs (Dant, 2008), the level of autonomy they have may not fulfill their entrepreneurial desires (Cochet et al., 2008; Dant, 2008). This could lead to dissatisfaction and a loss of motivation among franchisees.

As a solution to risks and governance problems stated above, franchisees might consider investment in a franchise instead single-unit franchise. In this franchise model, franchisees invest capital and choose to either manage the business themselves or have the franchisor's management team oversee it. Even when the franchisee manages the business, they still hire a team to handle the day-to-day operations. The objective is to earn a return on their investment and realize capital gains. Hotel, large restaurant, and some retail and gym franchises are typical examples of investment franchising (Simpson, 2022).

This study compares single-unit franchises with investment franchises, focusing on small investors. Instead of taking on the full risks and responsibilities of owning a single-unit franchise, investing in a share of one, managed by the franchisor, might be a more efficient approach. Most franchise literature focuses on single-unit or multi-unit franchisees. Although investment franchises are less prevalent, this research aims to shed light on this model and its potential benefits for investors.

Methodology

This study used secondary data about investment franchises. Qualitative and quantitative data based on franchise literature in journal papers, mass media, and sectoral reports, industrial magazines from emerging markets, mainly from Türkiye, are investigated and analyzed. Due to the lack of decent sources available in Türkiye, sources in other emerging market settings were also used to reveal the research topic.

Findings

Examples of investment franchises are commonly found in the hotel and gastronomy sectors. As a new approach to traditional franchising ownership structure, the investment franchise model offered by Avane Cloud Kitchen, each branch of the restaurant chain is established as a separate legal entity. So the franchisor can offer shares to potential investors. This innovative concept not only promotes the growth of the restaurant chain but also makes franchising more accessible by allowing individuals to become shareholders with a minimal investment of just 10%. Avane Kitchen declares model as a partnership model for its branches (UFRAD, 2024). This lower financial barrier enables a broader range of investors to participate in the success of the restaurant chain without assuming full operational responsibility.

The founder and CEO of the company states that "In the 'Partnership Model for Avane Branches,' we offer franchise owners the opportunity to become partners with Avane branches that operate under the direct management of Avane with small investments. With this model, where daily operations are completely carried out by Avane, franchise owners can have a profitable investment options" (UFRAD, 2024a). The company predicts a 24–30 months ROI depending on the location of the business, which is claimed to be a unique and incomparable ROI period.

Another finding that came out of the investigation is the difference in the application of the investment franchise model in developed and emerging markets. Franchisees in developed markets are typically corporate investors with experience in the relevant industry, and they may invest huge amounts. In emerging markets, small investors prefer the model of limited investments and limited risks. Moreover, due to the economic stability of the developed markets, investors might be interested in stocks of the mature franchising brands instead of investing a small portion of a franchise unit. This difference might result from the limited experience in the franchising sector and related legal and practical differences developed in different markets.

Hotel, healthcare, fitness, and restaurant sectors are prominent in investment franchising because they require significant capital amounts for the initial investment. These franchising units require a high investment in fixed assets like tools, equipment, kitchens, and other expensive facilities. As a result, franchisors tend to meet their financial requirement through the investment franchise model.

Distribution of decision and ownership rights has always been a discussion issue in franchising networks. From the franchisors' perspective, by investment franchising, franchisors keep all decision rights and prevent the free riding problem. Central management guarantees the reliability and quality in all units. Moreover, this model helps franchisors to cope with the capital scarcity problem. However, the franchisor should have a proven business or a reliable and perceived brand name to get satisfactory investment.

Bulakh et al. (2020) claim that investment franchising brings out a new type of ownership. Companies, investment groups of individuals have the opportunity "to create a regional franchise network using employed staff." Moreover, a franchising business owned and run by a commercial organization, looks for "long-term interests on the invested capital rather than only regular income" (Bulakh et al., 2020) by franchisees. This longstanding aim might increase the expected lifetime of a franchise unit.

Gürkan (2024) claims that investment franchising decreases the franchisee's risk, and they can easily concentrate on their income with fewer financial risks. In the case of Avane Cloud Kitchen, the franchisor, has the responsibility to cover the financial loss. However, in this model, the number of shareholders is greater compared to the traditional one, and Gürkan (2024) claims that it might be challenging for the central management to align the shareholders' interest. However, shareholders usually have a short-term view, and this might show up as a challenge for the central management.

The positioning of investment franchises can differ based on the legal frameworks of various countries. In traditional franchising, businesses are typically organized as C corporations. However, some hotel companies operate as Real Estate Investment Trusts (REITs). The primary distinction between the two models is in taxation. REIT stockholders are exempt from corporate taxes for the dividends distributed, while C-corporation hotels are subject to corporate taxes for distributed dividends (Dogru, 2017). A similar nuance might exist in different legal systems that might affect the preference for an investment franchise or traditional model.

Conclusion and Implications

This research stands as a valuable contribution to the existing literature by forging an important path in the examination of investment franchise in franchising networks, using a comprehensive framework. While the distribution of ownership rights has been explored in previous studies (Callaci et al., 2020), our research mainly focuses on a new approach in the context of franchising governance. In addition to enriching the understanding of the investment franchise, our examination also unveils the differences between the traditional model.

Investment franchising has drawbacks and benefits compared to the traditional model. However, these differences might be different in various markets. The difference in the market might depend on the market's franchising experience, legal developments and field practices (Dant et al., 2008).

Despite variations across different markets, investment franchising generally offers lower financial risks through smaller investment requirements for franchisees, greater transparency through regular financial reports and meetings, and consistent dividend distribution.

Our study offers important insights with compelling managerial implications for the franchising sector, especially franchisees who want to invest in a franchise with limited financial resources. It is apparent that investing in a valuable brand with long experience requires a high amount of capital. On the other hand, valuable brands apply tough selection processes at the beginning, and strict control and monitoring activities as long as the business continues. Investment franchising might solve the obstacles on both sides through offering more transparent activities with fewer capital requirements.

For managers seeking to broaden their business in the franchising sector, an investment franchising model can be a strategic decision. Because, as an emerging market, the share of online sales in the restaurant sector in Turkey is around 25%, which is indicated as low compared to the world ratio of 75% (UFRAD2024), and this is a vital sign showing that the sector will grow in the near future.

Furthermore, this study investigates the unique dynamics of franchising governance within emerging markets, offering new insights to the business field. With the increasing focus on emerging markets, our findings highlight the ownership problems faced by franchisors and franchisees in countries like Turkey.

Limitations and Future Research

While this research has generated useful insights through literature review, it is important to consider its limitations. First, the number of franchisors offering the model is limited in emerging as well as in developed markets. The lack of empirical analysis in this study might prevent getting the complexities of the franchising environment. Moreover, practical examples from a few country settings might lead to an unsatisfactory representation of the franchising market setup, which requires further field research with multiple franchise networks.

Finally, future empirical research investigating investment franchise applications in other emerging and developed country settings could facilitate meaningful comparisons. This might lead to valuable insights and enhance the applicability of the findings in a broader framework.

Bibliography

Arturs Kalnins, & Kyle J. Mayer, (2004) Franchising, ownership, and experience: A study of pizza restaurant survival. *Management Science 50*(12), 1716–1728. <https://doi.org/10.1287/mnsc.1040.0220>.

Blair, Roger D. (2005). The economics of franchising. Cambridge University Press.

Bozagcı, E. C., & Çevik, A. (2022). Bulut Mutfak Modeli Üzerine Nitel Bir Araştırma: Avane Cloud Kitchens. *Ordu Üniversitesi Sosyal Bilimler Enstitüsü Sosyal Bilimler Araştırmaları Dergisi, 12*(2), 675–688. <https://doi.org/10.48146/odusobiad.1091100>.

Bradley, Bill (2015). *Franchise Turnover Rates.* <https://smallbizclub.com/startup/franchise-center/franchise-turnover-rates/>.

Bulakh, T., Plakhotnikova, L., & Hromadskyi, R., (2020). НАУКОВИЙ ВІСНИК НАЦІОНАЛЬНОЇ АКАДЕМІЇ СТАТИСТИКИ, ОБЛІКУ ТА АУДИТУ, Nº 3.

Business Research Insights (2024). *Franchise Market Report Overview.* <https://www.businessresearchinsights.com/market-reports/franchise-market-108346>.

Callaci B., (2021). Control Without Responsibility: The Legal Creation of Franchising, 1960–1980. *Enterprise & Society, 22*(1), 156–182. <http://doi.org/10.1017/eso.2019.58>.

Cochet, O., Dormann, J., & Ehrmann, T. (2008). Capitalizing on Franchisee autonomy: Relational forms of governance as controls in idiosyncratic franchise dyads. *Journal of Small Business Management, 46*(1), 50–72.

Dant, R. P., & Kaufmann, P. J. (2003). Structural and strategic dynamics in franchising. *Journal of Retailing, 79*(2), 63–75.

Dant, R. P. (2008). A futuristic research agenda for the field of franchising. *Journal of Small Business Management, 46*(1), 91–98.

Dant, R. P., Perrigot, R., & Cliquet, G. (2008), A cross-cultural comparison of the plural forms in franchise networks: United States, France, and Brazil*. *Journal of Small Business Management, 46*, 286–311. <https://doi.org/10.1111/j.1540-627X.2008.00244.x>.

Dogru, T. (2017). C-corporation hotels vs. hotel-REITs: A theoretical and practical comparison. *Boston Hospitality Review, 5*(1).

Gorovaia, N., & Windsperger, J. (2018). The choice of contract duration in franchising networks: A transaction cost and resource-based view. *Industrial Marketing Management, 75*, 125–133.

Gürkan, G. (2024). *Vergleich zwischen traditionellem Franchising und Shareholder-Franchising: Wie ist es besser?* (Bachelor Thesis, Turkisch-German University).

Hadfield, G. K. (1989). Problematic relations: Franchising the law of incomplete contracts. *Stan. L. Rev., 42, 927.*

Kidwell, R. E., Nygaard, A., & Silkoset, R. (2007). Antecedents and effects of free riding in the franchisor-franchisee relationship. *Journal of Business Venturing, 22*, 522–544.

Lafontaine, F., & Blair, R., (2009). The evolution of franchising and franchise contracts: Evidence from The United States. *Entrepreneurial Business Law Journal*, 3(2), 381–434.

Lefler, Jeff, (2016). *5 Years of Franchisee Turnover Rates.* <https://www.franchisegrade.com/reports/article/5-years-of-franchisee-turnover-rates>.

McDermott, Martin J., & Jackson, Jason. (2023). The ranking order of factors that influence purchasing a franchise business: Qualitative study. *International Journal of Business Research and Information Technology; New York City, 10*(1), 74–88.

Mumdziev, N., & Windsperger, J. (2011). As extended transaction cost model of decision rights allocation the case of franchising. *Conference Proceedings EMNet 2011.*

Oxenfeldt, A. R., & Thompson, D. N. (1968). Franchising in perspective. *Journal of Retailing, 44*(4), 3–13.

Park, K., & Jang, S. (Shawn) (2018). Is franchising an additional financing source for franchisors? A Blinder–Oaxaca decomposition analysis. *Tourism Economics, 24*(5), 541–559. <https://doi.org/10.1177/1354816618757561>.

Rubin, P. H. (1978). The theory of the firm and structure of the franchise contract. *Journal of Law and Economics, 21*(1), 223–233.

Simpson, Fiona, (2022). The Five Different Types of Franchise. *Forbes*. <https://www.forbes.com/sites/fionasimpson1/2022/10/17/the-five-different-types-of-franchise/>.

Soliman, Mohamed (2022). Why franchising is a smart business model: a comprehensive review. *ScienceOpen Preprints.*

UFRAD (2024). Franchise Rehberi, UFRAD Franchising Derneği. <https://ufrad.org/wp-content/uploads/rehber/2024rehber.pdf>.

UFRAD (2024a). *Franchise Dünyasi* (56).

Windsperger, J. (2002). Allocation of decision and ownership rights in franchise relationships. *Journal of Marketing Channels, 10*(2), 19–38. <https://doi.org/10.1300/J049v10n02_03>.

Windsperger, J., & Dant, R. P. (2006). Contractibility and ownership redirection in franchising: A property rights view. *Journal of Retailing, 82*(3), 259–272.

Windsperger, J., & Yurdakul, A. (2007). The governance structure of franchising firms: A property rights approach. In G. Cliquet, M. Tuunanen, G. Hendrikse, & J. Windsperger, (Eds.) *Economics and Management of Network* (pp. 69–95). Heidelberg: Springer.

9. Marketing Public Goods to Citizens: A Psychological Ownership Perspective on Urban Parks

Moritz Martin Botts[*,a] *and Ömer Hurmacı*[*,b]

ABSTRACT

Sustainable urban parks cannot be achieved without the support of citizens. Their efforts help governments to save urban parks for the use of future generations. In this conceptual paper, we offer a research model to better understand how psychological ownership can lead to pro-environmental behaviors. After a thorough literature review, we identify three factors that could increase citizens' psychological ownership toward urban parks, namely environmental self-efficacy, environmental knowledge, and similarity to other visitors. Moreover, we propose ascribed responsibility and attitude toward pro-environmental behaviors as the consequences of psychological ownership of urban parks. In turn, we claim that the two can increase citizens' pro-environmental behaviors. The paper ends with recommendations for scholars and public managers.

Keywords: Psychological ownership, Sustainability, Pro-environmental behaviors, Ascribed responsibility, Urban parks, Environment

Introduction

In a world with increased concern for a clean and sustainable environment, it remains unclear as to what individuals and the public can actually do to support public goods such as a green neighborhood. Green spaces are vital to reduce the heat of urban areas and provide outlets for citizens to connect with nature and pursue an active life (WHO, 2016). Problems arise when people engage with a public good that lacks a recognizable owner, similar to the concept of private ownership. Each individual, with their own fallible egocentric views, may try to maximize their profits from nature. This, in their minds, can be achieved by taking advantage of natural resources since the

*Faculty of Economics and Administrative Sciences, Turkish-German University, Istanbul, Turkey.
[a]<https://orcid.org/0000-0003-2514-5065>
[b]<https://orcid.org/0000-0003-4213-0332>
Email: <botts@tau.edu.tr>

costs of doing so will eventually be shared by all (Young & Dhanda, 2012). This concept dates back as early as Adam Smith, and ultimately to Aristotle (Pawlas, 2009). The perceived diffusion of responsibility (Peck et al., 2021) toward the public good is a challenge for local and central governments regarding sustainability.

The marketing literature has had an uneasy relationship with the concept of sustainability, ranging from greener consumption to concepts such as no consumption, and from small changes to marketing management to calls for the transformation of the economic system (Jones et al., 2008; Kemper & Ballantine, 2019). While the concept of corporate social responsibility focuses on the role of the company and its stakeholders (Kolk, 2016; Söllner, 2014), other concepts have focused on the role of the consumer (White et al., 2019).

The focus of this paper is urban parks, a public good often neglected in the public consciousness. We selected urban parks because, unlike an abstract concept such as *the environment*, parks are discrete phenomena that are well understood by the people who benefit from them. Furthermore, parks can be influenced and indeed managed by local governments with reasonable ease. Urban parks are defined in this paper as areas smaller than national parks, named by and under the responsibility of either the local government or the central government, containing grass, trees, and walking paths. Turkish regulations concerning spatial planning dictate that urban green spaces should be planned according to a 500-meter walking-distance rule (Ergen, 2021). This calls for the protection of green spaces. However, there is a limit to what local and central governments can do to maintain these spaces. Therefore, scholars call for further research to understand the visitors of green spaces (Arslan & Kaymaz, 2020), especially their attitudes toward urban parks as opposed to national parks (Özgüner, 2011). Compared to park users in Western countries, Turkish citizens rather visit parks in groups although the benefits they derive from parks are the same, such as peace, relaxation, and calmness (Özgüner, 2011).

We inquire into the factors that lead to psychological ownership of nature and how feelings of ownership for nature can induce ascribed responsibility toward nature and enhance attitudes toward pro-environmental behaviors. We posit that ascribed responsibility toward nature and enhanced attitudes toward pro-environmental behaviors are key to pro-environmental behaviors. To alleviate the problem of the sustainability of urban parks, it is vital to understand how pro-environmental behaviors of citizens toward urban parks might be increased. We suggest that citizens' psychological ownership of urban parks is critical to induce citizens' ascribed responsibility toward urban parks and their favorable attitudes toward pro-environmental behaviors. In turn, increased ascribed responsibility and favorable attitudes toward pro-environmental behaviors will result in pro-environmental behaviors. Therefore, the aim of this paper is to propose a comprehensive research model that will help governments understand how psychological ownership of urban parks develops and how it leads to citizens' pro-environmental behaviors.

First introduced in the field of organizational behavior (Pierce et al., 1991), the theory of psychological ownership offers a new perspective on the interplay between psychological and legal ownership. Unlike legal ownership, psychological ownership is not protected by any legal system (Pierce et al., 2001). Psychological ownership is rather a feeling that is held toward an intangible or a tangible ownership target (Pierce et al., 2003). For instance, it could be toward an idea, like fairness, or an object, like sneakers. In this regard, there is no limit to the number and type of ownership targets one can feel psychological ownership toward. However, this does not mean that holding legal ownership of something guarantees psychological ownership. Both psychological and legal ownership can manifest in a person without the existence of the other (Li & Atkinson, 2020). For instance, one might legally own a hairpin without any feelings of ownership toward it. Conversely, sports fans often feel strong psychological ownership of their teams (e.g., *my team* or *our team*) that they have no legal claim over.

To this point, psychological ownership is discussed in the sense that it is felt toward the target as a whole. However, it can also exist in partial form (Pierce et al., 2001). Consider a birthday party for twin sisters. Both sisters can feel that a part of the party is theirs. Married people might feel that a part of their home is theirs. Residents of a neighborhood might feel that a certain proportion of the neighborhood is theirs. The magnitude of these partial feelings of ownership might depend on personal characteristics, the legal situation of the target, and the size or duration of the target. Research shows that narcissistic people feel more psychological ownership over shared targets and assume that everybody recognizes their ownership claims (Kirk et al., 2018). Therefore, a narcissistic twin sister might experience a stronger sense of psychological ownership over their birthday party than their non-narcissistic twin. Since local governments are legally responsible for certain aspects of streets, residents might feel less ownership over those areas than they otherwise would. If the size of a shared area is large enough, some people could feel a lesser degree of ownership. By the same token, if the duration of an event is long enough, the partial ownership feelings of participants might approach each other.

Another issue untapped to this point is collective psychological ownership (Pierce & Jussila, 2010). People can feel a collective sense of ownership toward targets, expressed in the words *this is ours*. Therefore, psychological ownership can be both an individual-level and a group-level phenomenon (Pierce & Jussila, 2010). Moreover, they can both occur toward the same target at the same time, such as one's perception of their country both as *mine* and *our* (Nijs et al., 2024). In brand communities, both levels of psychological ownership can emerge. Citizens can feel a sense of *our-ness* (Pierce & Jussila, 2010) toward their home city and also parts of their city, such as certain streets, districts, or urban parks.

In the following sections, we provide a comprehensive literature review on why possessions serve to meet some fundamental motives of humans, the process of how a sense of ownership toward objects occurs, the application of the psychological ownership theory in marketing research, and research related to nature. Building on these concepts, we propose a model for understanding the relationship between citizens' psychological ownership of urban parks and pro-environmental behaviors toward them. Finally, we conclude with suggestions about data collection and remarks on the importance of research in this area.

Literature Review

The literature has identified four roots (Jussila et al., 2015; Pierce et al., 2001), or motives (Jussila et al., 2015), for psychological ownership. These are efficacy and effectance, self-identity, having a place, and stimulation. These four roots later help form psychological ownership through three routes (Pierce et al., 2001), or causes (Jussila et al., 2015), which are the exercise of control, intimate knowledge, and investment of the self (Pierce et al., 2003). These roots and routes do not have to play a role simultaneously in order for a sense of ownership to emerge. On the contrary, any root is sufficient but not necessary to form psychological ownership of targets through the mentioned routes, which themselves are sufficient but not necessary (Pierce et al., 2003).

This section follows with an elaboration on the roots and routes of psychological ownership, as well as its application in marketing research, both in general and specifically in research related to nature.

Roots (Motives) of Psychological Ownership

Efficacy and effectance are related to confidence and joy that one feels for (a) knowing that they have the opportunity and means to accomplish a goal and (b) having accomplished a goal, respectively (Pierce et al., 2001, 2003; White, 1959). Effectance can also be interpreted as the joy that is derived from being the cause of a certain effect (Pierce et al., 2003). Humans feel high self-efficacy about possessions that they know how to utilize and perceive themselves to have control over them. Effectance may occur when humans change their environment with their possessions, such as mowing lawns with a lawnmower. Studies show that effectance can be observed as early as infancy when infants begin to be the cause of changes in their environment, such as throwing something to the ground and making it emit a sound (Furby, 1980). To be the cause of that sound gives joy to the infant. In adults, it can manifest through a variety of both tangible and intangible ownership targets, such as making a loud noise with a sports car or changing people's point of view by spreading one's ideas. Interestingly, humans feel psychological ownership of targets that they perceive to be affected by them (Prelinger, 1959). In these regards, objects play an instrumental role by allowing individuals to have control over them and achieve their goals with them (Pierce et al., 2003). However, they can also play symbolic roles.

Self-identity can be constructed by engaging with ownership targets according to one's own preferences, such as clothing, electronics, and favorite baseball team (Pierce et al., 2001, 2003). Through the possession of tangible or intangible ownership targets that have symbolic values to them and to society, people know who they are, show it to others, and feel a sense of continuity in their lives (Pierce et al., 2003). The emphasis on society is important because it determines the symbolic values of possessions. A novice piano player might purchase and share pictures of their piano on social media in order to be seen as a skillful person by their friends. This person knows that society perceives playing the piano as difficult and requiring specific skills. In this way, this person defines themselves as a skillful piano player and is able to show this to others. Possessions, however, can do much more than this. They can also reveal who a person was in the past and who they might become in the future. Moreover, a person who has owned a piano for 10 years feels a sense of self-continuity by reminiscing about the days they spent with their piano, interacting with the piano in the present time, and envisioning that their piano will be with them in the future (Pierce et al., 2003).

Having a place is thought to be an innate condition of humans (Pierce et al., 2003). In order to maintain their psychic and physical security, humans need a special place that they can call home. This place is to be cherished with those a person sees as their in-groups and to be protected from out-groups. In these regards, humans demonstrate territorial behaviors (Pierce et al., 2003). These territorial behaviors can especially be observed in the service industry, where consumers have a third place, that is, a place other than home and work (Joo, 2020). Imagine leaving your coat on *your* desk in a public library when you went to use the restroom. On your way back, you see that your desk is occupied by a stranger and your coat is elsewhere. In such a situation, leaving a coat is considered to be a territorial marking behavior (Pierce & Jussila, 2010). By leaving a personal item in a particular place, a person signals that the space belongs to them and should not be intruded upon. However, the intruder might also feel a sense of ownership toward the desk. The intruder does not know when or whether the owner of the coat is coming back. Moreover, the intruder might not respect the idea of reserving a space by leaving a coat there. The coat-owner might be offended by two things. First, the intruder's act is in violation of social norms (Kirk et al., 2018). If the intruder had asked for permission, it might have been enough for the original owner. Second, the intruder's act might be considered as a violation of the first owner's territorial rights, and this is where the situation is related to psychological ownership. Verbal or physical retaliation against both the intruder and the library (the service provider) might happen in response to this sort of violation. Nevertheless, home is not just about protection or marking territories. Home is decorated with an individual's and their loved ones' personal belongings. Moreover, home is a warehouse of a person's memories because of the events that happened there and the possessions that tell a story.

Stimulation is a later addition to the original three roots (Jussila et al., 2015). According to the activation theory, humans have a need for stimulation. Possessions are good sources of stimulation (Jussila et al., 2015). A smart light bulb produces entertaining visual stimulation for its user with its variety of colors and disco modes. Wind chimes make pleasant sounds, and science magazines provide interesting information. People tend to acquire objects that stimulate them physiologically or intellectually. The Mona Lisa could arise feelings of awe, an emotion that could lead to psychological ownership of objects (Wang et al., 2019). However, the relationship between the human need for stimulation and psychological ownership is not just about stimulation that arises from possessions with little or no involvement of the individual being stimulated. Engaging with possessions, whether by using them or even just thinking about them, provides stimulation. If you are bored and have nothing to do, you can always rearrange your furniture or contemplate how marvelous your toy car collection is.

These four roots pave the way for people to spend time with, or think about, current or prospective possession targets. In the psychological ownership theory, the time spent with or thinking about current or prospective possessions can be categorized into three routes that cause people to feel a sense of ownership over possession targets (Pierce et al., 2001). To restate the three routes, they are exercise of control over the ownership target, intimate knowledge of the ownership target, and investment of the self into the ownership target (Pierce et al., 2003). However, these routes interact with one another and should not be considered as being independent of each other (Pierce et al., 2001).

Routes (Causes) of Psychological Ownership

Exercise of control over the ownership target might be the most potent route to psychological ownership in most cases (Pierce et al., 2001). This stems from the importance of touching, or even imagined touching, when engaging with possession targets. Haptics are found to be significant determinants of ownership feelings (Bräsel & Gips, 2014; Shu & Peck, 2011). Research found that mere touching is enough to induce a sense of ownership (Peck & Shu, 2009). Through touch, humans can engage with objects by moving, using, or even altering them. The ability to do any of these gives a great sense of control over objects. Then, this great sense of control leads to considering the object as *mine* and as part of the self. *I touched it first, so it is mine* is a very strong argument in a child's world. However, there are other ways to control objects. For instance, the lightings in smart homes can be controlled via voice commands. Interestingly, we also feel psychological ownership of things that control us in some way (Prelinger, 1959).

Intimate knowledge of the ownership target requires more time spent with or learning about the target, compared to the almost instant sense of ownership one can experience from a controlling touch. As humans spend time with ownership targets, they come to know them at a deeper level (Pierce et al., 2001, 2023). Our cell phones might be the same brand and model, thus, look the same from a distance. However, each cell phone has small dents or flaws. Most of the time, only the owner knows which pixels are not working on their cell phone or where there is a small crack in the case, let alone the interface and software settings. Even this kind of knowledge can create a strong perceived connection between the person and the ownership target. Proximity to the target is not necessary when gathering or passively acquiring knowledge about it. A fan can collect information about a celebrity via the internet. With enough information about the celebrity, this fan might believe that they have more intimate knowledge of the celebrity than other fans. Therefore, they might feel that this celebrity *belongs* to them. At the workplace, this can be triggered by technical knowledge of the technological devices that are used in the office, such as a photocopier. An employee, whose technical knowledge is low, might feel less psychological ownership of these devices.

Investment of the self into the ownership target is the last route to psychological ownership. As intimate knowledge, it requires more time spent with or thinking about the target of possession. Investment of the self can occur through physical, mental, or financial effort from the *self* (Pierce et al., 2003). Every semester, lecturers spend mental effort to educate their students. By transferring intellectual knowledge of their *self* to the students, they feel as if these students are *their* students. If you take two random students, chances are that a professor will feel a greater sense of ownership toward the student they taught, rather than the one they did not teach. A citizen, acting out of their own benevolence, may clean up their neighborhood. In turn, by investing physical effort from their *self*, these citizens may feel a stronger sense of ownership of the neighborhood. Consumers exchange their money for goods and services, typically earned through their own labor. By trading something from their *selves*, that is, their labor, for these goods and services, they may feel as though they have invested a part of themselves. In their view, this process makes these goods and services theirs, both legally and psychologically. In the preceding examples, the targets already existed before any investment of the self was made. However, the creation of an ownership target allows for the most potent investment of the self. Consider a painter purchasing raw materials, working on their brush strokes, and after everything is done, naming their piece of art. In this example, one can observe several types of effort being spent on the creation of the possession. The financial effort is spent on buying raw materials, brush strokes require physical effort, and the painting is named through mental effort. Having invested various types of effort into the creation of the painting, the painter may feel a greater psychological ownership of it than the person who will later purchase it.

Psychological Ownership in Marketing Research

In marketing research, the theory of psychological ownership is applied to a wide range of areas. Mostly, it found a prevalent place in the sharing economy, helping scholars better understand peer-to-peer relationships, dynamics between peers and organizations, consumer preferences, consumer perceptions of tangible and intangible targets, and challenges posed by dematerialization. Other prominent topics are related to product design and haptics, with their special focus on technology and affordance principles. Moreover, the effects of augmented reality experiences on psychological ownership are investigated in the context such as shopping behavior. Individual differences, such as gender and consumer ethnocentrism, have garnered significant interest among marketing scholars in relation to psychological ownership. Along with conceptual papers, psychological ownership is applied in marketing across topics such as technology appropriation, financial decision-making, virtual communities, and place advertising.

In the context of the sharing economy, Baker et al. (2021) uncovered the relationship between engagement and psychological ownership. Their research focused on peer-to-peer relationships. In their research, a dynamic framework of psychological ownership and engagement is offered. They investigated interactions between peers at both dyadic and collective levels. A central claim of their paper was that individual and collective psychological ownership led to engagement in the dyadic and collective levels, respectively (Baker et al., 2021). Bhappu and Helm (2019) claimed a *zone of optimal distinctiveness* between peer-to-peer lodging service providers and their users. Online profiles of these service providers allow for personalization and signaling of their identities. Although participants identified themselves with the service providers through these personalized profiles, after a certain level of personalization, they became repulsed and felt a lesser sense of ownership toward the lodges (Bhappu & Helm, 2019). In a peer-to-peer context, Lee et al. (2019) investigated the relationship between an organization and its peer service providers in terms of managerial practices. They found that, compared to the attachment to peer hosts, the attachment to an organization was more effective at facilitating psychological ownership toward the organization, which resulted in organizational citizenship behavior. Their study also delved into the antecedents of attachment to organizations. Their findings indicated that honesty, transparency, and frequency of the organization's information sharing were significant influences on the peer service providers' attachment to the organization. A counter-intuitive finding was the negative correlation between the empowerment of peer service providers and their attachment to the organization (Lee et al., 2019). In a car-sharing context, Paundra et al. (2017) empirically demonstrated that high psychological ownership led to an increased preference for private cars over shared cars. This effect persisted despite the lower price of the shared cars (Paundra et al., 2017). Seo and Park (2020) conducted two experiments with crowdfunding projects as targets of ownership. In their first experiment, the results revealed that when investors received information about the average amount of money contributed by others, their level of psychological ownership toward the project changed depending on whether their investment was higher or lower than the average. Those who invested less felt a lower degree of psychological ownership. In their second experiment, they demonstrated that this effect did not persist in crowdfunding projects for intangible objects (Seo & Park, 2020).

Sinclair and Tinson (2017) examined the post-ownership economy, focusing on music consumption in a qualitative study. Their interviews indicated that, for consumers, music-streaming platforms offer greater tidiness of playlists, a wider choice of content, and improved reliability while enhancing accessibility and mobility. Moreover, the effort put into creating playlists has been observed to diminish customers' switching intentions. Visibility of these platforms seemed to enhance the ability to signal one's taste in music to others. These inferences align with the roots and routes of psychological ownership and suggest that this theory plays a role in this sort of consumption (Sinclair & Tinson, 2017). In order to tackle the problem of overconsumption, Fritze et al. (2020) posited that psychological ownership increases the substitutive value of non-physical goods over physical ones. Indeed, in an access-based consumption context, their study revealed that when consumers feel psychological ownership of access-based services, the perceived value of these services as substitutes increases. An increase in the substitutive value of access-based services then resulted in the reduction of material ownership (Fritze et al., 2020). Pasimeni (2021) investigated the extent to which fractional ownership and the sharing economy are related to each other. They underscored that, contrary to fractional ownership, ownership is not shared in the sharing economy and belongs to only one party. An additional claim was that the sharing economy poses a potential risk of increasing inequality by leading to a centralization of ownership (Pasimeni, 2021). Unlike most circular economy research that took a supply-side perspective, Rogers (2021) delved into the demand side of the problem, specifically, consumers. In line with other research on access-based consumption (Morewedge et al., 2021), Rogers (2021) identified several threats to psychological ownership, such as the short-term duration of agreements, restricted ways of usage, and not allowing consumers to personalize the target of psychological ownership.

Another area in which the psychological ownership theory has been applied is design research. Baxter et al. (2015) demonstrated how psychological ownership might be utilized in the design of products by utilizing affordance principles. Their research related roots to *be-goals*, routes to *do-goals*, and actions to realize the routes to *motor-goals*. Moreover, they identified psychological ownership as an antecedent to object attachment (Baxter et al., 2015). Lee and Chen (2011) provided additional support for the influence of self-investment and perceived control on psychological ownership in a virtual world design context. They expanded the nomological network of the psychological ownership construct by integrating it with the architectural quality model and landscape preference model (Lee & Chen, 2011).

Since the feeling of control over the ownership target remains the key to psychological ownership, scholars conducted studies on the role played by haptics. In an experimental study, Bräsel and Gips (2014) indicated the potent influence of haptics in psychological ownership. In an online shopping scenario, they investigated the influence of touchscreens, touchpads, and mice on ownership feelings. Two of their studies demonstrated that touchscreens fostered a greater sense of ownership of shopping products. Moreover, the effect was amplified when the consumer owned the device used for online shopping. The research also demonstrated that this effect was stronger for products with higher haptic importance (Bräsel & Gips, 2014). Shu and Peck (2011) replicated some studies on the endowment effect and conducted new studies by utilizing psychological ownership and affective reaction as mediators. They demonstrated how these constructs influenced product valuation and choice. The effects of psychological ownership and affective reaction were found to be independent of one another. In the context of an unpleasant touching experience caused by the rough-textured object, sellers reported higher psychological ownership while reporting lower affective reaction (Shu & Peck, 2011).

Scholars investigated how new technologies such as augmented reality might be utilized in forming psychological ownership toward various targets. Using augmented reality devices in their study, Carrozzi et al. (2019) found that augmented reality holograms induced psychological ownership. Customization via augmented reality devices facilitated this relationship. Moreover, social identity needs of assimilation and differentiation were revealed as antecedents to psychological ownership in the usage of shared and personal augmented reality devices, respectively (Carrozzi et al., 2019). Song et al. (2020) probed into consumer shopping decisions, examining the effects of try-on augmented reality experiences. They dimensionalized augmented reality experiences as environmental embedding and simulated physical control. Their findings suggested that previous experience with the technology mitigated the effects of augmented reality experience on immersion. Interestingly, rather than immersion mediating the relationship between augmented reality experience and psychological ownership, it is found that augmented reality experience affected psychological ownership directly. Decision comfort, a widely used construct in augmented reality research, was influenced by psychological ownership (Song et al., 2020). Yuan et al. (2021) demonstrated through empirical evidence that attributes of augmented reality positively influenced flow experience, which, in turn, increased psychological ownership. Moreover, brand attachment moderated the relationship between consumer perceptions regarding augmented reality and flow experience (Yuan et al., 2021).

To understand the role played by individual differences in psychological ownership, Folse et al. (2012) conducted an experimental study on gender. Their research revealed that women were more apt at detecting advertising messages that have manipulative intent. On the other hand, men were more likely to take credit for the falsely promoted ownership of success in alleviating the damages caused by a natural disaster through donations that they never made. However, women's less favorable attitudes toward manipulative ads were mitigated when they were under high cognitive load and unable to elaborate on the ad's message (Folse et al., 2012). To understand the relationship between psychological ownership and the country of origin of products, Gineikienė et al. (2017) created and tested a scale on consumers from different countries with different levels of import penetration. They found that domestic products were perceived to be more in the *ours* category in the consumers' minds than foreign products. Moreover, compared to consumer ethnocentrism, domestic psychological ownership was a better predictor of the willingness to pay more and the judgment of domestic products. An interesting finding in their research is that individuals scoring high on the domestic psychological ownership scale showed a bias for domestic goods even in the absence of dispraise for foreign goods (Gineikienė et al., 2017). Expanding the nomological network of the psychological ownership construct, Kamleitner and Feuchtl (2015) investigated its relationship with attachment and attitude constructs, providing evidence that these are indeed related but distinct constructs. More importantly, their research revealed that, among these three constructs, psychological ownership was the only one that predicted actual behavior. Lastly, they empirically demonstrated that imagery vividness and imagery elaboration influenced psychological ownership (Kamleitner & Feuchtl, 2015).

Lee and Suh (2015) demonstrated the effects of autonomy, membership duration, and self-discrepancy on psychological ownership, as well as the consequences of psychological ownership in a virtual community context. Their findings shed light on the ways to increase the sustainability of virtual communities with the help of psychological ownership theory. A counter-intuitive finding in their study was the insignificant relationship between membership duration and psychological ownership, challenging the perhaps naïve assumption that a long-term relationship with a virtual community would foster ownership feelings (Lee & Suh, 2015). However, others expected that, with time, feelings of ownership "will flatten off" (Hulland et al., 2015, p. 143).

Kirk et al. (2015) conducted a conceptual investigation on how psychological ownership is related to two types of pride within the context of consumer technology appropriation. Unlike the technology adoption and acceptance studies, their paper focused on how consumer technology appropriation facilitates value creation. They used authentic pride and hubristic pride as two different types of pride. Authentic pride is felt if a person thinks that they invested themselves into something in an effortful way. Hubristic pride is felt after an accomplishment is achieved, and it is more about how the achiever evaluates themselves compared to their social circle. To be specific, hubristic pride is associated with a sense of superiority to others about the cause of the achievement, *I achieved this because I am more talented in this than others*, compared to authentic pride, *I achieved this because I put a lot of effort into this*. Consequently, they suggested that authentic pride, being the result of an effortful process, is an antecedent to psychological ownership. On the flipside, hubristic pride, a consequence of psychological ownership, is hypothesized to moderate the relationship between psychological ownership and evaluation of the possessed target (Kirk et al., 2015).

Li and Atkinson (2020) empirically demonstrated that consumers achieve happiness through higher psychological ownership, especially in experiential products. They designed experimental scenario conditions in which the target of psychological ownership (a hard-copy book) was purchased, borrowed from a person, or borrowed from a library. The findings suggested that, irrespective of how they acquired their books, subjects felt increased happiness in books that they perceived as theirs. Therefore, the authors provided evidence for the idea that legal ownership is not a necessary condition to enjoy products. In their second experiment, they used a scenario in which subjects purchased gifts either for themselves or for their friends. The results revealed that, regardless of who would receive the gift, subjects felt happiness if the gift was customizable (Li & Atkinson, 2020).

Sharma et al. (2021) investigated the psychological ownership of debt. They showed that structurally identical types of debt might induce different levels of psychological ownership because of different semantic properties. Specifically, subjects felt greater psychological ownership for debt types that included the term *credit* compared to *loan*. Moreover, individuals were more likely to perceive a line of credit to be their money in their bank while viewing a loan as money that they owe to their bank. The effect of semantics was diminished when the offer was provided with words and sentences that are inherently lower in psychological ownership, such as money that belongs to the bank (Sharma et al., 2021).

In an advertising context, Wei et al. (2023) empirically demonstrated the mediating effect of psychological ownership between homesickness advertising (vs. non-homesickness advertising) and hometown brand citizenship behavior. They also provided evidence of the moderating effect of place attachment on the relationship between homesickness advertising (vs. non-homesickness advertising) and psychological ownership (Wei et al., 2023). Amani (2022) presented evidence of the influence of social media brand engagement on ownership feelings toward destination brands. In turn, psychological ownership of destination brands led to voice behavior of local residents (Amani, 2022).

Karahanna et al. (2015) developed formative scales for measuring the motives of psychological ownership and conceptualized a variable of psychological ownership motivation. Their approach to self-identity needs is quite elaborate in that it has three dimensions, which are the need for coming to know the self, the need for expressing self-identity, and the need for maintaining the continuity of self-identity. Besides these, they successfully linked psychological ownership motives to social media use (Karahanna et al., 2015).

Alongside empirical studies, marketing scholars also undertook conceptual inquiries, addressing potential problems and areas for development in psychological ownership research. The dual-process model of Morewedge (2021) is an attempt to explain the interplay between legal and psychological ownership. In their model, psychological ownership occurs via three routes (control, self-investment, and knowledge) with the addition of self-congruity as another route. These routes are considered to provoke implicit judgments about psychological ownership. In turn, these implicit judgments are corrected by explicit judgments about legal ownership. Explicit judgments are made if the person has motivation, ability, and opportunity to contemplate their status regarding legal ownership (Morewedge, 2021). Hulland et al. (2015) criticized the psychological ownership theory. First, they state that the target attributes as defined by Jussila et al. (2015) give a false *the more is merrier* impression. Second, they claimed that psychological ownership theory cannot explain why consumers dispose of goods or discontinue using services. Lastly, they pointed out a need for a high-quality measurement scale for the psychological ownership construct (Hulland et al., 2015). Jussila et al. (2015) also discussed the overemphasis on *my* and the lack of *part of me* aspect in psychological ownership scales.

Furthermore, Morewedge et al. (2021) scrutinized how technological developments affect the psychological ownership of consumers. They investigated this issue in regard to two trends: Moving from legal ownership to legal access and moving from material goods to experiential goods. Three effects of technological innovations that apply to both trends are the threat to psychological ownership, the transfer of psychological ownership to other targets, and the creation of new opportunities to maintain it. In the first trend of legal ownership to legal access, threats to psychological ownership are identified as fractional ownership and impermanence. Moreover, psychological ownership is transferred from one's own goods to collective goods. As opportunities to preserve psychological ownership, the increase in perceived control thanks to large assortments provided by access-based consumption, and new modes of self-expression provided by access-based consumption are given as examples. In the second trend of moving from material to experiential goods, threats to psychological ownership are identified as intangibility and reduced evaluability. Moreover, psychological ownership is transferred from material goods to higher categories such as devices (e.g., traditional board games to the computers that are used to play online board games), platforms, and brands. As an opportunity to preserve psychological ownership, enhanced self-identification is provided as an example (Morewedge et al., 2021).

Psychological Ownership and Nature

Wang et al. (2023a) developed and validated measures for individual and collective psychological ownership of nature, the need for which had been pointed out in the previous literature (Wang et al., 2022). Wang et al. (2023a) provided evidence that both measures are distinct from nature-relatedness and place attachment, which are considered to be proximate to the psychological ownership of nature. Moreover, the influence of individual psychological ownership on civic pro-environmental behaviors was fully mediated by place attachment (Wang et al., 2023a).

Felix and Almaguer (2019) extended the psychological ownership theory to the planet Earth within the context of pro-environmental behaviors. Moreover, they measured psychological ownership at both the individual and the collective level to better understand the driving forces of pro-environmental behaviors. Their results suggested that both levels of ownership are related to recycling intentions and the intention to buy green products. Furthermore, the relationship between materialism and pro-environmental behaviors was mediated only by individual psychological ownership (Felix & Almaguer, 2019). In a tourism study on destination sustainability, Xu et al. (2023) demonstrate how higher destination psychological ownership led to increased pro-environmental behaviors of tourists. In addition, they found that ascribed responsibility partially mediated this relationship. Moreover, perceived effectiveness moderated the effects of destination psychological ownership and ascribed responsibility on pro-environment behaviors of tourists (Xu et al., 2023). Note that most previous studies used effectiveness as an antecedent to psychological ownership. As a novel antecedent to psychological ownership of nature, Shekari et al. (2024) examined childhood nature-based recreation experiences within the context of pro-environmental behaviors. Their results confirmed that childhood nature-based recreation experiences influenced adults' environmental knowledge and connectedness to nature, but not their psychological ownership of nature. They attributed this insignificant relationship to psychological distance that is caused by temporal distance. In addition to these, psychological ownership, environmental knowledge, and connectedness to nature were found to be significant influencers of pro-environmental behaviors (Shekari et al., 2024). She et al. (2022) extended the concept of psychological ownership to the natural environment by examining three routes (pro-environment investment, environmental self-efficacy, and environmental knowledge) as antecedents of environmental psychological ownership. In contrast to most previous research that found or hypothesized control as the strongest correlate of psychological ownership, environmental knowledge was found to have the strongest influence on environmental psychological ownership in their research. Furthermore, environmental psychological ownership influenced pro-environment intentions (She et al., 2022).

Mishra et al. (2023) examined sustainable purchasing behavior in fashion by young consumers in both a scenario-based experiment and a survey. In their first study, their findings revealed that ecological consciousness influenced sustainable purchasing behavior through the mediating effect of psychological ownership of the environment. In contrast to this, their second study found a direct effect of ecological consciousness on sustainable purchasing behavior (Mishra et al., 2023). Wang et al. (2019) empirically examined awe, an emotion, as an antecedent to psychological ownership of nature within the framework of green consumption. They showed that, among some neutral and positive emotions, awe was the only emotion that influenced green consumption behaviors. Moreover, this effect was partially mediated by psychological ownership of nature. Awe resulted in higher psychological ownership when the interdependent (vs. independent) self-construal of participants was activated (Wang et al., 2019).

Kuo et al. (2021) provided evidence for the mediation of psychological ownership in the relationship between place attachment (measured by two sub-constructs of place identity and place dependence) and environmentally responsible behavior. Their findings corroborated that environmentally responsible behavior is directly influenced by both place identity and place dependence. They also directly affected destination psychological ownership. Moreover, destination psychological ownership partially mediated the relationship between place attachment and environmentally responsible behavior (Kuo et al., 2021). Liu et al. (2022) empirically investigated the relationships among perceived justice, psychological ownership, and environmentally responsible behavior intention. Their findings suggested that perceived justice in a community tourism destination affected both psychological ownership of the community and environmentally responsible behavior intention. Moreover, they found a positive relationship between the length of residency and intentions to conduct environmentally responsible behavior. As expected, higher psychological ownership toward the community led to a higher environmentally responsible behavior (Liu et al., 2022). Via several experimental studies, Ding et al. (2021) demonstrated that shape anthropomorphism and linguistic anthropomorphism in packaging led to higher recycling intentions through the mediating role of empathy. To elaborate on this, the influence of shape anthropomorphism was greater than linguistic anthropomorphism. Moreover, findings suggested that psychological ownership moderated the relationship between anthropomorphic design and empathy (Ding et al., 2021).

Through a series of studies, Peck et al. (2021) showed how to foster stewardship behaviors (both physically and financially effortful) toward public goods by increasing psychological ownership via allowing visitors to nickname public goods, see signs that contain possessive pronouns, and plan their route with the help of a map. In addition, their findings suggested that psychological ownership led to greater feelings of responsibility. However, when visitors were aware of others' use of the public goods, they had lower stewardship behaviors due to the diffusion of responsibility (Peck et al., 2021).

Gupta and Singh (2024) showed that psychological ownership of residents fosters destination advocacy behaviors. Surprisingly, residents' knowledge of their hometown was the only significant influence on psychological ownership, with experienced control and self-investment having an insignificant effect. They attributed the reasons for these insignificant effects to the target of ownership and the newfound emergence of the destination, respectively (Gupta & Singh, 2024).

Utilizing self-categorization theory, Nijs et al. (2024) investigated collective psychological ownership of countries, neighborhoods, and local parks. Their findings suggested that collective psychological ownership led to exclusive determination rights, which increased the exclusion of outsiders. Collective psychological ownership also increased the group responsibility, in turn, higher group responsibility led to higher intentions to engage in stewardship behavior (Nijs et al., 2024).

Wang et al. (2023b) studied individual differences regarding views of the environment within the framework of psychological ownership and pro-environmental intentions. Their results suggested that higher psychological ownership led to participants' higher pro-environmental intentions. However, an unexpected finding was that both high and low environmentally oriented participants showed similar results in terms of their felt individual ownership and its association with civic behaviors (Wang et al., 2023b). One implication of this result could be the implementation of standardized advertisements targeting individuals regardless of their environmental orientation.

Wang et al. (2022) conceptually examined the feasibility of nature as a target of psychological ownership and asserted that it is a viable target. They criticized existing and adapted measures of psychological ownership and called for developing new measures for both individual and collective psychological ownership of nature. Moreover, they maintained that psychological ownership of nature may be more effective for people with anthropocentric worldviews compared to those with ecocentric worldviews. They further argued that natural environments that are close in psychological distance are more likely to induce psychological ownership, given that people experience them throughout their lifetime. Additionally, they provided a comprehensive list of concepts related to nature that are somewhat similar to psychological ownership, although distinct from it (Wang et al., 2022).

The exploratory study by Matilainen et al. (2017) provided a detailed analysis of the conflict between privately owned natural resources (forests) and common natural resources (wild animals). In-depth interviews indicated that tourism entrepreneurs claimed to be more knowledgeable about forests than the forest owners themselves. This sense of knowledge of the target led them to believe that they had the right to use the forest. On the other side, forest owners built their identity as forest owners, either belonging to a generation of forest owners or as members of a community who own forests. The most important inference made in their work is that psychological ownership may not always help resolve conflicts. However, it could be a tool to predict and manage these conflicts (Matilainen et al., 2017).

Guan et al. (2024) developed and tested a scale of community-based psychological ownership in the context of rural tourism. The dimensions of this scale are as follows: self-identity, self-efficacy, community responsibility, community belongingness, community possession, and territoriality. Their findings suggested that, except for community possession, all other dimensions influenced participation in the community (Guan et al., 2024).

Proposal for a Model

Self-efficacy is one of the roots of psychological ownership (Pierce et al., 2001). It motivates people to take actions that will foster their psychological ownership. Controlling the target is one way to satisfy this root. The effect of control on psychological ownership has been investigated in several contexts such as virtual worlds (Lee & Chen, 2011), online shopping (Bräsel & Gips, 2014), augmented reality (Song et al., 2020), and the environment (She et al., 2022).

Proposition 1: Environmental self-efficacy of citizens positively influences their psychological ownership of urban parks.

Knowledge is one of the routes to psychological ownership (Pierce et al., 2003). Through intimately knowing a target, people develop psychological ownership of it. The relationship between the knowledge of the target and psychological ownership toward it is the least researched relationship among the routes to psychological ownership. However, studies in pro-environmental behaviors suggest the influence of environmental knowledge on environmental psychological ownership (She et al., 2022; Shekari et al., 2024). Moreover, previous research identifies environmental knowledge as the most potent predictor of environmental psychological ownership among the routes (She et al., 2022).

Proposition 2: Environmental knowledge of citizens positively influences their psychological ownership of urban parks.

Self-identity is one of the roots that urge people to take actions to foster psychological ownership of possessions (Pierce et al., 2003). Self-identification is a need that motivates people to connect with others and possessions that they perceive to be similar to themselves. Similarity to peers is used in the literature in the context of psychological ownership (Lee et al., 2019). It is expected that if people perceive themselves to be similar to other well-behaved users of urban parks, their psychological ownership of the park will be increased.

Proposition 3: Citizens' perceived similarity to other visitors of urban parks positively influences their psychological ownership of urban parks.

Once people feel a sense of ownership toward a target object, they evaluate it more favorably (Pierce et al., 2003). Scholars investigated the relationship between psychological ownership and attitude (Gupta & Singh, 2024; Lee & Suh, 2015). The influence of psychological ownership on attitude toward a pro-social behavior is empirically shown in a nonprofit service organization context (Ainsworth, 2020). It is expected that psychological ownership of urban parks will result in favorable attitudes toward pro-environmental behaviors.

Proposition 4: Psychological ownership of citizens toward urban parks positively influences their attitude toward pro-environmental behaviors.

Responsibility is conceptualized as a factor leading to psychological ownership (Pierce et al., 2003). However, research shows that perceived and ascribed responsibility is induced by psychological ownership toward natural targets (Nijs et al., 2024; Peck et al., 2021; Xu et al., 2023) and pro-social activity (Kang & Baker, 2022). It is expected that people who develop a sense of ownership toward urban parks will eventually feel a sense of responsibility toward them.

Proposition 5: Psychological ownership of citizens toward urban parks positively influences their ascribed responsibility toward urban parks.

Attitude is an important predictor of pro-social behaviors (Ainsworth, 2020; Gupta & Singh, 2024). Positive attitudes are hypothesized to increase destination advocacy behaviors (Gupta & Singh, 2024) and volunteering intentions (Ainsworth, 2020). Based on these, the influence of attitude toward pro-environmental behaviors on actual pro-environmental behaviors is expected.

Proposition 6: Citizens' attitude toward pro-environmental behaviors positively influences their actual pro-environmental behaviors.

Responsibility leads to care for the target of ownership (Pierce et al., 2003). Previous research corroborates the influence of responsibility on natural targets regarding pro-environmental behaviors (Nijs et al., 2024; Peck et al., 2021; Xu et al., 2023).

Proposition 7: Ascribed responsibility of citizens toward urban parks positively influences their actual pro-environmental behaviors.

To summarize, as depicted in Figure 13, our research model includes the antecedents of psychological ownership and its consequences. These antecedents are the routes to psychological ownership. Here, ascribed responsibility and attitude toward pro-environmental behaviors are used as direct outcomes of psychological ownership. In turn, ascribed responsibility and attitudes toward pro-environmental behaviors are proposed to enhance pro-environmental behaviors of citizens toward urban parks.

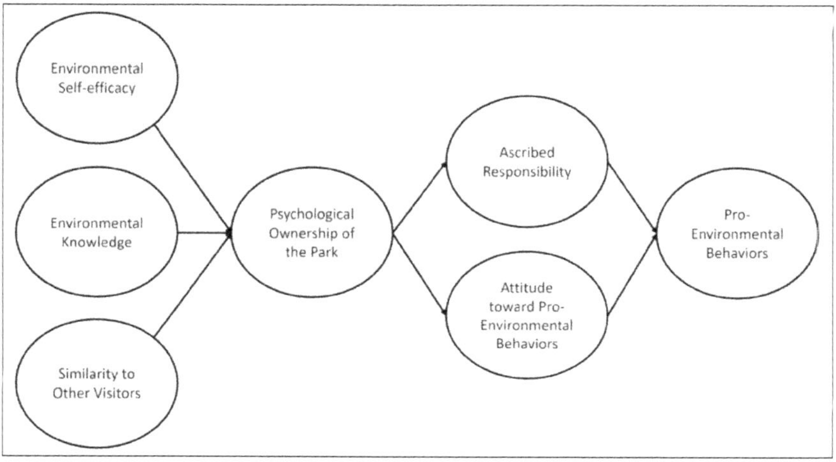

Figure 13: Proposed research model.

Conclusion

Urban parks are essential assets of urban life. However, their sustainability poses substantial problems for local and central governments. Their efforts alone might not be sufficient to maintain the sustainability of urban parks. Citizens should be motivated to engage in pro-environmental activities. Therefore, taking a psychological ownership perspective on the sustainability of urban parks, we scrutinize the factors that lead to pro-environmental behaviors of citizens who frequent urban parks.

Our literature review shows that several ownership targets related to the environment have previously been investigated, such as parks, lakes, and even the planet Earth. Moreover, various types of samples were used, such as residents, tourists, and visitors to green spaces. Research looked into individual differences in psychological ownership of natural targets such as environmental orientation. Scholars also demonstrated that psychological ownership of targets related to nature is different from place attachment and connectedness to nature. Most importantly, new scales have been developed in order to better capture the essence of psychological ownership when the target object is related to nature.

After the literature review, both on the application of psychological ownership theory in the marketing literature and on the investigation of nature as a target for psychological ownership, we propose a comprehensive research model. This model will help both scholars and public managers understand the relationship between psychological ownership and pro-environmental behaviors. Therefore, they will be able to leverage psychological ownership to promote pro-environmental behaviors among citizens. We identify environmental self-efficacy, environmental knowledge, and similarity to other visitors as important antecedents to psychological ownership. Moreover, we highlight ascribed responsibility and attitude toward pro-environmental behaviors as key mediators of the relationship between psychological ownership and pro-environmental behaviors.

To empirically test the model, we suggest collecting survey-based quantitative data among the population of either two major Turkish cities or two different neighborhoods of the metropolis of Istanbul. Turkey as a case is interesting, because the local government promotes a clean environment and wants to further citizenship engagement toward this goal (İBB, 2023). Moreover, the current marketing campaign of İstanbul Metropolitan Municipality is İstanbul is yours—be a volunteer, which uses a possessive pronoun. With a study about the psychological ownership of urban parks, these marketing communication activities can be examined in more detail.

Results of this study will benefit the advancement of marketing research and public policy regarding the sustainability of green spaces. The concept of psychological ownership will be tested in the Turkish case. It can be assumed that the basic concept would also apply to Turkish respondents, although nuances might vary compared to other samples. For instance, the aspect of sustainability might be less important in Turkish civil society than having a place to socialize while barbecuing (Özgüner, 2011). Furthermore, the specific environmental application of urban parks has not garnered much attention from scholars.

Considering practical applications, the findings can help guide local governments on how to support community engagement with public goods, particularly urban parks. Public managers can refine their marketing communication efforts, which try to increase the citizens' engagement with nature. Therefore, a future study of psychological ownership of urban parks will have both scientific as well as practical value. In combination with other recommendations for sustainable consumer behavior (White et al., 2019), these suggestions can lead to consumers' and, therefore, citizens' practical changes toward a greener environment.

Bibliography

Ainsworth, J. (2020). Feelings of ownership and volunteering: Examining psychological ownership as a volunteering motivation for nonprofit service organisations. *Journal of Retailing and Consumer Services*, *52*, 101931.

Amani, D. (2022). It's mine, that's why I speak: Destination brand psychological ownership as a mediator of the link between social media brand engagement and local residents' voice behavior. *Cogent Business & Management*, *9*(1), 2031432.

Arslan, E. S., & Kaymaz, I. (2020). Visitor perception of recreational ecosystem services and their role in landscape management of Gölcük Nature Park, Turkey. *International Journal of Sustainable Development & World Ecology*, *27*(3), 202–213.

Baker, J. J., Kearney, T., Laud, G., & Holmlund, M. (2021). Engaging users in the sharing economy: individual and collective psychological ownership as antecedents to actor engagement. *Journal of Service Management*, *32*(4), 483–506.

Baxter, W. L., Aurisicchio, M., & Childs, P. R. (2015). A psychological ownership approach to designing object attachment. *Journal of Engineering Design*, *26*(4–6), 140–156.

Bhappu, A. D., & Helm, S. (2019). Zone of optimal distinctiveness: Provider asset personalization and the psychological ownership of shared accommodation. In *Advances in Service Science: Proceedings of the 2018 INFORMS International Conference on Service Science* (pp. 73–81). Cham: Springer.

Brasel, S. A., & Gips, J. (2014). Tablets, touchscreens, and touchpads: How varying touch interfaces trigger psychological ownership and endowment. *Journal of Consumer Psychology*, *24*(2), 226–233.

Carrozzi, A., Chylinski, M., Heller, J., Hilken, T., Keeling, D. I., & de Ruyter, K. (2019). What's mine is a hologram? How shared augmented reality augments psychological ownership. *Journal of Interactive Marketing*, *48*(1), 71–88.

Ding, Z., Sun, J., Wang, Y., Jiang, X., Liu, R., Sun, W., Mou, Y., Wang, D., & Liu, M. (2021). Research on the influence of anthropomorphic design on the consumers' express packaging recycling willingness: The moderating effect of psychological ownership. *Resources, Conservation and Recycling, 168*, 105269.

Ergen, M. (2021). Using geographical information systems to measure accessibility of green areas in the urban center of Nevşehir, Turkey. *Urban Forestry & Urban Greening, 62*, 127160.

Felix, R., & Almaguer, J. (2019). Nourish what you own: psychological ownership, materialism and pro-environmental behavioral intentions. *Journal of Consumer Marketing, 36*(1), 82–91.

Folse, J.A.G., Guidry Moulard, J., & Raggio, R. D. (2012). Psychological ownership: a social marketing advertising message appeal? Not for women. *International Journal of Advertising, 31*(2), 291–315.

Fritze, M. P., Marchand, A., Eisingerich, A. B., & Benkenstein, M. (2020). Access-based services as substitutes for material possessions: The role of psychological ownership. *Journal of Service Research, 23*(3), 368–385.

Furby, L. (1980). The origins and early development of possessive behavior. *Political Psychology, 2*(2), 30–42.

Gineikienė, J., Schlegelmilch, B. B., & Auruskevicienė, V. (2017). "Ours" or "theirs"? Psychological ownership and domestic products preferences. *Journal of Business Research, 72*, 93–103.

Guan, J., Zhu, D., Cheng, S., & Li, Q. (2024). "It is my place": residents' community-based psychological ownership and its impact on rural tourism participation. *Journal of Sustainable Tourism*, 1–27. <https://doi.org/10.1080/09669582.2024.2346779>.

Gupta, A., & Singh, V. (2024). Destination advocacy behaviour of residents: Examining the role of psychological ownership. *Journal of Hospitality and Tourism Insights*. Ahead-of-print. <https://doi.org/10.1108/JHTI-11-2023-0778>.

Hulland, J., Thompson, S. A., & Smith, K. M. (2015). Exploring uncharted waters: Use of psychological ownership theory in marketing. *Journal of Marketing Theory and Practice, 23*(2), 140–147.

İBB. (2023). *İstanbul Sustainable Energy and Climate Action Plan*. <https://cevre.ibb.istanbul/wp-content/uploads/2024/04/ENG-SECAP-v04.pdf>.

Jones, P., Clarke-Hill, C., Comfort, D., & Hillier, D. (2008). Marketing and sustainability. *Marketing Intelligence & Planning*, *26*(2), 123–130.

Joo, J. (2020). Customers' psychological ownership toward the third place. *Service Business*, *14*(3), 333–360.

Jussila, I., Tarkiainen, A., Sarstedt, M., & Hair, J. F. (2015). Individual psychological ownership: Concepts, evidence, and implications for research in marketing. *Journal of Marketing Theory and Practice*, *23*(2), 121–139.

Kamleitner, B., & Feuchtl, S. (2015). "As if it were mine": Imagery works by inducing psychological ownership. *Journal of Marketing Theory and Practice*, *23*(2), 208–223.

Kang, Y. A., & Baker, M. A. (2022). Which CSR message most appeals to you? The role of message framing, psychological ownership, perceived responsibility and customer altruistic values. *International Journal of Hospitality Management*, *106*, 103287.

Karahanna, E., Xu, S. X., & Zhang, N. (2015). Psychological ownership motivation and use of social media. *Journal of Marketing Theory and Practice*, *23*(2), 185–207.

Kemper, J. A., & Ballantine, P. W. (2019). What do we mean by sustainability marketing? *Journal of Marketing Management*, *35*(3–4), 277–309.

Kirk, C. P., Peck, J., & Swain, S. D. (2018). Property lines in the mind: Consumers' psychological ownership and their territorial responses. *Journal of Consumer Research*, *45*(1), 148–168.

Kirk, C. P., Swain, S. D., & Gaskin, J. E. (2015). I'm proud of it: Consumer technology appropriation and psychological ownership. *Journal of Marketing Theory and Practice*, *23*(2), 166–184.

Kolk, A. (2016). The social responsibility of international business: From ethics and the environment to CSR and sustainable development. *Journal of World Business*, *51*(1), 23–34.

Kuo, H. M., Su, J. Y., Wang, C. H., Kiatsakared, P., & Chen, K. Y. (2021). Place attachment and environmentally responsible behavior: The mediating role of destination psychological ownership. *Sustainability*, *13*(12), 6809.

Lee, Y., & Chen, A. N. (2011). Usability design and psychological ownership of a virtual world. *Journal of Management Information Systems*, *28*(3), 269–308.

Lee, J., & Suh, A. (2015). How do virtual community members develop psychological ownership and what are the effects of psychological ownership in virtual communities? *Computers in Human Behavior*, *45*, 382–391.

Lee, H., Yang, S. B., & Koo, C. (2019). Exploring the effect of Airbnb hosts' attachment and psychological ownership in the sharing economy. *Tourism Management*, *70*, 284–294.

Li, D., & Atkinson, L. (2020). The role of psychological ownership in consumer happiness. *Journal of Consumer Marketing*, *37*(6), 629–638.

Liu, Y., Qu, Z., Meng, Z., & Kou, Y. (2022). Environmentally responsible behavior of residents in tourist destinations: the mediating role of psychological ownership. *Journal of Sustainable Tourism*, *30*(4), 807–823.

Matilainen, A., Pohja-Mykrä, M., Lähdesmäki, M., & Kurki, S. (2017). "I feel it is mine!"—Psychological ownership in relation to natural resources. *Journal of Environmental Psychology*, *51*, 31–45.

Mishra, S., Malhotra, G., Chatterjee, R., & Kareem Abdul, W. (2023). Ecological consciousness and sustainable purchase behavior: The mediating role of psychological ownership. *Asia Pacific Journal of Marketing and Logistics*, *35*(2), 414–431.

Morewedge, C. K. (2021). Psychological ownership: Implicit and explicit. *Current Opinion in Psychology*, *39*, 125–132.

Morewedge, C. K., Monga, A., Palmatier, R. W., Shu, S. B., & Small, D. A. (2021). Evolution of consumption: A psychological ownership framework. *Journal of Marketing*, *85*(1), 196–218.

Nijs, T., Martinovic, B., & Verkuyten, M. (2024). The two routes of collective psychological ownership: Rights and responsibilities explain intentions to exclude outsiders and engage in stewardship behavior. *Personality and Social Psychology Bulletin*, *50*(2), 270–284.

Özgüner, H. (2011). Cultural differences in attitudes towards urban parks and green spaces. *Landscape Research*, *36*(5), 599–620.

Pasimeni, F. (2021). The origin of the sharing economy meets the legacy of fractional ownership. *Journal of Cleaner Production*, *319*, 128614.

Paundra, J., Rook, L., van Dalen, J., & Ketter, W. (2017). Preferences for car sharing services: Effects of instrumental attributes and psychological ownership. *Journal of Environmental Psychology*, *53*, 121–130.

Pawlas, A. (2009). Diskussionsbeitrag zur betriebswirtschaftlichen Ethik—Adam Smith, Ethik und Marktwirtschaft. *Zeitschrift für Betriebswirtschaft*, *79*(5), 663–680.

Peck, J., & Shu, S. B. (2009). The effect of mere touch on perceived ownership. *Journal of Consumer Research*, *36*(3), 434–447.

Peck, J., & Kirk, C. P., Luangrath, A. W., & Shu, S. B. (2021). Caring for the commons: Using psychological ownership to enhance stewardship behavior for public goods. *Journal of Marketing*, *85*(2), 33–49.

Pierce, J. L., & Jussila, I. (2010). Collective psychological ownership within the work and organizational context: Construct introduction and elaboration. *Journal of Organizational Behavior*, *31*(6), 810–834.

Pierce, J. L., Kostova, T., & Dirks, K. T. (2001). Toward a theory of psychological ownership in organizations. *Academy of Management Review*, *26*(2), 298–310.

Pierce, J. L., Kostova, T., & Dirks, K. T. (2003). The state of psychological ownership: Integrating and extending a century of research. *Review of General Psychology*, *7*(1), 84–107.

Pierce, J. L., Rubenfeld, S. A., & Morgan, S. (1991). Employee ownership: A conceptual model of process and effects. *Academy of Management Review*, *16*(1), 121–144.

Prelinger, E. (1959). Extension and structure of the self. *The Journal of Psychology*, *47*(1), 13–23.

Rogers, P. (2021). Rented but MINE! Application of psychological ownership theory to access-based consumption and the circular economy. *Circular Economy and Sustainability*, *1*(2), 719–744.

Seo, B. G., & Park, D. H. (2020). Did you invest less than me? The effect of other's share of investment on psychological ownership of crowdfunding projects. *Sustainability*, *12*(5), 2025.

Sharma, E., Tully, S., & Cryder, C. (2021). Psychological ownership of (borrowed) money. *Journal of Marketing Research*, *58*(3), 497–514.

She, S., Li, S., Xu, J., & Yang, B. (2022). Exploring the concept, antecedents, and consequences of environmental psychological ownership. *International Journal of Environmental Research and Public Health*, *19*(19), 12621.

Shekari, F., Azizi, F., & Ghaderi, Z. (2024). Adults' pro-environmental behaviours and childhood experiences: The mediating role of nature connectedness, psychological ownership, and environmental knowledge. *Current Issues in Tourism*, *27*(22), 3849–3865

Shu, S. B., & Peck, J. (2011). Psychological ownership and affective reaction: Emotional attachment process variables and the endowment effect. *Journal of Consumer Psychology*, *21*(4), 439–452.

Sinclair, G., & Tinson, J. (2017). Psychological ownership and music streaming consumption. *Journal of Business Research*, *71*, 1–9.

Söllner, A. (2014). Globalization, greed, and exploitation. How to break the baleful path? *Journal of Business Economics*, *84*(9), 1211–1235.

Song, H. K., Baek, E., & Choo, H. J. (2020). Try-on experience with augmented reality comforts your decision: Focusing on the roles of immersion and psychological ownership. *Information Technology & People*, *33*(4), 1214–1234.

Wang, X., Fielding, K. S., & Dean, A. J. (2022). Psychological ownership of nature: A conceptual elaboration and research agenda. *Biological Conservation*, *267*, 109477.

Wang, X., Fielding, K. S., & Dean, A. J. (2023a). "Nature is mine/ours": Measuring individual and collective psychological ownership of nature. *Journal of Environmental Psychology*, *85*, 101919.

Wang, X., Fielding, K. S., & Dean, A. J. (2023b). Psychological ownership of nature: Relationships with pro-environmental intentions in less environmentally-oriented individuals. *Personality and Individual Differences*, *213*, 112304.

Wang, L., Zhang, G., Shi, P., Lu, X., & Song, F. (2019). Influence of awe on green consumption: The mediating effect of psychological ownership. *Frontiers in Psychology*, *10*, 2484.

Wei, C., Wang, C., Sun, L., Xu, A., & Zheng, M. (2023). The hometown is hard to leave, the homesickness is unforgettable - The influence of homesickness advertisement on hometown brand citizenship behavior of consumers. *Behavioral Sciences*, *13*(1), 54.

White, R. W. (1959). Motivation reconsidered: The concept of competence. *Psychological Review*, *66*(5), 297–333.

White, K., Habib, R., & Hardisty, D. J. (2019). How to SHIFT consumer behaviors to be more sustainable: A literature review and guiding framework. *Journal of Marketing*, *83*(3), 22–49.

WHO. (2016). Global Report on Urban Health: Equitable, Healthier Cities for Sustainable Development. Project Report. World Health Organization, Geneva.

Xu, Z., Yang, G., Wang, L., Guo, L., & Shi, Z. (2023). How does destination psychological ownership affect tourists' pro-environmental behaviors? A moderated mediation analysis. *Journal of Sustainable Tourism*, *31*(6), 1394–1412.

Young, S. T., & Dhanda, K. K. (2012). *Sustainability—Essentials for Business*. Los Angeles, CA: Sage.

Yuan, C., Wang, S., Yu, X., Kim, K. H., & Moon, H. (2021). The influence of flow experience in the augmented reality context on psychological ownership. *International Journal of Advertising*, *40*(6), 922–944.

List of Contributors

Hilmi Berkay Abbasoğlu
Turkish-German University, berkay.abbasoglu@tau.eu.tr

Abdulrahman AlAbdeh
TouristPay, abdeh@touristpay.com.tr

Ela Sibel Bayrak Meydanoğlu
Turkish-German University, meydanoglu@tau.edu.tr

Moritz M. Botts
Turkish-German University, botts@tau.edu.tr

Serdar Salih Durmuşoğlu
Fonksiyonel Holding, Serdar.durmusoglu@pt.bogazici.edu.tr

Angelina Egbers
Bielefeld University of Applied Sciences and Arts, angelina_fabiene.egbers@hsbi.de

Alexander Förster
Bielefeld University of Applied Sciences and Arts, alexander.foerster@hsbi.de

Ömer Hurmaci
Turkish-German University, omer.hurmaci@tau.edu.tr

Lia Bo Josephs
Bielefeld University of Applied Sciences and Arts, lia_bo.josephs@hsbi.de

Tim Kampe
Bielefeld University of Applied Sciences and Arts, tim.kampe@hsbi.de

Alina Neumann
Bielefeld University of Applied Sciences and Arts, alina_marie_chiara.neumann@hsbi.de

Hüseyin Hayri Nuroğlu
Turkish-German University, h.nuroglu@tau.edu.tr

Mehtap Öner
Marmara University, mehtap.oner@marmara.edu.tr

Mehmet Hakan Özdemir
Turkish-German University, hakan.ozdemir@tau.edu.tr

Judith Quiring
Bielefeld University of Applied Sciences and Arts, judith.quiring@hsbi.de

Ferhat Sayın
Turkish-German University, ferhat.sayin@tau.edu.tr

Jan Schilling
Bielefeld University of Applied Sciences and Arts, jan.schilling@hsbi.de

Eliza Starke
Bielefeld University of Applied Sciences and Arts, eliza.starke@hsbi.de

Manuel Stegemann
Bielefeld University of Applied Sciences and Arts, manuel.stegemann@hsbi.de

Margareta Teodorescu
Koblenz University of Applied Sciences, teodorescu@hs-koblenz.de

Tolga Tuzcuoğlu
Robert Bosch GmbH, tolga.tuzcuoglu@de.bosch.com

Andreas Uphaus
Bielefeld University of Applied Sciences and Arts, andreas.uphaus@hsbi.de

Dorothee Wilm
Bielefeld University of Applied Sciences and Arts, dorothee.wilm@hsbi.de

Erencan Yavrucu
Turkish-German University, erencan.yavrucu@tau.edu.tr

www.ingramcontent.com/pod-product-compliance
Ingram Content Group UK Ltd.
Pitfield, Milton Keynes, MK11 3LW, UK
UKHW021014120926
8556IPUK00040B/1135

9 783631 938485